Same-Sex Marriage

The Personal and the Political

Also by Kathleen A. Lahey:
Are We 'Persons' Yet? Law and Sexuality in Canada

Also by Kevin Alderson:
Beyond Coming Out
Breaking Out

Same-Sex Marriage

The Personal and the Political

Kathleen A. Lahey
and Kevin Alderson

INSOMNIAC PRESS

Edited by Richard Almonte
Copy edited by Adrienne Weiss
Interior design by Marijke Friesen

National Library of Canada Cataloguing in Publication Data

Lahey, Kathleen Ann
    Same-sex marriage : the personal and the political / Kathleen A. Lahey and Kevin Alderson.

Includes bibliographical references and index.
ISBN 1-894663-63-2

    1. Same-sex marriage. I. Alderson, Kevin George, 1956- II. Title.

HQ1033.L34 2004   306.84'8   C2004-900485-9

The publisher gratefully acknowledges the support of the Canada Council, the Ontario Arts Council and the Department of Canadian Heritage through the Book Publishing Industry Development Program. We acknowledge the support of the Government of Ontario through the Ontario Media Development Corporation's Ontario Book Initiative.

Printed and bound in Canada

Insomniac Press
192 Spadina Avenue, Suite 403
Toronto, Ontario, Canada, M5T 2C2
www.insomniacpress.com

THE CANADA COUNCIL | LE CONSEIL DES ARTS
FOR THE ARTS | DU CANADA
SINCE 1957 | DEPUIS 1957

ONTARIO ARTS COUNCIL
CONSEIL DES ARTS DE L'ONTARIO

To Marguerite Russell, who inspires me in all things.
—Kathy

To Dr. Gary Sanders, who taught me the meaning of love.
And to my parents, who gave me a chance to experience all of this.
—Kevin

Table of Contents

Introduction

The twenty-first century has brought with it the dramatic opening of marriage to same-sex couples in Europe and North America. Beginning in the Netherlands in 2001, continuing in Belgium and two Canadian provinces in 2003, and then in areas of the United States and Quebec in 2004, thousands of same-sex couples have taken advantage of this fundamental civil right. Although same-sex couples were permitted to marry in some U.S. states in the mid-1970s, and although some African cultures such as the Nuer and Ibo have always celebrated woman-woman marriage in exactly the same way as man-woman marriage, the marriage bar has been the one legal right that has been most consistently denied to lesbian, gay, bisexual, transgender and transsexual persons who would marry a person of the same sex.

This book documents the extension of civil marriage from two perspectives: through the experiences of same-sex couples who have been among the first to marry, often after long personal involvement in the marriage movement, and from the perspective of the legal and political struggles that have made same-sex marriage possible. Part I of this book was written by Kathleen Lahey, a lesbian law professor who has litigated the marriage issue in Canada as well as having been involved in queer scholarship and law reform. These chapters trace the queer marriage movement from its origins in history and early queer consciousness through to the 1970s U.S. marriages, the resulting political backlash, and then to the dramatic legal and constitutional breakthroughs of the last decade. Chapter Two outlines how political opposition to same-sex marriage has led to the creation of legal and political barriers that are designed to stave off same-sex marriage: the secularization of religious doctrine; the enactment of 'man-woman' definitions of marriage; express prohibitions on same-sex marriage in statutes and even in constitutions; and segregated alternatives to civil marriage for same-sex couples. Chapters Three through Five examine how litigants, activists, courts and legislators have overcome these barriers to achieve the extension of civil marriage to same-sex couples in Europe, Canada and the U.S. While the precise combination of factors that opened marriage in each jurisdiction is unique, one factor is common everywhere: recognition that same-sex couples have equal rights to the equal protection of the law—including the equal right to civil marriage.

What emerges from the telling of each of these stories of legal and political struggle is a simple fact: as lesbian, gay, bisexual, transgender and transsexual people have asserted their right to full human dignity, it has become impossible for the state to maintain the second- and even third-class status of same-sex couples. Neither the outmoded 'heterosexual presumption' that has led courts and officials to conclude that same-sex couples cannot be 'any two persons' referred to in neutral marriage laws nor narrow readings of equal protection laws have survived the queer marriage movement.

Part II of this book was written by Dr. Kevin Alderson, professor of counselling psychology and author of two books on gay identity. Dr. Alderson presents the personal stories based on interviews he conducted of sixteen lesbian and gay couples who have already married or are awaiting their wedding day. These couples are not cloaked with pseudonyms, which is the usual practice in research. Instead, they have used their real names and provided photographs in order to give voice and image to same-sex marriage.

Each couple has an incredible story to tell. Many of them have made history by being among the first couples to be able to marry in their country or state, by being instrumental in winning the right to marry in their state, by being able to marry in a legally valid religious marriage, by travelling great distances—one couple from Hong Kong—to marry in Canada, or by becoming marriage 'freedom riders' who have gone home as legally married couples, perhaps some day to raise questions there about the validity of their marriages.

Opposite-sex couples can learn a lot from these married lesbian and gay couples. Forced into extended courtships, the fact that these same-sex couples are still together after all these years without the legal obligations of marriage, and in some cases, without having children, speaks strongly to the fact that they stayed together because they wanted to.

The structure of the interviews in Part II arises from the methodology employed, which is the qualitative social science inquiry of phenomenology. The goal of the interviews was to examine the human phenomenon of same-sex marriage by learning about it from the people who have experienced it. The goal of phenomenology is to understand the essence or core of the phenomenon under investigation. This was done with a team of eleven research assistants working with Dr. Alderson to extract the core of what same-sex marriage means to those living it. Guiding this process of discovery was the question "What is the experience of being married to a person of the same gender?" The actual language used by the interview subjects when recounting their lived experience has been retained in these interviews. Some of the interviews begin with Dr. Alderson's own personal observations of the lead-up to the interview, and in some cases, he finishes with a few additional observations to enable readers to see the research process through his eyes as he experienced it.

The political and religious debate over same-sex marriage will no doubt continue for some time to come. But the key breakthroughs in the marriage bar discussed in this book have transformed this debate from the abstract theoretical 'what if' type of discussion into the unfolding of a genuinely new chapter in human history. For the first time in the history of the marriage movement, this debate now involves not just the idea of queer marriage, but the realitites of same-sex couples who have chosen to marry. It is our fervent hope that those who are concerned with this issue will come to see that in the end, what really matters in life as well as in law is mutual respect, tolerance, and, where it can thrive, genuine love.

The law is stated as at March 21, 2004.

PART I

The Political and Legal Struggle for Marriage

CHAPTER ONE

History, *Loving*, Stonewall and the Queer Civil Rights Movement

Introduction

The high profile marriage cases in the United States and Canada that have been heard over the last ten years have given the false impression that the concept of civil marriage for lesbian and gay couples is some newfangled notion that is just too novel and untested for careful governments to take seriously.

Nothing could be further from the truth. Historical and anthropological evidence shows that same-sex couples have formed intimate long-term relationships since time immemorial, not just in Greek and Roman society, but in societies all around the globe. While the nature of what we would today call 'marriage' has changed over the millenia, one thing that has not changed is that same-sex couples have the same need for personal intimacy, close relationships and social acceptance that is expected of opposite-sex couples.

This chapter outlines the historical record of queer relationships and marriages, and then links the contemporary demand for legal marriage for queer couples to three important developments that took place in the 1960s: the 1967 decision of the United States Supreme Court in *Loving* v. *Virginia*, which swept aside the long-standing prohibitions on interracial marriages that had been brought to the U. S. colonies from England; the Stonewall Rebellions in Greenwich Village, New York, in 1969; and the queer civil rights movement that erupted as queers around the world began to seize 'pride.'

Queer Marriage in History

The best-known account of queer marriage in history is undoubtedly that of John Boswell, who published *Same-Sex Unions in Pre-Modern Europe* in 1994. Some of the specific interpretations Boswell gave medieval religious texts and records remain hotly debated by scholars. However, Boswell's main discovery has never been disputed: that same-sex couples in early Modern Europe used a variety of religious ceremonies to obtain Catholic blessing for marriages that closely resembled heterosexual marriages. In addition, Boswell threw new light on the openness with which same-sex unions were celebrated in Roman and Greek law and society.[1] Historical records, artifacts and research indicate that since earliest recorded history, same-sex couples have often enjoyed social and even formal recognition of their relationships. Although 'marriage' would have been different then than today, the list of times and places where same-sex couples have received such recognition includes, at a minimum: Egypt, Ancient Greece (Athens, Thebes, Crete and Sparta), Ancient Rome, China (from at least the 1500s to the present in Guangzhou, Fujian and Fuzhou), Japan, South East Asia (Malay and Bali), Australia (Aboriginal peoples), India (Bhopal, 1987), South America, Central America, North American Indigenous peoples, Medieval Eastern Europe, Portugal (1500s), Early Modern Europe, Balkans (early 1800s), England, Italy, the Netherlands, Canada (cross-dressing women in the 1800s), United States (cross-dressing couples in the 1900s), and Africa (continuously until the present day).[2]

Recognition of same-sex relationships in history not only spans huge time periods and geographical areas, but also relates to widely diverse social contexts. The fact that records of same-sex relationships and marriages are found in so many different times and places indicates that even though Euro-American marriage laws and religious beliefs may have presumptively linked the concept of 'marriage' with heterosexuality, the concept and practice of same-sex marriage has never been entirely suppressed.

Loving v. *Virginia* (1967)

The 1960s saw growing awareness of civil rights with the U.S. racial liberation movement. Despite the famous decision of the U. S. Supreme Court in *Brown* v. *Board of Education of Topeka, Kansas*[3] in 1952, which declared racial segregation in public eduction to be unconstitutional, many states still refused to extend equal voting rights to African-Americans, continued to prohibit interracial marriage, and resisted racial integration of schools and other public facilities.

When considered in the context of this atmosphere of continuing discrimination, the U.S. Supreme Court decision in *Loving* v. *Virginia*[4] drew wide attention as a reaffirmation of the historic anti-segregation ruling in *Brown v. Board of Education.*

The *Loving* decision had a special resonance with lesbian and gay people in 1967. When the Court declared that 'The freedom to marry has long been recognized as one of the vital personal rights essential to the orderly pursuit of happiness by free men,' many queers saw in this simple statement the promise that they too could expect to enjoy this vital personal right. Already in some of the U.S. states same-sex sexual contact had begun to be decriminalized as the result of the recommendations of the English Wolfenden Report. The Netherlands had decriminalized 'homosexuality' shortly after the French Revolution; Illinois took the lead in the U.S. in 1961; and Canada followed suit in 1969. As decriminalization became an acceptable policy option, many queers began to come out of the closet and attempted to exercise some of their basic civil rights.

It is also significant that as lesbian and gay people started turning to the law to frame their dreams of civil rights for queers, the *Loving* decision created a real sense of hope that constitutional guarantees of equality and liberty might someday be extended to their relationships.

Stonewall and the Queer Civil Rights Movement
The June 27-28, 1969, Stonewall Rebellions in Greenwich Village, New York, galvanized growing awareness of queer oppression in a way that neither the *Loving* decision nor the decriminalization movement had achieved. Now celebrated around the world as 'Pride Day,' the Stonewall Rebellions ignited queer refusal to be relegated to the margins of existence when the queer patrons of the Stonewall Bar fought back against routine police harassment and raids in their neighbourhood.

One of the most immediate consequences of the Stonewall uprising was that queers in the U.S., Canada, Europe and elsewhere, immediately began coming out of the closet in unprecedented numbers. At the same time, they began to demand full civil rights—equal rights to employment, custody of their children, equal property rights, and, not surprisingly, the right to marry. In Canada, the 1969 decriminalization of same-sex sexual activity between two consenting adults in private coincided with the Stonewall Rebellions and accelerated the expectation that queers were entitled to all the same ordinary rights enjoyed by other Canadians.

The New Queer Marriage Movement
Literally on the heels of the Stonewall Rebellions, queer couples in Europe, Canada and the U.S. immediately began applying for marriage licences as

part of their new expectation that they should enjoy ordinary civil rights. At first, the applications were successful as municipal and county officers looked at gender-neutral marriage laws and saw that they almost invariably merely referred to 'any two persons' who apply to marry.[5] For example, on January 7, 1975, a county clerk in Phoenix, Arizona, issued a marriage licence to two men after checking the legislation and regulations to see if there existed a prohibition on their marriage. The Boulder, Colorado county clerk Clela Rorex did the same thing on March 26, 1975, when she issued marriage licences to five couples. Finding nothing in the statutes or regula-tions to answer the question, Rorex had consulted a city district attorney. The district attorney gave her the opinion that in the absence of any laws specifically prohibiting same-sex marriage, the clerk had the administrative authority to determine whether these couples met the legal requirements for the issuing of a licence. In Rorex's Judgment they did. Thus, she issued the licences, the marriages took place, and several of the couples are still happily married.

Unfortunately, it did not take long for the interpretation of these laws to be tightened up. In Arizona, the legislature rushed through 'emergency legislation' to define marriage as being between a man and a woman, and the Arizona Supreme Court voided the queer marriage that had been performed. In Colorado, the Attorney General subsequently issued an opinion that the licences were invalid, and ordered county clerks not to issue them to any more lesbian and gay couples. The Colorado marriages were never nullified, although a federal court later ruled that the marriages were not valid for purposes of federal immigration laws.[6] Despite these responses, the demand for same-sex marriage accelerated in the late 1960s well into the 1980s. Diverse couples made applications all across the U.S., with documented applications made in California, Minnesota, Kentucky, Washington, Ohio, Maryland, Illinois and Washington, D.C. Applications were also made in Canada and in a number of European countries—particularly in the Scandinavian countries.

CHAPTER TWO

Blocking Queer Marriage:
Canada, the U.S. and Europe

The Heterosexual Presumption

In the 1960s and 1970s, most marriage laws looked more or less just like they do now. The typical marriage statute simply states something like: 'any two persons not under a legal disqualification to contract a marriage' may marry. Marriage laws usually contain minimum age requirements and rules about marrying first cousins, but some marriage laws require little more than that the parties each have the mental capacity to enter into the contract of marriage, be unmarried at the time they seek to marry, and have the money to pay the registry fees.

Until same-sex couples began to demand the right to marry in the late 1960s and early 1970s, marriage laws had been completely silent about the sexes of the 'two persons' who could marry. Once it became clear that queer couples expected to be treated like any other couple, however, most governments began to scramble to find ways to reinforce the unstated presumption that many politicians have had that marriage is for heterosexuals only. The fact that registry officials in Arizona and Colorado had issued marriage licences to queer couples because the laws simply referred to 'any two persons' was seen as creating a public emergency.

Four basic strategies were used to attempt to reinforce this heterosexual presumption:

• Appeal to courts to apply religious doctrine to prevent queer couples from marrying, including assumptions about the procreative purposes of marriage;

- 'Heterosexualize' neutral definitions of 'spouse' to create the impression that marriage has always been exclusively heterosexual;
- Enact 'defence of marriage' prohibitions on same-sex marriage;
- Create segregated legal structures to give some limited legal recognition to lesbian and gay relationships while keeping them out of the institution of marriage.

These strategies have made it extremely difficult to remove the heterosexual presumption from marriage law. Like the now-outmoded presumption that 'slaves' could not vote, marry or own property, or the presumption that women should not be allowed to work outside the home or hold public office, the heterosexual presumption treated the cumulative effects of centuries of prejudices as having legitimately relegated same-sex couples to a second- or third-class status—as alien 'Other.'

Each of these four strategies is designed to reinforce the heterosexual presumption attributed to marriage law. As governments have become more desperate to prevent queer couples from entering the state of marriage, they have sometimes deployed two, three or even *all* of these strategies to try to defeat the marriage movement.

This chapter discusses how each of these barriers attempted to reinforce the belief that only heterosexuals can marry, and how the nature of each barrier actually contributed to the overall process by which queer marriage finally became thinkable. It is fair to say that the real story of queer marriage will end up being the story of how traditional conservative values have had to give way to the constitutional values of freedom, liberty and equality among all persons. The breakthroughs in Europe, Canada and the U.S. illustrate the many ways in which these fundamental constitutional principles have finally overcome attempts to reserve marriage exclusively for heterosexuals.

Religious Doctrine
It is not at all surprising that the first line of defence against lesbian and gay marriage was religious doctrine. After all, the merger of state law and religious doctrine had resulted in the initial enactment of criminal sodomy laws in the Visigoth era, and early canon law and later ecclesiastical courts had incorporated the so-called 'procreative' purpose of marriage into both civil law and common law in the laws of England and other European countries.

European Countries
Denmark actually began discussing the issue of opening marriage to same-sex couples in 1968, nearly a year before the Stonewall Rebellions. During

consideration of a draft bill on marriage by the Danish Parliament in the fall of 1968, Poul Dam, a member of the left-wing party, introduced a proposal that Parliament should consider the needs of same-sex couples. This modest proposal disappeared from sight for five years, but in its 1973 report the Government Law Reform Committee on Marriage Laws actually addressed the issue of same-sex marriage.

According to Dr. Caroline Forder, Professor of Family Law at the University of Maastricht, the Netherlands, almost all the members of the Committee took the view that marriages between persons of the same sex would constitute such a decisive breach with 'traditional views on marriage' that they would not be accepted in other countries and could even bring *all* Danish marriages into disrepute.[7]

Sweden reached the same conclusion in its 1984 government report, *Homosexuella och samhellet (Homosexuals and Society)*. The Swedish report described marriage as 'a bridge too far' and also concluded that the entire institution of marriage could be damaged if same-sex couples were permitted to marry.

In each of these countries, the most vocal opponents of opening marriage to same-sex couples were right-wing political parties that openly associated themselves with organized religions. Even as the Dutch marriage bill was enacted in 2000, these parties continued their opposition on expressly religious grounds. As Dr. Forder has written, 'The Staatkundig Gereformeerde Partij-faction (very strict protestant) reacted with shock to the bill [because] the opening up of marriage to same-sex couples would conflict with their religious views.'[8] Most members of that party voted against the same-sex marriage bill, although it passed. As discussed in Chapter Three, members of that party are still pressuring the government to provide 'heterosexual-only' registries or registrars, and religious exemptions for registrars whose religious values conflict with same-sex marriage.

United States

Unlike in Europe, where religious doctrine was brought into the same-sex marriage debate through the legislative process, religious doctrine was first raised in the courts in the U. S. (and in Canada, as discussed below) as queer couples turned to the courts to gain access to civil marriage. Because most marriage laws in the United States used gender-neutral language, the courts had to take responsibility for deciding whether those gender-neutral terms included lesbian and gay couples or not. State governments quickly brought forward voluminous materials showing the alleged religious origins of marriage as a way to convince courts to rule against lesbian and gay couples.

Thus, the first same-sex marriage judicial decisions invariably relied directly on passages from the Christian Bible or on secular versions of biblical doctrine. In 1971, in *Baker* v. *Nelson*, a Minnesota court relied directly on religious doctrine in ruling that Richard John Baker and James Michael McConnell could not marry: 'The institution of marriage as a union of man and woman, uniquely involving the procreation and rearing of children within a family, is as old as the Book of Genesis.'[9] In Arizona, the state Supreme Court invalidated the Phoenix marriages retroactively, also citing passages from the Christian Bible.

Many U.S. state courts have continued to rely on religious doctrine. In the 1991 case of *Dean* v. *District of Columbia*,[10] a D.C. court was asked to rule on the gender-neutral marriage law strictly on the basis of the language used in the statute. No constitutional issues were raised. The D.C. Human Rights Commission sided with the couple, taking the position that the marriage bureau was violating city law by refusing to let two gay men marry. The court relied directly on the Christian Bible in that case, and also cited the older cases that had also based their decision on religious doctrine.

Not all of the early U.S. cases explicitly relied on religious doctrine in such a direct way. Secularizing religious doctrine as 'common knowledge' observations about marriage, other courts, such as the Washington court in *Singer* v. *Hara* (1974), simply concluded that John F. Singer and Paul Barwick were excluded from 'the nature of marriage itself' because 'two males cannot produce children.'[11] The Kentucky court in *Jones* v. *Hallahan* (1973) ruled in even more general terms that two women were 'incapable of entering into marriage as it is defined.'[12]

The fact that U.S. courts so easily adopted religious doctrine as the basis for prohibiting same-sex marriage is particularly alarming. U.S. state prohibitions on interracial marriage had also been militantly upheld by judges on the basis of religious doctrine. The Virginia trial court in *Loving* had upheld criminal convictions for interracial marriage by relying on attitudes about 'unnatural' relationships and biblical teachings:

> 'Almighty God created the races white, black, yellow, malay and red, and he placed them on separate continents. And but for the interference with his arrangement there would be no cause for such marriages. The fact that he separated the races shows that he did not intend for the races to mix.'

That court then sentenced the Lovings, who had gone over the Virginia state border to marry in a state that did not prohibit their marriage, to be exiled from Virginia for twenty-five years.

The U.S. Supreme Court resoundingly rejected this reasoning, and held that prohibitions on interracial marriage violated the U.S. constitution. Unfortunately, as the 1986 decision in *Bowers* v. *Hardwick*[13] (upholding sodomy laws on biblical grounds) and the 2003 decision in *Lawrence* v. *Texas*[14] (which finally overturned *Bowers*) reveal, it has taken much longer for courts to critically assess the relevance of religious doctrine in determining queer civil rights.

Canada

The same pattern can be seen in the early Canadian decisions on same-sex marriage. Richard North and Chris Vogel (read their interview in Part II) were the first two gay men in Canada to try to obtain a marriage licence. They were to be married in the Unitarian Church in their community, yet the Manitoba court that heard their case in 1974 (*Re North and Matheson*[15]) ruled against them on the basis of outdated English ecclesiastical law as represented in two cases: *Hyde* v. *Hyde,*[16] an 1866 case involving polygamy, and *Corbett* v. *Corbett,*[17] a 1970 case involving the marriage of a transsexual person.

The court in *Hyde* v. *Hyde* was required by English law to apply ecclesiastical law to the marriage in question. Thus, it ruled that polygamous marriage could not be considered valid in England because it violated Christian doctrine: '[M]arriage, as understood in Christendom, may…be defined as the voluntary union for life of one man and one woman, to the exclusion of all others.'

The court in *Corbett* was less obviously bound by ecclesiastical law. The court heard hours of expert evidence on the proper biological and scientific criteria to use in determining the legal 'sex' of a person, and devoted the greatest part of its decision to analyzing that evidence. Despite this veneer of scientific inquiry, however, the court actually based its decision on the obscure ecclesiastical concept of 'meretricious relationships,' and held that the marriage of a transsexual person was void from the beginning—there had never been any marriage in the eyes of the law because the transsexual spouse had never 'really' become a woman.

Until the breakthrough round of marriage litigation discussed in Chapter Five, the courts in Canada kept mechanically applying the 'one man and one woman' statement in *Hyde* and the ecclesiastical ruling in *Corbett* both to transsexual marriage cases and to lesbian and gay marriage cases. In the 1972 *Sherwood Atkinson (Sheri de Cartier)*[18] case and the 1992 case of *C.(L.)* v. *C.(C.)*,[19] the ecclesiastical ruling in *Corbett* was automatically applied to lawsuits challenging the validity of marriages involving transsexual persons.

The role of religious doctrine is even more evident in the 1993 Ontario decision in *Layland and Beaulne*,[20] in which two gay men challenged the denial of their right to marry on the basis that it violated their constitutional equality rights. The court not only reiterated religious doctrine as a reason for maintaining the prohibition on same-sex marriage, but also sought to attribute the already-outmoded canon law requirements that married couples be able to physically consummate their marriage and to procreate to 'the state' and to 'society': 'the institution of marriage is intended by the state, by religions and by society to encourage the procreation of children.'

Right up until the middle of 2003, the federal government in Canada continued to subscribe to this religious justification for the prohibition on same-sex marriage. Indeed, the federal government framed its entire case around the proposition that religious views of marriage have so permeated the institution of marriage that religious organizations are essential 'stakeholders' in deciding whether same-sex couples should be permitted to marry, and that the core character of marriage in Canada continues to be heterosexual procreative unions.

None of the three jurisdictions in which religious doctrine was brought into the debate over same-sex marriage ended up relying on that strategy alone. Each of them also took legislative steps designed to prevent same-sex couples from marrying. What is interesting is that each country devised its own unique strategy, with little crossover until recently.

Canada: Heterosexualizing 'spouse' and 'cohabitation'

Demands for same-sex marriage hit the national media in Canada right when the women's movement had succeeded in convincing the federal government that it should take definitive steps to rid federal laws of sexism. Acting on the recommendations of the 1970 report of the Royal Commission on the Status of Women,[21] the federal government introduced omnibus legislation in 1974 and 1975 to replace sexist terms such as 'husband,' 'wife' and 'common-law wife' with gender-neutral terms like 'spouse' and 'cohabitant.'

This omnibus legislation also expanded the uniquely Canadian policy of giving some of the benefits usually reserved for married couples to 'common-law wives.' Unlike many countries (notably the U.S.) which rarely recognize unmarried cohabitants, Canada had always given veteran's pensions to unmarried 'war brides' who lived with their common-law husbands without ever actually marrying them. ('War brides' often could not obtain documentation proving the divorce or the death of their first spouse, so they could not marry anyone else.) By 1970, the federal government had been persuaded to extend the Canada Pension Plan and Old Age Security benefits to unmarried couples as well. The 1974 and 1975 omnibus legislation added further benefits to that list.

The decision to replace gender-specific language in federal law with gender-neutral language created a problem: how to ensure that lesbian and gay couples would not be included in new gender-neutral terms like 'spouse' and 'cohabitant.'

'*Opposite-sex cohabitants*' *Deemed to be Spouses*

Apparently the drafters of these new laws were confident that defining 'spouse' as 'two persons who are married to each other' would be understood as referring only to heterosexuals. When it came to identifying the cohabitants who could qualify for spousal treatment, however, the phrase 'of the opposite sex' was added to make it perfectly clear that no queers need apply, even if they did cohabit for the same minimum period of time.

The expansion of 'spouse' to include cohabiting heterosexuals was an extremely important development in Canadian family law. Since the mid-1970s, this expanded definition has been inserted into literally hundreds of federal and provincial statutes.

Although there is no clear legislative record as to exactly why the drafters of federal laws decided it was important to insert the words 'opposite sex' into these new cohabitation clauses, it is clear that queers were never far from politicians' minds. In addition to worrying that giving benefits to unmarried couples would endanger family stability, politicians were already warning in 1974 about where this could lead: 'Once you open the door on a thing like this, then you open the door on common law marriages and the recognition of them *and a lot of other things*.'[22]

By the mid-1980s, politicians had become more blunt about the purpose of these heterosexualizing clauses. For example, when the Ontario government added 'sexual orientation' to the Ontario Human Rights Code in 1986, it apparently thought that it could prevent the courts from treating lesbian and gay couples as 'spouses' or as 'cohabitants' by inserting the 'opposite-sex' definition of spouse into thirty-three Ontario statutes—one of which was the definition of 'spouse' in the Human Rights Code itself.

Ian Scott, then Attorney General of Ontario, stated in no uncertain terms that adding 'sexual orientation' to the Human Rights Code would not enable lesbian and gay couples to be treated as spouses or as opposite-sex cohabitants. "The government," he said, "has no plans to redefine the family in Ontario legislation to include unmarried couples of the same sex."[23] As another member of the government put it,

'The Code is very clear on the meaning of family, marriage and spouse in its definition sections. It leaves no room for doubt. There is no ambiguity in the words used in terms of the opposite sex. The amendment can in no way impair the clarity of these definitions, nor will it.'[24]

In the short term, the 'opposite-sex cohabitant' clauses inserted into statutory definitions of 'spouse' strongly reinforced the assumption that marriage has always been exclusively for heterosexuals. Also in the short term, these definitions initially induced Canadian courts to enforce the human rights of *individual* queers but to treat *queer couples* as having no relationship rights. Thus, individual lesbians and gays could turn to human rights commissions with complaints of employment discrimination, for example, but the commissions turned complaints about the denial of spousal benefits away year after year. (The story of Rich North and Chris Vogel's attempt to obtain spousal employment benefits after they were denied the right to marry illustrates how difficult it has been for queer couples to attain even such simple rights. See their interview in Part II.)

In comparison with other methods used to block same-sex marriage, the strategy of adding heterosexualizing cohabitant clauses to gender-neutral definitions of 'spouse' was far less difficult for couples to overcome than the more aggressive anti-queer marriage statutes and constitutional amendments used in the U.S. However, it did divert queer energies away from seeking the right to marry for nearly fifteen years after the Charter came into effect. This is because both the federal and provincial governments enacted literally hundreds of these 'opposite-sex' clauses beginning in the 1980s. Every time lesbian or gay couples sought some sort of relationship rights, whether they were the right to family medical coverage or the right to tax or pension benefits reserved for spouses, they were met with the fact that such cohabitant benefits were expressly limited to couples 'of the opposite sex.'

Thus, the history of lesbian and gay relationship rights in Canada is the history of battling these ubiquitous clauses—one clause at a time. The Supreme Court of Canada was in no hurry to strike them down, either. As late as 1995, the Supreme Court of Canada ruled in *Egan and Nesbit*[25] that such 'opposite-sex' definitions of spouse did not violate the Charter of Rights because queer relationships were still so 'novel.' Although the Court did rule in that case that same-sex couples are protected by section 15 of the Charter of Rights, it agreed that the government could exclude them from a benefit designed to meet some of the special economic needs of married and unmarried heterosexual couples.

The *Egan and Nesbit* case was greeted with skepticism by many lower courts, some of which refused to follow that Supreme Court of Canada ruling even in 1995. Indeed, some lower courts had already ruled some of the opposite-sex cohabitation clauses to be unconstitutional before 1995. However, these opposite-sex clauses were enacted faster than they could be litigated, and right up until the middle of 1999, they remained in effect in hundreds of statutes. (For information on how these opposite-sex clauses were finally invalidated by the Supreme Court of Canada in *M.* v. *H.*,[26] see Chapter Five.)

'Man-woman' Definitions of Marriage

In the last decade, a few governments in Canada have made some attempts to directly heterosexualize the term 'marriage' through legislation. Neither of the federal provisions have any actual legal effect, and there is general consensus that neither the Quebec nor the Alberta provincial provisions have any effect either, because provinces do not have the legislative competence to define capacity to marry.

Well after the Charter challenges to the queer marriage bar discussed in Chapter Five had been filed, the federal government took two steps that were designed to make it look as if federal law had always defined marriage in strictly heterosexual terms. When Parliament was enacting the Modernization of Benefits and Obligations Act to extend spousal benefits to same-sex cohabitants, it added section 1.1, which states: 'the amendments made by this Act do not affect the meaning of the word "marriage," that is, the lawful union of one man and one woman to the exclusion of all others.' It was openly recognized from the outset that this provision was not drafted in a form that could amount to a binding statutory definition of marriage.

The second reference to 'man-woman' marriage in federal legislation appears in section 5 of the Federal Law-Civil Code Harmonization Act. This provision was also developed and passed after same-sex marriage cases had been filed in 2000 in Ontario, B.C. and Quebec. Section 5 purports to 'harmonize' the new man-woman definition of marriage in the 1994 Quebec Civil Code with federal law. The problem with this supposed harmonization was that there was no man-woman definition of marriage in federal law with which the Civil Code definition could be 'harmonized.' Since the Supreme Court of Canada had already held that harmonization legislation like this was merely interpretive and not binding, this federal statute also had no actual legal effect.

The 1994 insertion of a reference to 'a man and a woman' into the Quebec Civil Code is similar to Alberta's definition of marriage as being between a man and a woman. Under the British North America Act, 1867, the basic document of the Canadian constitution, the federal government has constitutional authority over marriage and divorce, and the provinces can only regulate solemnization of marriage. Thus, the Quebec and Alberta definitions violate the constitutional division of powers between the federal and provincial governments, and thus do not have the effect they claim to have.

When compared with the U.S.-style of 'defence of marriage' acts, it is clear that Canada has generally approached the entire issue quite obliquely, and certainly not with the political will exhibited in the U.S. statutes and constitutional amendments.

United States: 'Defence of marriage' Laws

The strategy of enacting legislation or even constitutional bars to same-sex marriage has so far been largely limited to the U.S. The U.S. has essentially adapted the old unconstitutional anti-miscegenation laws to prohibit same-sex marriage. These prohibitions on same-sex marriage are much more aggressive than milder 'man-woman' references to marriage.

Legislation that expressly prohibits same-sex marriage originated in the U.S. in reaction to the news of the first queer marriages. When news that a gay couple had received a marriage licence in Phoenix in 1975 reached the Arizona state government, the government immediately asked the legislature to pass 'emergency' legislation to ensure that the courts would have to define marriage in 'man-woman' terms. Arizona later joined the dozens of states that now prohibit same-sex marriage in much the same terms as interracial marriages had been prohibited before the U.S. Supreme Court ruling in *Loving* v. *Virginia*: 'Marriage between persons of the same sex is prohibited [and void] even if contracted in a jurisdiction in which they are valid.'[27]

These 'defence of marriage acts,' referred to as DoMAs, were designed to 'solve' the problem of sex-neutral marriage statutes in the same way that Virginia had prohibited interracial marriages: 'All marriages between a white person and a colored person shall be absolutely void without any decree of divorce or other legal process.'[28]

As had happened with the anti-miscegenation statutes earlier in the century, other states quickly adopted the language of the Arizona legislation. This process accelerated sharply after 1993, when the Hawaii courts finally broke through the barriers posed by older judicial rulings in the U.S. and held that it was unconstitutional to prohibit same-sex couples from marrying.

These DoMA statutes have now been enacted by the federal government and a total of thirty-seven states. Many of these states have gone further by embedding their DoMAs in their state constitutions. Constitutionally-embedded DoMAs are thought to be out of the reach of ordinary courts and legislatures—only subsequent constitutional amendment can remove a constitutional DoMA. These statutes range from simple statements like that enacted in Arizona to long and detailed bills like that adopted in Washington, which outlines the legislature's intent to prohibit same-sex marriage, to adopt the federal DoMA, and to preclude recognition of same-sex marriages even if validly performed or recognized elsewhere.

With the opening of same-sex marriage in Massachusetts as of May 2004 and the marriage of thousands of same-sex couples in San Francisco, New York, New Mexico and Oregon beginning in early 2004, many state legislatures are taking another look at whether they should strengthen their prohibitions on same-sex marriage. Other states are looking at new legislation or at backing their DoMAs up with constitutional amendments. There are some indications that new legislation will be even more wide-sweeping than existing DoMAs. For example, Ohio, which has until now refused to enact prohibitions on same-sex marriages, is rushing through a bill that would not only prohibit same-sex marriage and withhold recognition from same-sex marriages validly performed elsewhere, but would also ban civil unions (such as those permitted under Vermont and Quebec law) and domestic partnerships (such as those permitted under various municipal laws in the U.S. and in Nova Scotia) that extend medical insurance and other legal benefits of marriage to same-sex couples. At least a half-dozen other states are considering adding bans on same-sex marriage to their constitutions.

Segregated Legal Structures (RDPs and Civil Unions)

Another unique political and legal strategy for barring queer couples from marrying was devised by several European countries, which developed segregated 'non-marriage' legal structures that would give lesbian and gay couples some legal status at the same time that they continued to prohibit their same-sex marriages. First crafted in Denmark and Sweden under the general name of 'registered domestic partnerships' (RDPs), these structures were enacted as early as 1989 in Denmark. The French version, which was enacted in 1999, is called the 'pacte civil de solidarité' (PaCS).

Segregated legal structures have also been used in the U.S. and Canada to attempt to reinforce the barriers to same-sex marriage. Unlike the European countries that have enacted RDPs and civil unions, however, North American governments have invariably enacted them at the eleventh hour when faced with court rulings declaring the marriage bar or the denial of spousal treatment to be unconstitutional.

Same-Sex Marriage

The spread of RDP and civil union statutes in North America offers an excellent map of political reaction to the demand for same-sex marriage. The more immediate the perceived threat that a state court might remove the 'heterosexuals-only' limits on marriage, the more willing politicians in that state become to consider extending various elements of spousal treatment to queer couples. However, it is important to emphasize that despite the rhetoric of equality and acceptance surrounding the enactment of these segregated legal structures, not one RDP or civil union statute anywhere in the world actually extends the full array of rights and obligations associated with marriage to same-sex couples. RDPs and civil union statutes are all discriminatory in both form and substance.

Denmark

The notion of limited 'registered partnerships' was conceived in Denmark shortly after queer activists began to seek access to civil marriage in 1968. Registered partnerships emerged conceptually as it became clear that civil marriage was not an option. Although contemporary commentators make it seem as if the development of RDPs was a huge step forward greeted with celebration by lesbians and gays across Denmark, this is not an accurate picture.

It is much more accurate to say that the concept of RDPs emerged as the government grudgingly accepted that it faced far too much opposition to leaving lesbian and gay couples without any form of legal recognition at all. Activists saw the RDP proposal for what it was: a second-class status segregated from civil marriage designed to make it look like the government had done all that needed to be done for queer couples.

As Dr. Forder has recounted, Poul Dam's 1968 proposal that the rules on domestic relationships be applied to lesbian and gay couples was referred to the Government Law Reform Committee on Marriage Laws. In its 1973 report, this Committee recommended against opening marriage to lesbian and gay couples, and that appeared to be the end of the matter. In 1980, the same Committee recommended that some housing provisions be extended to lesbian and gay couples, but that recommendation did not go anywhere. During all this time, activists continued to lobby for the right to marry.

In 1984, the Danish government established a Commission on the Situation of Homosexuals to be chaired by Poul Dam. The government became interested in a segregated 'alternative' to marriage for queer couples, and requested that the Commission on the Situation of Homosexuals consider this approach. Activists attempted to block this process, and proposed that the only legislation that urgently needed to be enacted related to inheritance rights of same-sex couples. These changes were made in 1986, but they were not made in the form of RDP legislation.[29]

Activists opposed the RDP proposal that was finally considered by the Commission. This opposition was partly successful, because the majority of the Commission actually opposed registered domestic partnerships in its final report. However, the government pushed the legislation through over this opposition.

The Danish RDP came into effect in 1989. While RDPs enacted subsequently by other European countries all differ in various respects, the pattern was set in the Danish legislation. RDPs are segregated legal structures that confer many, but not all, of the incidents of marriage on registered partners. The Danish RDP is exclusively for same-sex couples, and civil and religious marriage are exclusively for heterosexuals. Denmark has no cohabitation regimes like those developed in Canada or Sweden.

The incidents of marriage extended to couples by the Danish RDP legislation include: the obligation of partners to support each other; community-property rules; insurance rules; the right to the home; social security benefits; pensions; tax treatment; and rules relating to dissolution of the relationship. The differences between RDPs and marriage are, however, numerous and significant:

- an RDP is not considered to be a form of marriage;
- registration can only be performed by public authorities, therefore, couples cannot be registered in a religious ceremony;
- at most, individual priests can decide for themselves whether they will unofficially bless RDPs, but there are no authorized religious ceremonies for this blessing;
- RDPs are executed in separate government offices where no marriages are processed;
- because RDPs are purely civil relationships, registered couples have no claim to mediation performed by the clergy;
- only citizens and residents of Denmark can register their relationship;
- RDPs are available only to same-sex couples and are not to heterosexuals;
- queer couples were not permitted to adopt jointly, but had to use step-parent adoption procedures (this has now been changed);
- lesbian couples were prohibited from using reproductive technologies to have children.

Activists in Denmark have continued to push for changes on all of these points, but change has been slow in coming. Since 1999, it has been legally possible for a child to have two mothers or two fathers, and step-parent adoptions by such couples have become more acceptable. Further changes are being sought.

Other European Countries

During the 1990s, several other European countries enacted RDPs along the same lines as the Danish RDP includeding Norway (1993); Sweden (1995); Greenland and Iceland (1996); the Netherlands, Belgium and Spain (1998); and France (PaCS, 1999). Although each of these RDPs have their own unique features, and while some are more comprehensive than others, none of them offer all the incidents of marriage to registrants, and none of them have the kind of automatic recognition, filiation provisions or recognition associated with marriage.[30]

As outlined in Chapter Three, it was the discriminatory nature of RDPs that finally led the Netherlands to extend marriage to same-sex couples—in the name of equality.

United States

Unlike Canada and European countries, the U.S. has been extremely reluctant to recognize any kind of non-marital status even for heterosexuals, let alone for same-sex couples. In recent years, some states have started to move in that policy direction for heterosexuals on limited issues, but that movement is minute when compared with the sweeping 'opposite-sex cohabitant' movement that began in 1974 in Canada.

As is outlined in Chapter Four, however, as soon as the appellate courts in Hawaii, Vermont and Massachusetts ruled that denial of the right to marry violated the constitutional rights of same-sex couples, the legislatures in those states moved with amazing speed to enact various kinds of 'alternative' statutory structures for queers. This was done for the same reason that RDPs were initially devised in Denmark: to give enough of an appearance of caring for the legal needs of same-sex couples and their families to prevent the courts from ordering that same-sex couples be permitted to marry.

Thus, there are a few isolated statutory alternatives in the U.S. Hawaii replaced its RDP bill with a watered-down 'reciprocal beneficiaries election' after a new constitutional amendment blocked the threat of queer marriage. This election provides but few useful benefits, and there are few registered elections. The Vermont civil union bill gives those who are civilly united most, but not all, of the features of marriage. And fortunately, as outlined in Chapter Four, the Massachusetts appellate court ruled that if the state government were to enact Vermont-style civil union legislation, it would still order that same-sex couples be permitted to marry as of May 2004. The only other RDPs in existence in the U.S. are mainly at the municipal level; full-scale RDPs appear to be enacted only to stave off queer marriage.

Canada

Two statutory regimes have been enacted in Canada: Nova Scotia has enacted an RDP statute, and Quebec has provided for the status of 'civil union' in the Quebec Civil Code. Both of these statutes were adopted in the wake of the Supreme Court of Canada decision in *M. v. H.*, which held that limiting spousal benefits to opposite-sex cohabitants only violates section 15 of the Charter.

Neither the Nova Scotia nor the Quebec bills give all the rights and obligations of married couples to same-sex couples. The Quebec bill was enacted right as the trial in the Quebec marriage challenge was starting, resulting in additional hearings to determine whether it in any way affected the Quebec couple's suit for marriage. The court held that it did not precisely because civil union was not marriage.

With the exception of the Nova Scotia RDP, which provides for some marital-like inheritance rights, the growing numbers of same-sex cohabitant provisions that have been enacted in response to the Supreme Court of Canada's decision in *M. v. H.* are all extensions of the benefits already given to opposite-sex cohabitants. They are frankly not conceived as alternatives to marriage at all. They simply confirm that the 'opposite-sex' limits on those benefits have now been removed.

Conclusion

This amazing array of statutory and constitutional bars to same-sex marriage demonstrates perhaps better than any poll ever could, just how deeply homophobic attitudes have invaded the legal imagination. It is obvious that legislators in Canada, Europe and the U.S. have found it far more palatable to devote substantial 'law reform' efforts to the creation and enactment of RDPs, 'opposite-sex' limits on cohabitant benefits, civil unions, statutory and constitutional bans on same-sex marriage, and complex beneficiary elections than to simply face the necessity of permitting same-sex couples to marry.

Fortunately there are courts in all these countries. As will be seen in the next three chapters, if it were not for the courts—and if it were not for equality guarantees in the constitutions of many of the U.S. states, Canada and the Netherlands—same-sex couples would still be at the mercy of the prejudices of elected politicians.

CHAPTER THREE

European Breakthrough: The Netherlands and Belgium

From a North American perspective, the Netherlands seems an unlikely place for civil marriage to have been formally extended through legislation to lesbian, gay and bisexual couples. As a civil code country, the Netherlands is governed largely by its Parliament. Thus, courts play more of an advisory role than in North America. They generally see themselves as offering advisory opinions to the government in human rights cases instead of striking down laws they find to be discriminatory, as is done under the U.S. Bill of Rights or the Canadian Charter of Rights and Freedoms.[31]

The Netherlands certainly has a history of social tolerance and even activism. Homosexuality was decriminalized in 1811 under French rule when the Napoleonic Code applied geographically to the Netherlands and Belgium. After the French withdrew, the Dutch government never recriminalized same-sex sex. When the Dutch government began to enact legislation to extend some selected marital rights to unmarried cohabitants in the 1980s, the legislation was expressed in gender-neutral terms that were never construed as excluding lesbian and gay cohabitants.

When the Netherlands did enter into the process of enacting legislation to recognize lesbian and gay couples, which it did late compared with other countries, the legal context was largely neutral and was even becoming increasingly inclusive of queer couples. This neutrality was reinforced by the adoption of strong constitutional prohibitions on discrimination in 1983, the basket clause of which was understood to prohibit discrimination on the basis of sexual orientation. Like section 15 of the Canadian Charter of

Rights and Freedoms, the new Dutch provision prohibits discrimination on grounds such as sex and race as well as 'on any other ground whatever.'

Before any legislative steps to recognize same-sex relationships were even contemplated in the Netherlands, same-sex couples had already turned to the courts to seek the right to marry. Indeed, the first queer case to reach the Dutch Supreme Court was a marriage case. The seriousness with which that Court considered the marriage issue helped open the issue to widespread public and political debate at the same time that the question of legislative recognition of same-sex couples began. Because the Dutch Supreme Court case was surprisingly favourable to same-sex marriage, the issue of marriage was given serious consideration at the same time that RDPs were considered. This had a profound impact on both the purpose and the effect of the new RDP law. Instead of being designed to block demands for same-sex marriage, the Dutch RDP bill was seen as part of the larger legislative process of removing discriminatory barriers to same-sex couples in family law. Thus, the marriage bill and the RDP bill were developed more or less at the same time, and the marriage bill was introduced just one year after the new RDP law was enacted.

As a result of this sequence of events, the Netherlands opened marriage to queer couples on April 1, 2001. A few days later, Belgium, which had enacted limited 'statutory cohabitation' legislation in 1998 at about the same time the Dutch RDP law had come into effect, announced that it would extend marriage to queer couples as well. The new Belgian marriage law came into effect in June of 2003.

The Dutch Marriage Cases

Two 1990 marriage cases put the issue of same-sex marriage squarely on the political agenda. Neither case resulted in a judicial order that lesbian and gay couples be permitted to marry. However, both cases *did* open up public and political debate in terms that ultimately resulted in legislation to permit same-sex couples to marry.

Interpreting Neutral Marriage Law

These two cases began in exactly the same way the U.S. and Canadian cases had begun: by asking the courts to rule that as in other Dutch laws, the absence of sex-specific language in the marriage law meant that same-sex couples could marry. On this issue the two courts reached much the same conclusion as had the North American courts. They found that there was an implicit presumption in marriage law: that it applied only to heterosexual couples.

There was one notable difference between these two cases and their U.S. and Canadian counterparts: despite the fact that North American courts had been citing religious doctrine and even passages from the Christian Bible for the last twenty years when ruling that same-sex marriage was prohibited, the Dutch courts took a more moderate cultural approach to the issue.

Even though the Dutch government had been treating same-sex couples as being included in new gender-neutral laws extending some of the benefits of marriage to unmarried cohabitants for the past ten years, and despite the widespread assumption that the new 1983 constitutional anti-discrimination provision prohibited discrimination on the basis of sexual orientation, both courts concluded that the history of marriage was relevant to the interpretation of that word in the civil code. Thus, the neutral marriage law was not extended to lesbian and gay couples.

In the first case, *Boele-Woelki and Tange*,[32] the Amsterdam District Court held in February 1990, that at the time the marriage law had first been enacted, only opposite-sex couples could marry. Thus, the court held that even though there was no express prohibition on same-sex marriage in the words used in the law, the legislators who enacted the law must have intended to limit marriage to couples of the opposite sex.

In the second case, *EAAL and EAA*,[33] the Dutch Supreme Court reached the same conclusion in October 1990. The Supreme Court agreed that because of the historical tradition of heterosexual-only marriage, it could not read the neutral marriage law as literally permitting same-sex couples to marry. The Supreme Court went further than had the District Court, however, and also stated that if changing social conditions were relevant to the couple's right to marry, such a change should come from the government. The Court confirmed that it could only render an advisory opinion on such a point.

This second point did not have the negative impact similar judicial statements had been having in the U.S. and Canada because of important fundamental differences in the nature of the legal systems in the Netherlands and North America. The Netherlands legal system is classified as a 'civilian legal system' because it is based on a civil code, a detailed statement of the law the format of which is attributed back to the Roman Justinian Code. Judges in civil code countries cannot adapt the law as it is written in the civil code to changing social conditions. Instead, they are expected to simply apply the law as they find it and to leave major adaptations or refinement of issues to the government. Civilian judges can make recommendations to the government as to points that might need to be changed, but they cannot make those changes themselves.

In most of the U.S. and Canada, the legal systems are classified as 'common law legal systems' based on the common law system imported from England during the colonial period. (Quebec and Louisiana are largely civil code systems.) The common law legal system is based heavily on judicial interpretation and application of laws on a case-by-case basis. Under the common law, judges have the power to adapt both common law rules (judge-made rules) and the interpretation of unclear statutory provisions to changing social conditions. Legislatures can change the law by amending or adopting statutes, but judges have pervasive powers that enable them to adapt the law even if the legislature will not and has not acted. This is a power totally unlike that of civilian judges.

Thus, the Dutch Supreme Court's suggestion that only the government could bring the marriage law into line with changing social conditions was not a cop-out, but a serious statement of how change on this point ought to proceed. Particularly when coupled with the Dutch Supreme Court's ruling on the human rights issues raised in these cases, Dr. Forder has reported that this decision sent an important message to the government.

Application of Human Rights Provisions

The second issue raised in each of the two Dutch marriage cases was whether denying these couples marriage licences infringed rights guaranteed to them by the European Convention on Human Rights and the International Covenant on Civil and Political Rights. The same-sex couples who brought these cases relied on Articles 8, 12 and 14 of the European Convention and on Articles 23 and 26 of the International Covenant, which guarantee the freedom to marry and have a family, and prohibit discrimination. The couples were able to base their marriage claims on these provisions of international law because the Dutch Constitution makes all of the Netherlands' international obligations binding at the domestic level (Articles 93 and 94 of the Dutch Constitution). In the Dutch Supreme Court case, the couple also claimed that the Dutch constitutional prohibition on discrimination 'on any ground' guaranteed that they could marry.

Both courts refused to accept these arguments. Again, however, these rulings have to be read in the context of the fundamental differences between courts in civil code systems and courts in common law systems. Both courts emphasized that it was up to the government to act on the issue of marriage rights.

In many regards, the Dutch Supreme Court's decision on the human rights issues also tracked what the U.S. and Canadian courts had been saying for the last fifteen years. The Dutch Supreme Court consulted the case law of the European Court of Human Rights as it stood in 1990, and found that it had refused to apply anything except a 'traditional concept of marriage' in its cases. It then reasoned that the International Covenant family provisions must also be referring to 'traditional marriage involving persons of opposite sexes' and that the anti-discrimination provisions of both treaties had to be understood as assuming this traditional concept of marriage.

Like the early Canadian decisions, the European decisions that the Court relied on had involved transgendered individuals who sought to marry. As in Canada, these gender identity cases were treated as deciding the issue of same-sex marriage for lesbian and gay couples as well as for transgender and transsexual persons. Indeed, the language with which the Court disposed of this issue sounds like the cultural reasoning used in the U.S. constitutional cases of that era:

> 'Civil marriage is since time immemorial understood to be an enduring bond between a man and a woman to which a number of legal conse-quences are attached, which partly relate to the difference in sex and the consequences connected therewith for the descent of children. Marriage has these characteristics not only in the Netherlands but in many countries. Moreover, it cannot be said that the general opinion in the legal community has developed such that the considerations just mentioned do not justify the distinction in treatment on the grounds of sexual orientation, which can manifest itself in the impos-sibility to enter a relationship-like marriage with a person of the same sex as oneself.'[34]

While the Dutch Supreme Court did not follow the U.S. and Canadian judicial decisions that had been quoting religious doctrine ever since the early 1970s, it did express exactly the same universalized presumption of heterosexuality set out in those cases. The Court reasoned that it flew in the face of biological reality to think that the presumption of parentage flowing from the legal status of marriage could be applied to two lesbian women, because two women cannot physically procreate with each other.

According to Dr. Caroline Forder and Nancy Maxwell, Professor at Washburn University School of Law and co-director of the Molengraaff Institute of Private Law, the Netherlands, the real significance of the Dutch Supreme Court decision is that the Court went on, after delivering these fairly conservative reasons, to state that it nonetheless recognized the 'possibility' it might not be justifiable to deny other benefits of marriage to same-sex couples. Thus, the Court implied that it may be discriminatory to deny these other benefits to same-gender couples. The Court added that this particular question had not been raised directly in that case, and again reiterated—because of the more limited role of the courts in the Netherlands—that a 'question of this kind…could only be addressed by the legislature.'[35]

Both Forder and Maxwell agree that this last point sent a strong 'signal' to the government, and within two weeks of the decision a government committee began considering the legal status of lesbian and gay relationships. Also within a short period of time, over 130 local authorities began to offer to register lesbian and gay couples in semi-official registries. The resulting lesbian and gay registry movement gave the issue of same-sex marriage an even higher public and political profile, and helped attract growing support for the legal recognition of same-sex relationships.

The Dutch Marriage Law

As the Dutch government began to consider the issue of the legal status of lesbian and gay relationships, it became clear that public opinion was in advance of political will—at least until the conservative government was replaced with a more progressive government in 1994. Thus RDP legislation moved along a somewhat faster track than did same-sex marriage legislation.

Segregated RDPs Unacceptable

Within two weeks of the Dutch Supreme Court decision in the *EAAL and EAA* case in October 1990, the government formed the Advisory Commission for Legislation (also known as the first Kortmann Commission) to investigate and report on what law reform might be needed to address the needs of diverse family forms.

In its December 1991 report the Commission recommended the development of a registration system which the Commission indicated should be available to all couples who were not legally permitted to marry. As initially envisioned, this group would have included lesbian and gay couples as well as close family members such as brother and sister, or parent and child—groups never before contemplated within the scope of marriage laws. At this point, the bill was called the Registration of Cohabitation Bill.

A more progressive government was elected in 1995. The new government issued a policy memorandum entitled *Changing Family Forms* in which it recommended that registration should be available to *all* couples, not just to same-sex couples and close relatives. The reference to relatives was removed, and the bill was opened up to all conjugal couples. As Dr. Forder has observed, the reason for opening the RDP bill to all couples was to make it clear that RDPs were not being established as a 'ghetto institution.'

RDPs Not a Substitute for Marriage

Extending RDPs to heterosexuals did not satisfy the demands of lesbian and gay couples, who still wanted to be able to marry. From the perspective of lesbian and gay couples, extending RDPs to heterosexuals would give that privileged group a *third* relationship status to choose from—marriage, RDPs or cohabitation—while doing nothing to remedy the discrimination still faced by queer couples. As Dr. Forder has recounted, in a 1999 study, over 80% of lesbian and gay couples wanted to be able to marry, and were not satisfied with being restricted to choosing RDPs.

Nancy Maxwell has reported that the general population did not support such segregation either. A public opinion poll carried out in 1995 demonstrated that 73% of respondents thought that lesbian and gay couples should be permitted to marry, and civil marriage was rated much higher than limiting lesbian and gay couples to parallel partnership registration laws.[36]

As a result of strong public support, and while the RDP bill was still pending in the spring of 1996, the Dutch Parliament passed a motion requesting the government to investigate the extension of civil marriage to same-sex couples. The express reason given for this motion was that limiting lesbian and gay couples to RDPs alone violated the principle of equality. The motion passed, and the government created a new commission to investigate the extension of marriage to same-sex couples.

The RDP bill was eventually passed in 1997, before the report on marriage could be released. During the legislative process, the legal rights of registered partners were expanded considerably. However, important differences between marriage and RDPs still existed:

- the law only applied to citizens or residents of the Netherlands;
- partners could terminate their RDP without going to court;
- RDPs did not give registered partners any legal relationship with their partner's children;
- RDPs did not give registered partners joint custody of their partner's children;
- RDPs did not give registered partners the legal right to adopt their partners' children:
- immigration sponsorship was still denied;
- and, differences in pension rights still existed.

Further legislation introduced in 1998 ameliorated some of these differences, but did not eliminate them completely.

In the end, the Dutch RDP legislation bore out the fears of lesbians and gays. Despite the fact that heterosexual couples could elect to enter into RDPs, lesbian and gay couples were still segregated from heterosexual couples in 'separate and not even equal' institutions.

The Marriage Bill

The second advisory commission was established in 1996. (Also known as the second Kortmann Commission.) The Commission was charged with investigating the legislative options for extending marriage to lesbian and gay couples and for assessing the likely impact of such a change. It is interesting to note that the chair of the Commission was a Professor of Law at the Catholic University of Nijmegen (the Catholic Church being one of the most outspoken opponents of same-sex marriage from the outset).

The second Kortmann Commission released its report on marriage in October 1997. This report recommended that lesbian and gay couples be permitted to marry. The majority based their recommendation on the principle in *Brown* v. *Board of Education* (the famous U.S. Supreme Court decision banning segregated schools) that separate treatment is not equal treatment.

However, there was a minority report opposing same-sex marriage. The minority was of the view that despite the differences between the incidents of RDPs and the legal consequences of marriage, RDPs were sufficient for queer couples. The minority appeared to be motivated primarily by the perception that same-sex couples do not reproduce in the same way as heterosexual couples, but also noted concern that such marriages might not be recognized in international private law.

Nonetheless, both the majority and minority of the Commission agreed that the existing provisions relating to the parent-child relationship should be improved so that both members of lesbian and gay couples could become the legal parents and legal custodians of their children. Thus, the Commission recommended that joint adoption by lesbian and gay couples should be permitted, that registered partners would be considered to have joint custody of their children, and that obligations of parents with joint custody be extended.

Unfortunately, the government of the day was not prepared to put the majority report into effect. Thus, the marriage recommendations languished until another change in government in 1998.

Following the 1998 election, the new government announced that it would extend marriage to lesbian and gay couples. The new government explicitly acknowledged the importance of eliminating marriage discrimination and ensuring that lesbian and gay couples are given public recognition as being as worthy of state recognition as heterosexual couples. The government rejected the contention that limiting lesbian and gay couples to RDPs would be considered to extend them equal treatment.

The new marriage law proposed for enactment did make one distinction between heterosexual and lesbian and gay couples. Reflecting the preoccupation with lesbian procreation that so concerned the Dutch Supreme Court in its 1990 decision in the *EAAL and EAA* case, the government accepted the Kortmann Commission's recommendation that the presumption of paternity based on marriage not be extended to same-sex couples. Ignoring the obvious fact that this presumption is itself a legal fiction designed to replace biological reality with social relations, the second Kortmann Commission had declared:

'It would be pushing things too far to assume that a child born in a marriage of two women would legally descend from both women. That would be stretching reality. The distance between reality and law would become too great. Therefore this bill does not adjust chapter 11 of Book 1 of the Civil Code, which bases the law of descent on a manwoman relationship.'[37]

The Commission felt that the parent-child relationship would be adequately protected by extending joint custody to married queers, permitting second-parent adoption, and attaching the right of inheritance to joint authority. Not all of these changes have been implemented, and in this regard, the Dutch marriage laws lag far behind Canadian (British Columbia) and U.S. parent-child decisions that have extended the presumption of parentage to the lesbian partner of the birth mother. However, this one point of distinction did not perturb the Dutch Parliament.

The Dutch marriage bill finally came under parliamentary debate in 2000. It passed in the first stage of the parliamentary process by a margin of 109 to 33 in a free vote. It passed the second stage on December 19, 2000, was signed into law on December 21, 2000, and came into effect on April 1, 2001.

The Dutch marriage bill is simple in the extreme, amending Article 30, Book 1 of the Civil Code to define marriage as follows:

1. A marriage can be contracted by two persons of different sex or of the same sex.
2. The law only considers marriage in its civil relations.

The first lesbian and gay marriages under this new law were performed right after the stroke of midnight in the first few moments of April 1, 2001. Nearly four hundred marriages of lesbian and gay couples were registered in the first month of the new law.

Religious Objectors

During parliamentary debates over same-sex marriage and during its implementation, Dr. Forder reports that several issues surrounding religious objectors have emerged. To date, the Dutch government has indicated that churches can still refuse to bless or celebrate same-sex marriages, and that testators can make distinctions between same-sex and opposite-sex spouses.

More contentious has been the question of whether individual civil status registrars should be permitted to refuse to register marriages of same-sex couples, or whether heterosexual couples would be entitled to demand that some registrars register opposite-sex marriages only. The government initially took the position that civil employees had to do their jobs, but there has been confusion about what the position is. One member of the government appeared to agree that the government would make amendments to permit such religious exemptions; another stated that exemptions would not be available, but that local offices should make sure that they had enough staff to service all needs if a registrar were not available.

In the one reported case of religious objection on the part of a local registrar, the matter went to a court for decision. In that case, the District Court ruled that dismissal of the registrar was unjust. The Court reinstated her contract and awarded her damages. The decision remains somewhat in question as the policy is still not firmly established. No cases have arisen out of the demand for 'untainted' religious-objecting registrars who marry only heterosexual couples, but Dr. Forder does not expect this to produce any change in policy.

Some religious organizations have developed rituals for same-sex weddings, but these remain optional with the individual church within the subscribing denominations, and cannot be demanded as a matter of legal right.

Belgium

Shortly after the Netherlands proposed its legislation to extend marriage to same-sex couples, Belgium announced that it would do the same. In 2003, the second house of the Belgian Parliament passed the new marriage bill by 91 to 22 votes, and it came into effect in June 2003.

Reflecting many of the same biases that have surrounded the Netherlands' marriage legislation, the Belgian marriage law did nothing to deal with the fact that same-sex couples did not have the right to adopt children, and it also limited its application to residents of Belgium and the Netherlands. Unlike the Netherlands, however, extending marriage to same-sex couples was a huge leap forward for queers in Belgium. Before gaining the right to marry, they had limited relationship rights under a 1998 statutory cohabitation law that extended only a small number of legal benefits to both same-sex and opposite-sex cohabiting couples.[38]

CHAPTER FOUR

Changing Social Realities: From Hawaii to Massachusetts and Beyond

As the 1970s and 1980s passed, lesbian and gay couples in the U.S. continued to apply to courts to enforce their fundamental constitutional rights to equality, liberty, due process and freedom of association. These constitutional challenges were invariably defeated as the courts persisted in applying both religious doctrine and secular variants of the 'procreative purpose' of marriage claimed by government lawyers.

During the 1970s and 1980s, however, the realities of queer existence were undergoing massive changes in the U.S. Decriminalization of queer existence had begun in 1961 in the U.S. After the Stonewall Rebellions, and Alfred Kinsey's meticulously-researched books on queer sexual behaviour received heightened attention, queers all across the country began to organize, to come out, and, while their legal rights remained on hold in most places, to become more open about their relationships.

As the realities of queer existence underwent these dramatic changes, perhaps one of the biggest changes occurred in relationship expectations. By the end of the 1970s, large numbers of lesbian women and gay men had begun to form families as part of living their lives openly. Queers created diverse family forms. Many queers became more involved in the lives of their children from heterosexual marriages, became co-parents with their partners, formed families assisted by medical reproductive technologies, informal sperm donation and reproductive agreements, fostered and/or adopted children.

These developments were not limited to the U.S. Lesbians in Melbourne, Australia, had access to artificial insemination in the mid-1970s; sympathetic doctors in Canada, the U.K. and various European countries were giving lesbian women increasing access to a range of reproductive technologies. Everywhere queers had begun to contest the claim often hurled at them in custody litigation that as homosexuals they were 'unfit' to have custody or even to have visitation with their own children.

In the U.S. in the early 1990s, these changing social realities became the new focus of queer marriage litigation. The courts were provided with detailed personal information on the client couples, their families, and their reasons for wanting to be able to marry. This information was backed up with expert evidence from leading academic researchers who had been studying queer families from sociological, psychological, economic and statistical perspectives. Exhaustive lists of the many legal and economic benefits that were given only to couples who marry were also produced, enabling courts to appreciate the magnitude of the injustice being done.

With this shift in emphasis, U.S. litigators managed to focus judges' attention onto the functional realities of marriage, cohabitation and raising families, and to de-emphasize the abstract intellectual issue of 'biological procreation.' This 'social realities analysis' displaced traditional religious and biological reasoning relied upon in earlier marriage cases, and enabled courts to conclude that unless the state could produce some compelling justification for continuing to discriminate against queer couples, they ought to be permitted to marry.

For nearly a decade after beginning the 'social realities' wave of marriage litigation, it looked as if historic ruling after historic ruling would continue to fall short of opening marriage to queer couples. As soon as politicians began to grasp the implications of the 1993 rulings in the *Baehr* cases in Hawaii, intense political backlash resulted in the swift enactment of state statutes and even constitutional amendments designed to deprive the courts of the power to actually order the issue of marriage licences. The Hawaii government used all of those strategies to prohibit same-sex marriage shortly after the Hawaii courts ruled that queers could not be constitutionally prohibited from marrying. Even today, queer couples in Hawaii have only a few relationship rights.

This pattern has surrounded all the subsequent marriage cases in the U.S. In 1998, the state of Alaska amended its state constitution to block the favourable *Brause* decision. In 1999, the state of Vermont enacted a civil union statute in order to convince the *Baker* litigants to settle for this 'alternative to marriage' rather than press the court for an order that the state issue them marriage licences. And even after the Massachusetts Supreme Court made it abundantly clear in the November 18, 2003 *Goodridge* ruling in which the court ordered that same-sex couples be permitted to marry beginning mid-May 2004, the Massachusetts legislature immediately petitioned that court to consider whether a new segregated civil union would satisfy the ruling. (Hillary and Julie Goodridge are interviewed in Part II.)

Fortunately, the *Goodridge* decision was framed around such a strong constitutional analysis of discrimination that when the Massachusetts Supreme Court released its opinion on the proposed civil union bill on February 4, 2004, it flatly rejected this proposed resolution of the issues. Thus, that court cleared the way for lesbian and gay couples to marry in Massachusetts as of May 17, 2004. While efforts to amend the state constitution will probably continue for several years, this was a key ruling.

The *Goodridge* decisions also had a completely unexpected effect. One week after the February 4, 2004 *Goodridge* decision was issued, the Mayor of San Francisco concluded that prohibiting same-sex marriage violates the California constitution. Within weeks, thousands of couples were married in San Francisco under the auspices of this directive. County and city officials in Albuquerque, New Mexico, New Paltz and Nyack, New York, Asbury Park, New Jersey, and Portland, Oregon, quickly followed suit by performing marriages there, with more discussions underway at the local level all across the country. The San Francisco marriages numbered in the thousands within a week. Although very controversial, the 'marry now, litigate later' approach has shifted the issue. In the past, the question has been framed as 'why should they marry?' Since the San Francisco, Portland and New York marriages have taken place, the starting point of the discussion has now become 'what is the harm of queer marriage?' and 'denying same-sex couples marriage licences is unconstitutional.' At the same time, the flood of media images of ordinary queer couples celebrating their marriages have helped emphasize the ordinariness of the longing for queer marriage. Although courts have now put all of these new practices on hold—except in Oregon—couples are actively planning weddings to take place when the door is opened again.

This chapter outlines how the paradigm shift that unfolded in the Netherlands and Belgium has shaped legal events in the U.S. As in the Netherlands and Belgium, decision-makers have gradually been given less and less scope for demanding that marriage be presumptively restricted to heterosexuals. At the same time, presenting the full picture of queer existences—and the nature of queer families—has enabled decision-makers to come to see queer couples as just one of many diverse family forms.

Hawaii: The *Baehr* Rulings

In 1991, Joseph Melillo and Pat Lagon, Genora Dancel and Ninia Baehr, and Tammy Rodrigues and Antoinette Pregil filed suit against the state of Hawaii after they had been denied marriage licences. They pleaded that the state had violated their rights under the Hawaii state constitution, including their rights to privacy, due process and sex equality.

Pretrial Rulings

The case got off to an unpromising start. The trial court basically dismissed the case before there could even be a trial. The state made a motion to dismiss the case on the basis that it lacked any real legal merit. The state argued that queers did not have any legally recognized constitutional right to marry, and that the state had good reason for prohibiting them from marrying. The trial court agreed and dismissed the case.

The couples appealed this dismissal to the Hawaii Supreme Court. The appellate court turned the case around and sent it back to the trial court, ordering the trial court to hold the trial.[39]

This Supreme Court decision completely broke with all the earlier cases on same-sex marriage. The state had argued before the Supreme Court that there was no legal basis for a trial: the state alleged that it is biologically impossible for same-sex couples to marry in the traditional heterosexual understanding of the term, and that queers are legally free to marry a person of the opposite sex. The appellate court rejected both of those contentions, relying—finally—on the U.S. Supreme Court decision in *Loving* v. *Virginia* on both points. The appellate court pointed out that for hundreds of years before the 1967 *Loving* decision, it was fervently believed that persons of different races could not marry, and that the state of Virginia had also tried to argue that both spouses in *Loving* had been legally free to marry persons of their same race.

Against both of those appeals to tradition, the Hawaii Supreme Court pointed to 'changing customs' and 'evolving social order' in contemporary society, both of which it declared were entirely relevant to deciding whether the constitutional equality rights of same-sex couples were now being violated.

With this resounding decision, the Supreme Court thus sent the *Baehr* case back to the trial court for a proper trial. It directed the trial court to subject the state's reasons for prohibiting same-sex marriage to 'strict scrutiny' and directed that the state had to present 'compelling justification' for this exclusion if it was to win the trial.

The Hawaii Supreme Court's ruling represented a rupture with the older discourse of religious doctrine and traditional heterosexual images of marriage. By forcing the parties to litigate the case within the framework of constitutional equality analysis, the Supreme Court prevented the state from making emotionally based arguments and required it to provide reasons that would be considered sensical in contemporary society. Likewise, by granting a presumptive right to equality to the couples, the Court ensured that the trial court's ruling would have to be based on the evidence and not on prejudices, beliefs and stereotypes.

The Trial

The *Baehr* trial ushered in a new era in queer litigation. Instead of stereotypes, abstract legal concepts, religious doctrine and age-old prejudices, the question of same-sex marriage was to be based on concrete evidence about the purposes and effects of marriage in contemporary society. It became crystal clear that the burden was on the state to justify continuing with this form of discrimination when Judge Kevin Chang, the trial judge, directed that unless the state could demonstrate a compelling state interest in denying lesbian and gay couples the right to marry, this exclusion would have to be found to be unconstitutional.

The state of Hawaii had a difficult time meeting this burden. It claimed that it had to prevent same-sex couples from marrying so that it could promote the optimal development of children; ensure that children would so far as possible be raised in a single home by their parents or at least by a married male and female; ensure that Hawaii marriages would continue to be recognized in other states and countries; and, protect state revenue by making sure that same-sex couples could not claim all the same benefits (such as tax benefits) given to married couples.

The state did not succeed in convincing the court that these claims had any validity. Not only did the state's own expert witnesses end up agreeing with the couples instead of with the state on key issues, but the couples brought expert evidence of their own that the court found far more relevant and credible.

State's witnesses: The trial court dismissed one of the state's experts completely, saying that it did not find him to be a credible witness. The other three state witnesses actually agreed that having same-sex parents does *not* impair a child's gender identity, and two of them agreed that same-sex parents can be excellent parents who raise healthy and well-adjusted children. The state witnesses also agreed with the couples that the benefits given to married couples would be as important for children with same-sex parents as they are for children whose parents are heterosexual, and that the social status of married couples can also benefit their children.

Couples' witnesses: Because the appellate court had placed the burden on the state to justify its position on same-sex marriage, the couples' lawyers did not technically have to call any witnesses at all—particularly since the state's witnesses had ended up agreeing with the couples. However, as has become the practice in same-sex marriage litigation, the couples' lawyers called the best and most respected experts they could find to give evidence in support of their affirmative claims: that same-sex couples are fit parents; that their sexuality does not impair their fitness to raise children; that children with same-sex parents develop just as well as those with heterosexual parents; that biological parenting is not in some way superior to non-biological parenting; and, that permitting lesbian and gay couples to marry would have benefits for their children as well as for the parents.

Judge Chang released his decision in 1996.[40] His findings of fact reflected all of the expert evidence provided by the couples:

'Same-sex couples can, and do, have successful, loving and committed relationships.'

'Lesbian and gay men share the same reasons for seeking to marry as heterosexual couples: emotional closeness; intimacy and monogamy; and to establish a framework for a long-term relationship that has personal significance for them, is recognized by society, and to have or raise children.'

'Lesbian [women] and gay parents and couples have children as foster parents, natural parents, adoptive parents, and through alternative conception. '

'Gay and lesbian parents and same-sex couples have the potential to raise children that are happy, healthy and well-adjusted.'

'Children of gay and lesbian parents and same-sex couples develop in normal fashion. '

'Permitting gay or lesbian parents and same-sex couples to marry may assist their children because children benefit from having parents with a nurturing relationship and from living in a nurturing environment'; 'their children may obtain certain protections and benefits that become available as the result of marriage'; and 'it would help eliminate the stigma that children of gay and lesbian parents face in society.'

On the basis of these findings, Judge Chang rejected the state's claim that same-sex parenting would impair the optimal development of children, and went on to hold that prohibiting the couples from marrying violated the Hawaii state constitution.

The state of Hawaii was not satisfied with Judge Chang's decision and immediately filed an appeal to the Hawaii Supreme Court. As is usual in such situations, Judge Chang refused to order the state to issue marriage certificates to the couples right then and there. Instead, his order was stayed pending the outcome of the state's appeal.

During the three years that the appeal was pending—and beginning even before the trial before Judge Chang had been held—the state had begun to search for legislative and constitutional strategies to block same-sex marriage from ever coming into effect in Hawaii. In 1995, the state established a Commission on Sexual Orientation and the Law which eventually recommended the development of RDP legislation as an alternative to same-sex marriage.[41] When that avenue was politically rejected, the state developed a new 'reciprocal beneficiaries election' at the same time that it obtained passage of a constitutional referendum item preventing the legislature from defining marriage other than heterosexually. The legislature also enacted legislation defining marriage as being only between a man and woman.

By the time the *Baehr* case came before the Hawaii Supreme Court again in 1998, that court ruled that the issue was moot because of the amendment to the state constitution. Thus, by 1999 the potential for same-sex marriage had been eradicated in Hawaii. The steps taken by state are outlined here in some detail because they have become typical state responses to rulings that have opened the door to same-sex marriage. The steps also confirm that in the hands of North American legislators, RDP-type legislation is almost always proposed in an effort to avoid having to extend marriage to lesbian and gay couples:

RDP proposal: The Hawaii Commission on Sexual Orientation and the Law recommended that the state either recognize same-sex marriage or enact RDP legislation that would extend all the rights and obligations of marriage to same-sex couples. The government submitted an RDP bill to the legislature, which appeared to be headed for adoption, but late-breaking right-wing opposition to extending such a 'marriage-like' status to lesbian and gay couples resulted in the non-passage of that bill. However, when the legislation was pending, it enabled the state to convince the Hawaii Supreme Court to defer the hearing of the appeal from Judge Chang's decision long enough to give the legislature a chance to enact the RDP statute.

Only heterosexuals can marry: With Judge Chang's ruling barely a year old, the Hawaii legislature passed a measure declaring that the state's policy did not include marriages of same-gender couples. Until the state constitution was amended to give the legislature the power to enact such a provision, however, this statute had no effect because Judge Chang's ruling was a constitutional ruling that took precedence over such a statute.

Reciprocal beneficiary election: The proposal for a limited 'reciprocal beneficiary election' was made in 1997 so that the state could show some progress toward enacting legislation that would meet the needs of same-sex couples. The reciprocal beneficiary statute was originally intended to apply only to lesbian and gay couples, but religious and moral objections to using the term 'same-sex' in state legislation resulted in removal of this language. The statute now permits any two adults to register as reciprocal beneficiaries. They do not have to be involved in a conjugal relationship or be related to each other in any way at all—two tennis buddies are as entitled as anyone else to file an election.

Reciprocal beneficiaries have only some of the hundreds of rights and responsibilities given to married couples. These rights include joint medical insurance coverage; hospital visitation rights, mental health commitment approvals and notifications, family and funeral leave; joint property rights; inheritance and other survivorship rights; and legal standing for wrongful death, victims' rights, and domestic violence family status.

Nancy Maxwell has reported that the reciprocal beneficiary legislation is widely regarded as being 'ineffective and futile.' By the end of 1999, only 435 reciprocal beneficiary elections were on file (out of a state population of 1.1 million), and the legislation has not had much impact on access to medical insurance coverage or other important benefits. Nor is the election particularly durable: it can be terminated by merely filing a form no more complex than the election form. Originally enacted for a two-year trial period—just long enough to take the state past the hearing of the *Baehr* appeal—the election does appear to have been renewed.

Amendment to the state constitution: Also in 1997, the Hawaii legislature passed an amendment to the state constitution that gave the legislature the power to 'reserve marriage to opposite-sex couples.' In 1998, this amendment was confirmed by a state referendum by an overwhelming majority of voters. Shortly after the constitutional referendum, the Hawaii Supreme Court requested the litigants in *Baehr* to file supplemental briefs explaining the legal effect of the new constitutional amendment on the disposition of the case.

Proposed RDP bill: While the government waited for the decision in the *Baehr* appeal, it proposed a new and extensive RDP bill. Once the court granted the state's appeal in 1999, however, the RDP bill was allowed to die and was not revisited—the government no longer had any need to convince the Supreme Court that it was extending the full array of marital rights and obligations to same-sex couples. The very limited reciprocal beneficiary election was considered to be good enough.

Hawaii Supreme Court Decision

On December 9, 1999, the Hawaii Supreme Court unanimously reversed Judge Chang's decision[42] and the state of Hawaii ultimately won. The Court based its decision on the new amendment to the Hawaii state constitution, saying that the amendment took the issue 'out of the ambit of the equal protection clause of the Hawaii Constitution.' In essence, the Court refused to give precedence to its earlier constitutional ruling, but treated the new constitutional amendment as having a retroactive effect—completely eradicating the constitutional rights it had recognized in 1993. The Court treated the new amendment to the constitution as having cured the uncon- stitutionality of the heterosexual-only marriage law that had been challenged in *Baehr.*

The message of the *Baehr* case was not lost on other legislatures. By 2000, some thirty-five states and the federal government had enacted some version of the legislative or constitutional provisions developed in Hawaii during the *Baehr* appeal period. That number has continued to grow as further litigation on same-sex marriage has built on the successes of *Baehr.* It is interesting to note that approximately the same number of anti-miscegenation statutes had been enacted before *Loving* struck them down. The pattern that developed in *Baehr* has continued to be played out each time same-sex couples have obtained favourable rulings from state courts.

Alaska: The *Brause* Case

The next successful same-sex marriage challenge brought in the U.S. was *Brause* v. *Bureau of Vital Statistics,*[43] a decision of an Alaska trial court. The challenge was brought by two gay men who had initially applied to the Bureau of Vital Statistics for a marriage licence in 1994. They were denied the licence on the basis of the Alaska 'defence of marriage act' (DoMA), which defined marriage as being permitted only to a man with a woman. They brought their suit on the basis of the rights of privacy and equal protection guaranteed by the Alaska state constitution.

Jay Brause and Gene Dugan obtained a sympathetic hearing of their and the state's pretrial motions for summary judgment. The court readily concluded that 'marriage, i.e., the recognition of one's choice of a life partner, is a fundamental right' under the Alaska constitution. The court reasoned that, 'The relevant question is not whether same-sex marriage is so rooted in our traditions that it is a fundamental right, but whether the freedom to choose one's life partner is so rooted in our traditions. [T]he court finds that the choice of a life partner is personal, intimate, and subject to the protection of the right to privacy....' The court also concluded that the prohibition on sex discrimination was also implicated in this case. Thus, the court declared that the state would have to show a compelling reason for its current marriage law or the law could not stand.

During the pendency of the trial, the Alaska legislature responded with speed to the perceived threat to heterosexual marriage and approved a constitutional amendment defining marriage as the union of a man and a woman: 'To be recognized in this State, a marriage may exist only between one man and one woman.' Like the Hawaii amendment upon which it was modelled, the amendment was approved by an overwhelming majority of voters in 1998. A year after this amendment was adopted, the trial court dismissed the case.

Brause and Dugan later attempted to challenge the other aspect of the Alaska DoMA, which prohibited extension of marital benefits conferred by state law to couples of the same sex. In a 2001 decision of the Alaska Supreme Court, their constitutional challenge to the validity of this clause was dismissed too.

The message in the *Brause* case is that same-sex marriage claims can defeat DoMAs, but that constitutional amendments can defeat same-sex marriage rulings. And once same-sex marriage is blocked by constitutional amendments, the extension of marital rights or obligations becomes a matter of legislative *largesse*, as was seen in the *Baehr* case. Why bother enacting RDPs if same-sex marriage has already been blocked through constitutional amendment?

Vermont: The *Baker* Decision

The Vermont same-sex marriage litigation was more or less directly inspired by *Baehr* as Vermont couples responded with dismay to the Hawaii legislature's reaction to Judge Chang's ruling. Brought by a group of lesbian and gay couples, many with children, the *Baker*[44] case was initially unsuccessful. The Vermont trial court ruled that neutral marriage laws had to be interpreted in light of the assumption that marriage had always been a heterosexual institution. The trial court concluded that Vermont's 'common benefit clause' did not prevent the state from giving heterosexual couples benefits denied to same-sex couples because marital benefits rationally furthered the state's interest in promoting 'the link between procreation and child rearing'—one of the eight justifications the state had given the trial court.

The Vermont Supreme Court took a very different view of the state's justifications for heterosexuals-only marriage. The state had contended that it was permitted to 'send a message that procreation and child-rearing are intertwined,' and that there is a 'link between procreation and child-rearing.' The Court found this justification to be seriously under-inclusive and over-inclusive in that many people raise children who did not physically bear them, and many people receive the benefits of marriage who never procreate. The Court concluded that denying same-sex couples the benefits of marriage on such reasoning was detrimental to the interests of queer families.

The Court also concluded that the state's justifications contradicted existing state policy. Noting that it was now state adoption policy that lesbian and gay parents were considered perfectly acceptable parents, the Court could not find any basis for denying any of the benefits of marriage to those couples. The Court thus held that the plaintiffs had proven their case.

Unfortunately, the Court had stated at the outset that the *Baker* case was not about the right to obtain a marriage licence, but about the right to receive all the benefits accorded to married couples under Vermont law. Thus the Court ruled that the plaintiffs were entitled to receive 'the same benefits and protections afforded by Vermont law to married opposite-gender couples.'

However, the Court expressly stated that it would be up to the legislature to decide whether those benefits and protections were to be extended to lesbian and gay couples and their families by including them within the marriage laws of Vermont, or by extending them through a 'parallel "domestic partnership" system of some equivalent statutory alternative.' The Court provided an incentive to the legislature to act quickly by noting that the plaintiffs could petition the Court under its continuing jurisdiction for the 'remedy they originally sought,' which had been the issue of marriage licences.

Given the history of determined opposition to same-sex marriage in the U.S., it did not surprise anyone that the Vermont legislature quickly opted to enact some form of statutory alternative to formal marriage.

One judge dissented from this resolution of the *Baker* appeal. Judge Denise Johnson contended in her concurring decision that the denial of the right to marry ought to be seen as gender discrimination, and that the only appropriate remedy would be for the Court to order the issue of marriage licences to the plaintiffs. Her words were not heeded in Vermont, but perhaps they helped convince the Ontario Court of Appeal a few years later when, in the *Halpern* decision, that Court ordered the immediate issue of marriage licences to the applicants in that case.

Vermont Civil Union Law

The Vermont civil union law is widely heralded as being the most inclusive and comprehensive non-marital legislation relating to same-sex relationships enacted anywhere. However, that it is still discriminatory legislation cannot be doubted. As the Vermont legislature enacted the new civil union law, it also made 'findings' that civil marriage is 'a union between a man and a woman.' While the new civil union is open to both same-sex and opposite-sex couples, it would not exist if it had been up to heterosexual couples to demand it. It was obviously devised strictly as a way to avoid having marriage extended to same-sex couples by the Vermont Supreme Court.

The new legal relationship created by the Vermont legislation is termed a 'civil union.' As an 'alternative' to marriage, it is really just a variant of the RDP. However, it does have some characteristics that differentiate it from RDPs.

Instead of listing all of the incidents of marriage that are extended to same-sex couples, the civil union law is framed as extending all statutory, regulatory, common-law, equitable and policy features of civil marriage to parties to a civil union. This is done by providing that parties to civil unions are to be included in any definition or use of terms such as 'spouse,' 'family,' or similar terms throughout Vermont law. This statutory language ensures that features of marriage such as parental status, access to reproductive assistance, or the right to apply to family court for divorce services will be available to those who are civilly united. Vermont has permitted lesbian and gay couple adoption for nearly twenty-five years, and the civil union statute will assure that couples who form a civil union will be permitted to adopt.[45]

Despite this inclusive structure, the Vermont civil union statute remains discriminatory. The civil union statute is clearly premised upon the continuing exclusion of lesbian and gay couples from formal marriage, and it also repeatedly affirms in the preamble and in various provisions that civil union is not a form of marriage. This segregation is built into the administration and registration of civil unions. Parties to a civil union apply not for marriage licences, but for civil union licences. While religious celebrants can perform civil unions, the entire system of recording and registering civil unions is rigidly segregated in 'civil union registries' and tabulated in returns of 'civil union statistics.' Small towns are permitted to intermix marriage records with civil union records, but each type of certificate must be carefully executed to reflect its status. Outside of small towns, civil unions are to be recorded in separate registry books. In addition, discrimination against queer couples who form a civil union will not be considered discrimination on the basis of marital status, but discrimination on the basis of civil union.

The Vermont Civil Union Act also established a second legal status: registered reciprocal beneficiaries. Like the Hawaii reciprocal beneficiary provisions, this permits non-conjugal pairs to form reciprocal beneficiary relationships in order to receive selected spousal benefits. Unlike the Hawaii statute, the Vermont statute applies only to two people who are related by blood or adoption. And unlike the Hawaii statute, the Vermont statute is primarily focused on health insurance and health matters: hospital visitation; medical decision-making; decision-making in relation to organ donations, funerals, and disposition of remains; power of attorney for health care, patient care, and nursing homes; and abuse prevention. A spouse will have priority over a reciprocal beneficiary, but other family members have lower priority.

The Vermont civil union gives lesbian and gay couples by far the most complete relationship rights of any statute, without, of course, the right to marry. In contrast, the Vermont reciprocal beneficiary status is narrow. It does not affect property, support or inheritance at all—not even property management. A separate Civil Union Review Commission has been established to supervise the implementation of both civil unions and reciprocal beneficiaries legislation for two years, and the commission has been charged with considering whether the legal incidents of reciprocal beneficiary relationships should be expanded in the future.

Massachusetts: The *Goodridge* Decision

The *Goodridge* case was filed in Massachusetts in 2001 after all the plaintiffs had been denied marriage licences at various locations in the state. As in the Vermont case, the plaintiffs had brought not only their own life stories and reasons for wanting to marry to the court, but also provided detailed expert evidence as to the social realities of their relationships, their families, and their children. This evidence made it clear that their dreams are no different in substance from those of heterosexual couples.

The trial court decision was unfortunately all too predictable. The court held that even though the Massachusetts marriage law was gender-neutral, the 'plain wording' of other laws made it clear that same-sex couples could not marry. The court also rejected all the plaintiffs' constitutional claims, ruling that denial of the right to marry did not violate the liberty, freedom, equality or due process provisions of the Massachusetts state constitution.

Although there had been a lesbian and gay baby boom all across Massachusetts for at least twenty years before the *Goodridge* case was heard, the court concluded that the state had a good reason for limiting marriage to heterosexual couples: prohibiting same-sex marriage rationally furthers the legislature's interest in safeguarding the 'primary purpose' of marriage, which the court found was 'procreation.' The trial court completely denied the social realities of queer families, ruling that same-sex and opposite-sex couples are completely different from each other because heterosexual couples are 'theoretically...capable of procreation,' 'they do not rely on "inherently more cumbersome" noncoital means of reproduction, and they are more likely than samesex couples to have children, or more children.'

Thus the trial court dismissed the plaintiffs' claims.

In the strongest U.S. decision ever written on same-sex marriage, the Massachusetts Supreme Court held that prohibiting same-sex couples from marrying violates both the equality and liberty guarantees of the Massachusetts constitution: '[W]e conclude that the marriage ban does not meet the rational basis test for either due process or equal protection.'

The *Goodridge* decision is even stronger than earlier U.S. decisions, because the court then went on to rule that the traditional legal definition of marriage as being between a 'man and a woman' had to be adapted by the court to remain consistent with changing social realities:

'We construe civil marriage to mean the voluntary union of two persons as spouses, to the exclusion of all others. This reformulation redresses the plaintiffs' constitutional injury and furthers the aim of marriage to promote stable, exclusive relationships.'

'[E]xtending civil marriage to same-sex couples reinforces the importance of marriage to individuals and communities. That same-sex couples are willing to embrace marriage's solemn obligations of exclusivity, mutual support, and commitment to one another is a testament to the enduring place of marriage in our laws and in the human spirit.'[46]

In giving its reasons for making this monumental adjustment to the meaning of marriage, the court emphasized that the government had failed completely to give it any good reasons for continuing to exclude same-sex couples from marriage:

'The department has had more than ample opportunity to articulate a constitutionally adequate justification for limiting civil marriage to opposite-sex unions. It has failed to do so. The department has offered purported justifications for the civil marriage restriction that are starkly at odds with the comprehensive network of vigorous, gender-neutral laws promoting stable families and the best interests of children. It has failed to identify any relevant characteristic that would justify shutting the door to civil marriage to a person who wishes to marry someone of the same sex.

'The marriage ban works a deep and scarring hardship on a very real segment of the community for no rational reason. The absence of any reasonable relationship between, on the one hand, an absolute disqualification of same-sex couples who wish to enter into civil marriage and, on the other, protection of public health, safety, or general welfare, suggests that the marriage restriction is rooted in persistent prejudices against persons who are (or who are believed to be) homosexual. ... Limiting the protections, benefits, and obligations of civil marriage to opposite-sex couples violates the basic premises of individual liberty and equality under law protected by the Massachusetts Constitution.'

The Court's Order as to remedy could not have been clearer:

'We declare that barring an individual from the protections, benefits, and obligations of civil marriage solely because that person would marry a person of the same sex violates the Massachusetts Constitution.'

The Court then gave the legislature 180 days from the date of the decision (which was on November 18, 2003) to 'permit the Legislature to take such action as it may deem appropriate in light of this opinion.'

Civil Unions Not an Adequate Substitute for Marriage
Despite the clarity and comprehensive reasoning in the *Goodridge* decision, the Massachusetts government immediately began to look for ways to avoid having to extend marriage to same-sex couples. After all, if the governments of Hawaii, Alaska and Vermont could stave off same-sex marriage, surely, the government thought, the same could be done in Massachusetts.

It became immediately apparent that unlike the states of Hawaii and Alaska, which had been able to rush through amendments to their state constitutions to prohibit same-sex marriage, nothing like that could be done in Massachusetts. That is because the rules for amending the Massachusetts

constitution would not have resulted in a valid amendment until 2006—
long after the date on which the court decision was to take effect in 2004.
The Massachusetts constitutional amending formula requires that a proposed
amendment must receive a majority of votes in joint sessions of the legislature
in two consecutive legislative sessions before it can then be put to a popular
vote at ballot. The earliest that this could be accomplished would be in 2006.

Thus, the Massachusetts legislature realized that its only option would be
to try to convince the appellate court to accept a 'marriage-like' civil union
law instead of full marriage for queers. The Massachusetts Senate quickly
developed Senate Bill 2175, a draft bill to extend all of the 'benefits, protections, rights, and responsibilities of marriage' to same-sex couples. The bill
also contained a DoMA clause, saying that the legislature confirmed that
same-sex couples could not marry. The government then put this civil union
bill before the Massachusetts Supreme Court, asking the court whether this
would be a constitutionally acceptable approach to extending the rights and
obligations of marriage to same-sex couples. The court had no choice but to
accept the government's request for an advisory opinion, and called for interested parties to submit *amicus curiae* briefs (friend of the court briefs) in
January 2004.

Court-watchers did not expect the proposed civil union bill to satisfy the
court. After all, in its first decision in November 2003, the court had made its
ruling in the strongest possible terms: 'The Massachusetts Constitution affirms
the dignity and equality of all individuals. It forbids the creation of second-
class citizens.' In addition, one of the dissenting justices had read the majority
of the court as having concluded that marriage and only marriage would
satisfy the court: '[T]he majority conclude[d] that a marriage licence cannot
be denied to an individual who wishes to marry someone of the same sex.'

On February 4, 2004, the appellate court released its advisory opinion.[47]
If anything, *Goodridge II* was even more forceful than *Goodridge I*. The court
zeroed in on the stated purpose of the civil union bill, which was 'to preserv[e]
the traditional, historic nature and meaning of the institution of civil marriage.'
The court agreed that preserving civil marriage is 'a legislative priority of the
highest order,' but went on to conclude that the bill 'does nothing to "preserve"
the civil marriage law, only its constitutional infirmity.' That is, the court
concluded that the civil union law was in no way designed to 'preserve'
marriage—the civil union law was intended to preserve discrimination.

The court then restated its main finding in *Goodridge I*:

'[T]he government aim [of marriage] is to encourage stable adult
relationships for the good of the individual and of the community,

especially its children. The very nature and purpose of civil marriage…renders unconstitutional any attempt to ban all same-sex couples, <u>as</u> same-sex couples, from entering into civil marriage.' [emphasis in original]

The court went on to find that the proposed civil union bill was even more constitutionally offensive than the gender-neutral marriage law had been:

'Segregating same-sex unions from opposite-sex unions cannot possibly be held rationally to advance or "preserve"…the Commonwealth's legitimate interests in procreation, child-rearing, and the conservation of resources. … [I]t continues to relegate same-sex couples to a different status. … The history of our nation has demonstrated that separate is seldom, if ever, equal.'

The court went on to point out that even if 'civil marriage' and 'civil union' can be considered synonymous, the only purpose behind having a separate civil union law for same-sex couples would be to keep the 'stain' and 'stigma' placed by the state on same-sex couples and their families in place. Thus, the court concluded that the proposed civil union bill violates the equal protection and due process clauses of the Massachusetts constitution because it 'maintains an unconstitutional, inferior, and discriminatory status for same-sex couples.'

The Massachusetts court was not the first court to reach the conclusion that the state could not offer queer couples segregated 'alternatives' to formal civil marriage. The Canadian courts discussed in the next chapter had already reached that conclusion in May and June of 2003 as they permitted lesbian and gay couples to marry as of mid-2003. What is historic about the *Goodridge* decisions is that instead of giving the state an open-ended period of time in which to cast around for ways to avoid having to let queers marry, the Massachusetts court followed the Canadian example and simply ordered that same-sex couples be permitted to marry by a fixed date: May 17, 2004.

The *Goodridge* decisions were met with howls of rage at every level of government. The Massachusetts government immediately tabled a proposed amendment to the state constitution that would limit marriage to opposite-sex couples. U.S. President Bush announced plans to introduce a similar amendment to the U.S. constitution. State officials plan to bring further legal proceedings to enjoin the issue of marriage licenses when the date appointed by the court arrives.

These efforts have all been fruitless. The only legal initiative that would clearly prevent the court's order from coming into effect would be the ratification of an amendment to the state constitution. Under the Massachusetts constitutional amending formula, however, such an amendment could not come into effect until 2006 at the earliest. Because the government has encountered so much opposition to such a step, it now appears that the earliest that an amendment could come into effect would be 2008.

Once the right to marry becomes fully effective in Massachusetts, it is unlikely to be legally possible to erase it. At that point, opponents of same-sex marriage would have to prove that queer marriage causes 'irreparable harm' or 'public harm.' Because queer marriages in the Netherlands, Belgium, Ontario and B.C. have not caused anything that could remotely be described as 'harm,' it is not likely that this legal test can be met.

San Francisco: Marry Now, Litigate Later!

At the very moment that the Massachusetts government began to realize that it would not be able to stop queer marriage from coming into effect in May 2004, the newly-elected Mayor of San Francisco reintroduced the original queer marriage strategy used in the 1970s—marry queers now, and litigate the validity of those marriages later.

This is the approach that was first used in Arizona and Colorado in the mid-1970s when city officials decided in the course of their duties that gender-neutral marriage laws obviously permitted same-sex couples to marry. Those officials just went ahead and issued licences to large numbers of same-sex couples. Unfortunately, there had been little litigation over the constitutional validity of same-sex marriage by that time. Thus, when state officials prohibited the issue of further licences, county officials had little choice but to comply with those directives or face discipline. However, it has never been fully accepted by couples who married then that state governments could erase their marriages.

This is also the approach that was used by the Metropolitan Community Church of Toronto in 2001 when it went ahead and performed banns marriages for same-sex couples as soon as the church became licenced to perform marriages in Ontario. 'Banns marriages' are a hold-over from the days when churches had a monopoly on performing marriages in the British colonies. Once a church had proclaimed banns according to its practices, it is (in Ontario) permitted to issue perfectly valid marriage licences as an agent of the province, to perform the marriage, to issue a marriage certificate, and to register that certificate in the church registry as well as with the government. When the validity of the MCCT marriages came before the courts in

Canada (discussed in Chapter Five), the courts held that it was constitutionally necessary to recognize those marriages.

The marriage laws in all these 'marry now, litigate later' contexts were all gender-neutral. So too was California law in the early 1970s—the California statutes at that time permitted any person who was 'an unmarried person' to marry. However, as part of the backlash against the Colorado and Arizona marriages in the mid-1970s, the California legislature enacted an additional provision that describes marriage as 'between a man and a woman' and prohibits 'persons of the same sex from entering into a lawful marriage.' Then in 2000, in reaction to the successful court challenges in the Hawaii case, California voters adopted Proposition 22 on March 7, 2000, by a margin of 61 to 39 to ensure that California courts would not be forced to recognize same-sex marriages performed elsewhere. This 'defence of marriage act' provides that 'Only marriage between a man and a woman is valid or recognized in California.'

San Francisco Mayor Gavin Newsom has said that when he heard President Bush announce in his 2004 State of the Union address that the Massachusetts *Goodridge* decision could not be permitted to come into effect, and that Bush intended to initiate a federal constitutional ban on same-sex marriage, he decided right then and there that this discrimination could no longer be tolerated. On February 10, 2004, Newsom instructed city employees to explore ways to enable same-sex couples to marry. When city officials heard that anti same-sex marriage groups were getting ready to file lawsuits to block this plan, they put the policy into effect on February 12, 2004.

According to the *San Francisco Gate*, Del Martin and Phyllis Lyon, famous as the authors of *Lesbian/Woman*, first published in 1972, were the first couple to marry. By the time the city was ready to act on February 12, officials had reprinted the marriage licence forms in gender-neutral language ('first applicant' and 'second applicant' instead of 'bride' and 'groom') and the officiants pronounced couples 'spouses for life' instead of 'husband and wife.'[48]

These San Francisco marriages touched off immediate litigation. The first round was launched by private individuals and conservative groups that asked the courts to issue restraining orders against the city. These suits failed. On February 17, 2004, Judge Warren of the California Superior Court refused to grant these injunctions.[49] (Judge Warren is the grandson of Chief Justice Earl Warren of the U.S. Supreme Court, the judge who wrote the famous decision in *Loving* v. *Virginia*.) On February 20, 2004, Judge Quidachay issued another order permitting the marriages to continue.[50] At that point, 'The Terminator,' Governor Arnold Schwarzenegger, ordered state Attorney General Bill Lockyer to file suit directly with the California Supreme Court. The City and County of San Francisco countered with its own petition for a declaration that it would be unconstitutional to prohibit same-sex couples from marrying. Additional suits were filed by private groups opposing same-sex marriage, and groups such as the American Civil Liberties Union and the National Center for Lesbian Rights have been granted intervener status in all these cases.[51]

Throughout these developments, the numbers of couples married in San Francisco continued to climb steadily. On February 27, 2004, comedian Rosie O'Donnell and Kelli Carpenter, proud mothers of four children, were the 3,327th same-sex couple to marry. On March 11, 2004, the California Supreme Court ordered a freeze on further marriages and on all of the other lawsuits that had been filed until it could rule on Attorney General Lockyer's suit. Couples who were within minutes of marrying when the freeze was issued immediately filed new suits not affected by the freeze. In the mean-time, city officials in Albuquerque, New Mexico (later shut down by the state) and New Paltz and Nyack, New York, as well as in Portland, Oregon (not shut down) also began marrying same-sex couples. Pressure on city officials in other centres has been building steadily. If the Oregon court hearing an emergency application on March 23, 2004, does not prohibit Benton county officials from issuing licences, then same-sex couples will also be able to marry in Corvallis, Oregon on March 24, 2004.

Like the MCCT marriages in Ontario, it may well take litigation to bring finality to the issues in California, New Mexico and New York. It is not clear whether the Oregon government will insist on litigation in that state. The Dutch experience over a decade ago suggests that the sheer numbers of couples seeking these marriages and the high level of media attention being showered on each development in this dramatic turn of events could well influence public opinion strongly in favour of same-sex marriage. Indeed, an ongoing poll by USA Today indicates that 82.43% of 432,786 respondents have said that they *oppose* a constitutional amendment banning same-sex marriage, and only 17.57% of the respondents support such a ban.[52]

Conclusion

Some U.S. queers have been able to marry since 2001 if they could meet the citizenship and residency requirements in the Netherlands. Thousands of U.S. couples have travelled to Canada since the summer of 2003 to get married since the Ontario and British Columbia courts opened marriage to same-sex couples. Two-thirds of the marriages performed in B.C. have been for couples from outside that province. (There are no citizenship or residency requirements in any of the Canadian provinces.) Within three weeks of opening marriage to same-sex couples in San Francisco, at least 3,400 couples married there, joined by dozen of marriages in New Mexico, New York and Portland in February and March 2004, and to be joined by Massachusetts in May 2004.

There is every indication that this will not be the end of this new beginning. Same-sex marriage cases are still pending in other state courts; *Lewis et. al.* v. *Harris et. al.* was filed in New Jersey in 2002 and is pending before that state's appellate court, and *Morrison et al.* v. *O'Bannon* was filed in Indiana in 2002. Local politicians such as Mayor Richard Daley of Chicago and city officials in Ithaca, New York, are seriously discussing how to break the barriers to same-sex marriage in their communities. The Massachusetts state government continues to attempt to initiate amendments to the state constitution to prohibit same-sex marriage in that state, but there are indications that such initiatives in other states are not being greeted with the enthusiasm opponents of same-sex marriage have perhaps been expecting.

These developments are not limited to large cities and areas known for their progressive politics. I was struck when reading the *Sycamore Daily Chronicle*, published in a small town in northwestern Illinois, by the eloquence of a local pastor's column in support of same-sex marriage:

'I have conducted services for gay and lesbian couples since 1994. Each time, I see in their eyes and hear in their responses their hope, hurt, fear and longing to be recognized as spiritual persons who can love with commitment. I am humbled by the courage I have witnessed, and I am acutely aware of the need now for justice, equality and civil rights.'

This pastor went on to explain why it would be anti-democratic to enact a constitutional prohibition on same-sex marriage:

'The document that granted freedom and full citizenship to African-Americans and gave women the right to vote must not be used as a weapon with which to attack the families of our country's gay and lesbian citizens.'[53]

As illustrated by the parallel history of prohibitions on interracial marriage, which were not finally eradicated until 1967, it may take a long time to open marriage to same-sex couples in all the states in the U.S. But with marriage now becoming available on both coasts as well as over the border in Canada, it can finally be said that the U.S. marriage movement—which began so brilliantly a decade ago in Hawaii with the *Baehr* cases—has finally been successful. The law is now beginning to catch up with the new social realities that emerged over half a century ago.

CHAPTER FIVE

Marriage in Canada:
Ontario, British Columbia and Quebec

When compared with the Netherlands and the U.S., the struggle for same-sex marriage in Canada seemed to take no time at all. The Ontario and B.C. cases that broke through the legal barriers in Canada were not filed until the middle of 2000; the trials were held in 2001; and the appellate decisions permitting couples to marry were released in June and July of 2003. The Quebec case began at about the same time, but got held up by procedural issues at the appellate level. However, the Quebec Court of Appeal followed the Ontario and B.C. rulings on March 19, 2004.

In contrast with the political reaction to same-sex marriage in the U.S. and even in the Netherlands at some points, governments in Canada have been surprisingly supportive of extending marriage to queers from the beginning of this round of litigation. As recounted in this chapter, the Ontario and B.C. cases started as government applications to the courts for clarification of whether gender-neutral federal marriage laws permitted them to issue marriage licences to same-sex couples. While neither the B.C. Attorney General nor the Toronto municipal government ended up actively supporting the couples' cases, neither did they oppose them. The federal government, however, defended heterosexual-only marriage with every argument it could muster.

Once the Ontario and B.C. appellate decisions were released in 2003, it became obvious to the federal government that it was not likely to win an appeal to the Supreme Court of Canada. After all, lesbian and gay couples had already begun marrying on June 10, 2003, the day the Ontario Court

Same-Sex Marriage

of Appeal issued its decision. The Minister of Justice, the Hon. Martin Cauchon, made the historic decision to drop his opposition to same-sex marriage and began the process of acquiescing in these appellate rulings.

A week after the Ontario Court of Appeal announced queer couples could marry as of June 10, 2003, the federal government announced that it was not going to appeal either the Ontario or B.C. decisions. On June 24, 2003, it consented to the lifting of the suspension on queer marriages in B.C., permitting couples to marry as of July 8, 2003, instead of having to wait until July 12, 2004, the date originally set by the B.C. Court of Appeal.

Also in July 2003, the federal government tabled a draft bill to confirm that the new federal law permitting same-sex marriage would be applied in all the provinces and territories in Canada. At the same time, the federal government asked the Supreme Court of Canada to rule in an advisory capacity on whether the proposed new law would be consistent with the constitution, including the Charter. In January 2004, the federal government then indicated to the Quebec Court of Appeal that it was no longer seeking a stay of that trial court's order, thus laying the basis for that court's order permitting marriage as of March 19, 2004.

Religious organizations and other proponents of heterosexual-only marriage howled with rage at each of these developments. Some religious groups even tried (unsuccessfully) to convince the Supreme Court of Canada to let *them* appeal the Ontario Court of Appeal decision to that court. It should be noted that the appeal to the Quebec Court of Appeal was brought by religious interveners. The court ruled that they should not be allowed to prosecute the appeal when the federal government has not itself appealed.

All in all, it took less than two years to get from the opening of the first trial in B.C. on July 27, 2001, to the first wedding in Ontario on June 10, 2003. The Ontario marriages and the B.C. marriages shortly after were the first civil marriages of lesbian and gay couples to be performed in North America with open governmental approval since marriage licences had been issued to queer couples in Arizona and Colorado in the 1970s.

The speed with which the Ontario, B.C. and Quebec courts have opened marriage to same-sex couples is not so much a reflection of the devotion to queer rights in Canada—although Canada has become unique in that regard—so much as it is the cumulative effect of the incredible changes that had already taken place over the last thirty years in the lives of ordinary queers in Canada and in Canadian laws relating to sexuality.

This chapter outlines some of the longer-term developments that made this swift and breath-taking breakthrough possible, and discusses how Canadian couples, lawyers and activists were able to build on the Dutch and

U.S. marriage movement to obtain the right to marry in three provinces in just a few short years.

Key Structural Developments—Human Rights Laws and the Charter

A number of key elements came together over the course of the twenty-five years following the rejection of Chris Vogel and Rich North's application for a marriage licence in *Re North and Matheson*. Each development contributed to achieving one central long-term goal: getting full-scale protection for queers under all the human rights laws of Canada. Throughout the 1970s and 1980s it was obvious that such protection would be needed to erase the layers of discrimination and invisibility surrounding queer existence in Canadian law and society.

Quebec Human Rights Law

One of the most important early developments in this process was the addition of 'sexual orientation' to the Quebec Charter of Human Rights and Freedoms in 1977. This step was possible because of the social and political links between Quebec and France; it was France under Napoleon that had first repealed the religious-based criminal prohibitions on same-sex sex.

This development was critical because it made it clear that as judges elsewhere in Canada refused to accept human rights complaints based on other grounds such as 'sex,' 'marital status' or 'family status,' the addition of those two little words to human rights codes could open the door to protection of queer human rights. It was also critical because it demonstrated what concrete steps courts could take to prohibit the many forms of discrimination faced by queers on a daily basis. The first human rights complaint brought under the Quebec sexual orientation clause was aimed at a Catholic Church that refused to rent space to a queer discussion group on the basis of 'morality.' The court held that the church could not offer its space to all outside groups except that one group, and ruled that doing so discriminated on the basis of sexual orientation.

Perhaps most importantly, the 'sexual orientation' clause in the Quebec Charter helped inspire queer activists to insist that sexual orientation be included in the bill of rights that was being proposed as a new addition to the Canadian constitution.

The Canadian Charter of Rights

The Canadian constitution was revamped in the early 1980s when it was 'repatriated' from the U.K. During this process, a bill of rights was inserted into the constitution under the name of the Canadian Charter of Rights and Freedoms. The drafting of the Charter of Rights formed a focus for disadvantaged groups, who insisted that a U.S.-style 'Equal Rights Amendment' be included to ensure that the Charter would apply to all historically-disadvantaged groups: women, disabled people, Aboriginal peoples, and others characterized by race, ethnic origin and/or religion.

Most of those groups were successful in their lobbying efforts. Queers were not. The best that queers could do was to obtain informal assurance from the federal government that it considered queers to be included in the general language of section 15, the provision that guaranteed the right to equality. This general language was intended to signal to the courts that they could apply section 15 to groups not specifically mentioned in section 15, so long as they were also historically disadvantaged in relation to the issue under consideration. The text of section 15 states:

'Every individual is equal before and under the law and has the right to the equal protection and equal benefit of the law without discrimination and, in particular, without discrimination based on race, national or ethnic origin, colour, religion, sex, age or mental or physical disability.'

This language made it possible for the courts to decide whether groups such as queers could be included in the phrase 'Every individual' who is 'equal before and under the law....' While the government had not been willing to add 'sexual orientation' to the list of the 'particular' grounds of discrimination in section 15, it quietly assured queer activists that it would make sure that the courts knew that the general language in section 15 was *intended* to apply to queers.

The Effects of the Charter

Even though 'sexual orientation' did not end up being listed in section 15, the adoption of the Charter had a profound impact on the legal status of queers in Canada. It laid the basis for individuals and couples to turn to the courts for the enforcement of their rights, and it also spurred legislatures to make statutory changes that otherwise would have been deferred much longer.

Effect on legislation: The Charter of Rights came into effect in 1982. However, the equality provisions in section 15 were put on hold for three years, known as the moratorium years. Cynics viewed this as a stalling tactic on the part of government, but the official line was that the moratorium was to give governments time to take a close look at all existing laws, practices and programs in order to identify changes needed to bring them into 'compliance' with the Charter. This three-year gap was filled with a lot of law reform activity, including hearings, study papers, independent scholarly and activist work, and preparation of draft legislation.

By the time section 15 came into effect, the only government to take any steps to deal with discrimination on the basis of sexuality was Ontario. The federal Parliamentary Committee on Equality had toured the country collecting data on discrimination of all kinds, and, prompted by Svend Robinson, a member of that committee, had recommended that with regard to queers, it would be necessary to at least add 'sexual orientation' to the federal human rights code. The federal government took no steps to do so until forced by the Ontario Court of Appeal in 1991 (discussed below), but the Ontario government added a clause to its omnibus 'compliance' statute that inserted 'sexual orientation' into the Ontario Human Rights Code.

It is significant that no government other than Quebec had taken any steps by 1985 to recognize the equality rights of queers, whether as individuals or in their relationships. Indeed, as section 15 came into effect, there was a rash of 'opposite-sex' amendments to legislation in several provinces as governments looked for ways to ensure that even if the Charter did look like it might apply to queers, it would be clear that it did not give queer *relationships* legal status.

Thus, as the Ontario Human Rights Code was amended in 1986 to extend its protection to sexual orientation, the government inserted the words 'opposite sex' into the expanded definition of spouse at the same time. When this change was made, Ian Scott, then the Attorney General of Ontario, stated that the new opposite-sex clause was intended to protect the 'traditional' concept of marriage—'traditional marriage' being a clear reference to 'heterosexual-only marriage.' The government's intention was obvious: to ensure that 'sexual orientation' clauses could not be used to give lesbian and gay couples access to the category of 'spouse' either through formal civil marriage or through extended definitions in which opposite-sex cohabitants were classified as 'spouses' and given a growing number of the rights usually reserved for married couples.

Despite the nod to 'traditional' notions of the family, the Charter nudged Ontario into taking the important legislative step of prohibiting discrimination on the basis of sexuality. In turn, seeing Ontario take action nudged three other governments—Manitoba, the Yukon and Nova Scotia—into adding 'sexual orientation' to their human rights codes as well. Without the Charter, it is doubtful whether this step would have been taken so soon. However, these were the last codes to be amended until the courts began forcing them to be amended in 1992, in the historic *Haig and Birch*[54] decision.

Effect on courts: If all that had been achieved via the adoption of the Charter had been the insertion of 'sexual orientation' into a few human rights codes in the late 1980s, it is doubtful whether queers could have gained access to marriage by 2003. Throughout the rest of the 1980s, despite the Charter and the slow expansion of human rights protection, only one court relied on equality principles in ruling in favour of queer applicants: the *Veysey*[55] case in 1989. And even that Charter-based victory was short-lived; the Federal Court of Appeal vacated the Charter part of that ruling the next year (it upheld the decision on other grounds).

By the beginning of the 1990s, both the legislatures and the courts seemed to have lost interest in dealing with discrimination on the basis of sexuality. No further human rights codes were being amended, and no favourable court or tribunal rulings were being produced.

The key development that broke through the dead weight of the past was the 1992 Ontario Court of Appeal decision in *Haig and Birch*. This case challenged the federal government's continued refusal to do what it had agreed in 1985 ought to have been done—insert 'sexual orientation' into the federal human rights code. The petitioners in the *Haig and Birch* case turned to the Charter to challenge the continued refusal to make that change. In an historic decision, the court ordered that from thenceforth the federal human rights statute should be read 'as if' the words 'sexual orientation' had been inserted into the text of section 15 of the Charter.

The *Haig and Birch* decision was historic because it broke through both the legislative and judicial barriers to queer equality simultaneously. It broke through the legislative log-jam by demonstrating that courts could and would use their broad powers under the Charter to bring discriminatory legislation into line with the Charter itself if the legislature were not willing to take that step. It broke through judicial barriers to queer equality by becoming the first appellate case (one step away from the Supreme Court of Canada) to declare that queers *are* protected by section 15 of the Charter even though they are not mentioned 'in particular' in the text of section 15 itself.

As the leading Charter ruling on queer equality of its time, the *Haig and Birch* decision unleashed two torrents of legal change. On the legislative front, the rest of the provinces quickly began to add 'sexual orientation' to their human rights codes either through legislation or litigation. At the same time, courts finally began to apply the Charter equality provisions to cases brought by queers. By 1995, the Supreme Court of Canada confirmed in *Egan and Nesbit* that 'sexual orientation' is a prohibited ground of discrimination under section 15 of the Charter, and had gone one step further than *Haig and Birch* by holding that 'opposite-sex' definitions of 'spouse' are discriminatory because they exclude same-sex couples. However, a bare majority of the *Egan and Nesbit* court went ahead to rule that this discrimination was 'justifiable.' In 1998 the Supreme Court of Canada unanimously confirmed in *Vriend* v. *Alberta*[56] the 1992 decision in *Haig and Birch*, and read 'sexual orientation' into the Alberta human rights statute. And in 1999, the Supreme Court of Canada ruled in *M.* v. *H.* that section 15 of the Charter entitles same-sex couples to the spousal rights extended to opposite-sex cohabitants. In this case, the Court was not at all ambivalent on whether this was a justifiable form of discrimination, and concluded that it is not.

Turning the Focus to Marriage

During the fifteen years between the coming into force of section 15 of the Charter and the 1999 Supreme Court of Canada ruling in *M.* v. *H.*,[57] literally hundreds of human rights complaints, labour grievances, and Charter challenges moved through the legal process in Canada. The focus of these cases ranged from spousal benefits (like dental benefits) under collective agreements and workplace regulations to employment discrimination; pension rights; property rights; the many issues surrounding the parent-child relationship (custody, access, parental status, second-parent adoption); and inheritance rights. Early recognition of the parent-child relationship during the queer baby boom and the key Ontario case of *Re K* in 1995 (a brilliant section 15 ruling authored by Mr. Justice Nevins), which gave lesbian and gay co-parents the right to second-parent adopt their children, helped emphasize that so far as queer families were concerned, social realities had changed long ago. Thus, much of the litigation during this period was aimed at trying to bring various practical bits of legal doctrine into line with these new social realities.

In retrospect, four key factors stand out as helping shape the decision on when, where and how to take the issue of same-sex marriage back to the courts again.

The 1993 Layland and Beaulne Case

The first development was the trial court decision back in 1993 (the *Layland and Beaulne*[58] case) in which two Ontario judges held that the 'traditional' notion of heterosexual marriage was not affected by the enactment of section 15 of the Charter—queers still could not marry.

The key aspect of this case was that a third judge—Madame Justice Greer—dissented vigorously from the backward-looking reasoning of the majority. Justice Greer ignored the appeals to 'history' and 'immemorial heterosexuality' and instead focused her analysis directly on the steps of the section 15 analysis that the Supreme Court of Canada had outlined in the first section 15 case to reach that court. Finding that denial of the right to marry was 'differential treatment' of a group that has suffered historical disadvantage, she concluded that this denial harms queer couples and their families, and therefore is discriminatory.

By applying section 15 of the Charter in this textbook fashion, Justice Greer demonstrated that appeals to 'tradition' and biological essentialism are simply artifacts of outmoded social prejudices that were already, by 1993, out of step with contemporary life in Canada. This dissenting opinion contains one of the most cogent legal explanations of why the Charter equality guarantees are violated by 'heterosexual-only' marriage. Thus, Justice Greer's opinion laid out a clear map for future litigants, and, in the intervening years, her application of the section 15 equality guarantees has been approved by numerous courts all over Canada when addressing other forms of discrimination on the basis of sexuality. Even the Supreme Court of Canada later applied the same analysis to three other legal issues before it in *Egan and Nesbit* (1995), *Vriend* (1998) and *M.* v. *H.* As the jurisprudence on queer equality rights evolved, it became obvious that Justice Greer, and not the majority justices, had approached the issue of same-sex marriage correctly.

Shifting Legal Concepts of 'sex'
The second development in the legal battle for same-sex marriage involved a group of cases involving the status of marriages of transgender or transsexual individuals. The old English ruling in the *Corbett* case, which had held that so far as the law was concerned, 'once a man always a man,' was slowly eroding in Canada as courts began to recognize that under some circumstances, a person could actually change their legal sex as part of the transsexual process. Part of this change had begun to emanate from legislation concerning transsexual persons, but courts had begun to notice that along with a change in legal sex went the possibility of acquisition of the legal capacity to marry.

While none of these cases ever resulted in rulings that persons of the same legal sex can marry each other, courts had definitely begun, in these cases, to accept that the supposed immutability of the legal categories 'male' and 'female' could themselves change with evolving social conditions.[59]

The Supreme Court of Canada Decision in M. v. H.
The third factor that would alter the legal course for same-sex marriage was the May 20, 1999 decision of the Supreme Court of Canada in the *M.* v. *H.* case. In that case, the Supreme Court of Canada had agreed with two lower courts that the province of Ontario had to amend its family law to extend the right to alimony to same-sex partners. The alimony provisions—like hundreds of other legal provisions in Ontario—had applied only to

'spouses,' and 'spouse' was defined as being limited to married couples and to cohabitants of the opposite sex. The breadth and depth of the Court's decision in *M.* v. *H.* made it clear that 'opposite-sex' definitions of 'spouse' were no longer constitutionally acceptable. By itself, this ruling formed the perfect basis upon which to begin same-sex marriage litigation. In this decision, the Court established that discrimination against same-sex couples violates section 15 of the Charter.

Governmental responses to the *M.* v. *H.* decision were obviously designed to forestall any further expansion of queer rights. The Court had given the province of Ontario six months to bring the offending alimony law into line with its decision in *M.* v. *H.* , or to let that Court's order go into effect. It is obvious from the text of the Court's decision that it fully expected the province to come out with a little amendment extending 'spouse' to include same-sex couples for purposes of alimony and a couple of related provisions, such as the provision that recognized the validity of cohabitation agreements between unmarried cohabitants.

What actually ended up happening was that the *M.* v. *H.* case triggered an avalanche of legislative amendments to the bulk of *all* Ontario law relating to unmarried cohabitants. This avalanche then spread to the greater part of *all* federal laws and then to large chunks of laws in various other provinces. Some provinces enacted fairly narrow statutes; others, like B.C., which had been moving quickly to extend spousal treatment to same-sex couples since 1995, made a few further changes; Nova Scotia and Quebec actually went the furthest by enacting RDP and civil union statutes for queers. Although none of these statutory responses extended *every* bit of spousal treatment to same-sex couples, all did extend at least a few new spouse-type provisions to queers, and most extended large numbers of spouse-type provisions to queers.

It is important to realize that the federal and provincial governments did not make all these legislative changes out of sympathy for the plight of queer couples. Nor did they take this step because they were so moved by the Supreme Court of Canada's decision in *M.* v. *H.* These statutory changes were conceived as damage control, as a way to make it look like they were accepting the new legal status of same-sex couples that had been so clearly acknowledged in the *M.* v. *H.* decision—but to acknowledge that new legal status in a way that would still contain and limit the expansion of same-sex legal rights as narrowly as possible.

Segregating Recognition
In other words, the legislatures that enacted this raft of new queer relation-ship rules carefully structured them so that at the same time they appeared

to acknowledge queer couples' legal status, they still kicked queer couples out of the category of 'spouse'—a right that the Supreme Court of Canada and earlier lower courts had just given them.

The Ontario government led the way in this process. Having defined 'spouse' as including both married couples and 'cohabitants of the opposite sex' for fifteen years, the moment the Supreme Court of Canada in *M*. v. *H*. directed the government to rewrite that definition to include same-sex cohabitants consistent with its decision, it created a new category of 'same-sex partners' for same-sex cohabitants and left both married couples and heterosexual cohabitants in the old category of 'spouse.'

The new Ontario category of 'same-sex partners' had the effect of segregating queer couples from other couples for purposes of hundreds of provisions in some sixty Ontario statutes. At the same time that it segregated queers, it extended all those marital rights and obligations to them. It even amended the human rights code to prohibit discrimination on the basis of 'same-sex partnership' to ensure that queer couples could not bring complaints under the heading 'marital status.'

Other governments enacted other types of segregating legislation. The federal government moved queer couples to a new category called 'common-law partners.' The Nova Scotia government set up limited RDPs for queers. Quebec enacted civil union legislation that was entirely separate from the rules relating to matrimony in the Civil Code. The only province that continued to leave queer couples in the category of 'spouse' was B.C., although the newest legislation began to use segregating language. Judges continued to make orders for access to the category 'spouse,' but as fast as legislatures could enact alternative 'marriage-like' categories, queers were moved out to them.

This rush to stave off further rulings like *M*. v. *H*. by extending hundreds of marital provisions to queers under other names also had an unintended consequence: it made it clear that virtually every government in Canada considered queer couples to be so 'spouse-like' and their relationships to be so 'marriage-like' that it became more difficult to explain just what was wrong with queer marriage. As much of the substance of marriage became available to queer couples, it became increasingly difficult for opponents of queer marriage to explain why the *form* of their relationships should remain different.

Ironically, even these new 'marriage-like' structures were not all that similar to marriage. Danish and other northern European RDPs and the Vermont civil union statute extended far more comprehensive marital rights and obligations to same-sex couples. In Canada, there continued to be so many differences between same-sex partners/common-law partners/registered partners/etc. when compared with married couples, that this system of segregated rights still looked highly discriminatory. For example, same-sex partners still lacked the ability to inherit from a deceased partner in the same way as do married spouses, or the ability to claim a share of family property on divorce.

Refusal to Override M. v. H.

One other feature of the political response to *M. v. H.* should also be considered. At no time did the federal government or any other government appear to consider using the constitutional power to override the courts by using the 'notwithstanding' clause in section 33 of the Charter. Nor did anyone attempt to get a movement together to amend the constitution to ban same-sex marriage, or even to define ordinary law so that 'spouse' could not include couples of the same sex. Those U.S.-style strategies were never employed. Even the federal Parliament's motion to define marriage heterosexually, and section 1.1 of the federal *M. v. H.* Bill that declared the 'man-woman' definition of marriage to not be affected by the bill, and section 5 of the Federal Law-Civil Code Harmonization Act were merely declaratory, not binding, and have been held to have at most an interpretive purpose.

Thus, the Canadian context in the early 2000s more closely resembled that of the Netherlands than the U.S., in that Canadian governments clearly have never been motivated to take these more aggressive U.S.-style steps to block same-sex marriage at any cost.

The U.K. Connection

In retrospect, it is clear now that the groundbreaking decisions on marriage in *Halpern; MCCT, Barbeau; Egale* and *Hendricks* gained tremendous impetus from the exchange of information and strategizing that occurred at Rob Wintemute and Mads Andenaes' conference on legal recognition of same-sex relationships in July 1999. Sponsored by King's College, University of London, the conference enabled lawyers and academics who had been struggling with barriers to legal recognition of same-sex couples in countries around the world to hear in detail exactly how common obstacles were being addressed and sometimes even being overcome elsewhere.

Most of the Canadian participants arrived fully convinced that the time had come to initiate new marriage litigation in Canada. It became obvious that Canada was likely one of the best places to bring constitutionally-based Charter challenges to the marriage bar. As Kees Waaldijk outlined the same-sex marriage legislation scheduled to be tabled in the Dutch Parliament within the next few days and Mary Bonauto outlined why she expected to obtain a favourable ruling from the Vermont courts in the *Baker* case, the

Canadian participants were able to sit down with Evan Wolfson (co-counsel in the Hawaii case), and other lawyers involved in these developments, to discover what they thought the key elements of their approaches had been. Canadian lawyers were also able to learn in detail from Danish, Swedish and other European lawyers how the issue of same-sex marriage had remained firmly blocked in those countries by RDP legislation.

At the same time, the Canadian participants experienced first-hand how not only lawyers but also judges at the conference looked up to Madame Justice Claire L'Heureux-Dubé—who presented several papers at the conference—and the rest of the Supreme Court of Canada because of their leading contribution to the emerging jurisprudence on substantive equality. In several sessions, the Canadian participants had the opportunity to listen as Madame Justice L'Heureux-Dubé drew the connections between her original dissent in the ill-fated *Mossop*[60] appeal to the Supreme Court of Canada in the early 1990s to the entire series of Supreme Court of Canada decisions on queer and marriage issues: her majority opinion in *Moge*, which embraced diversity in marriage in the early 1990s; her dissent in *Egan and Nesbit*, which inspired the expansion of equality doctrine in the 1999 *Law*[61] decision; and, most importantly, the majority decision in *M.* v. *H.*, which had been released along with the *Law* case just six weeks before the conference was held and was clearly based on her thinking.

The Canadian participants had already put the connections together: *M.* v. *H.* had already laid the doctrinal basis for prohibiting discrimination in the legal recognition of same-sex couples; the Canadian courts were likely to 'get' how this prohibition on queer marriage cuts to the core of human dignity; and, the Canadian courts had already begun, as long ago as 1994 in Mr. Justice Linden's dissenting decision in *Egan and Nesbit*, to reject 'separate and unequal' alternatives for queer couples. The Canadian participants included Martha McCarthy, who had been counsel in *M.* v. *H.*, Joanna Radbord, who had been Martha's junior in that case; Douglas Elliott, who acts for the Metropolitan Community Church of Toronto; Kathleen A. Lahey, who had just published *Are We 'Persons' Yet? Law and Sexuality in Canada*; Marguerite Russell, an out lesbian U.K. barrister and lawyer who had worked in this area for years; and, Laurie Arron, who was involved with Egale. Not surprisingly, it quickly became obvious that Ontario now provided an excellent jurisprudential setting for the next marriage challenge—after all, it had been the Ontario Court of Appeal that had generated both *Haig and Birch* and *M.* v. *H.* As counsel in the most recent of those cases, Martha McCarthy and Joanna Radbord would be the ideal litigators for this effort, and already had clients who wanted to challenge the marriage bar. As discussions unfolded, it also became obvious that the MCCT, which was soon to become licenced by the province of Ontario to issue marriage licences and perform marriages, would not want to have to refuse to marry its lesbian and gay congregants, and that MCCT's lawyer, Douglas Elliott, brought tremendous depth of experience in Charter litigation to the enterprise.

Newly confirmed in their decision to initiate same-sex marriage challenges, the Canadian participants quickly became networked with clients, lawyers and activists in B.C., Ontario and Quebec. But, unlike in previous same-sex marriage challenges, as clients began to go to registry offices to apply for marriage licences, this time, some members of government came out to meet them and two—the Attorney General of B.C., Andrew Petter and the City Clerk of Toronto—actually began litigation on behalf of same-sex couples.

Ontario, B.C. and Quebec—The Cases Begin

Three sets of Charter challenges to the federal government's prohibition on queer marriage were filed in the summer and fall of 2000. These challenges were brought in Quebec, Ontario, and B.C.

Quebec

The Quebec case had actually been initiated in the late 1990s by Michael Hendricks and René LeBoeuf (interviewed in Part II) who had been in a long-term relationship by the time of their application. They were turned down and had difficulty getting support for their suit until the Supreme Court of Canada decision in *M*. v. *H.* galvanized interest in the same-sex marriage issue again. Their original lawsuit was amended and refiled by their lawyers on June 19, 2002, although preparation for the hearing in their case had begun two years before.[62]

Ontario

The Ontario case was being prepared quietly as couples inspired by Martha McCarthy's victory in the *M*. v. *H.* case asked her to see if she could help them get married. Martha began sending these couples to their local registry offices in the spring of 2000 to see if they could get licences, and had recommended that they not make any sort of fuss, but just wait for the lawsuit to be filed. This plan more or less fell apart on May 12, 2000, when two of her clients, Michael Leshner and Michael Stark ('the Michaels'), got so upset at being turned down that they called the media to get the reasons for the refusal on record (The Michaels are interviewed in Part II). The other couples were Hedy Halpern and Colleen Rogers, Aloysius Pittman and Thomas Allworth, Dawn Onishenko and Julie Erbland, Carolyn Rowe and

Carolyn Moffatt, Barbara McDowall and Gail Donnelly, and Alison Kemper and Joyce Barnett.[63]

Much to everyone's amazement, the City Clerk did not turn the Michaels down flat when they returned with the media. Instead, the Clerk announced that the City of Toronto had decided to seek direction from the courts on whether federal law permitted them to issue such a licence. Thus, the City of Toronto took the lead in the Ontario case, although the couples represented by McCarthy and Radbord also filed their own suit. The Metropolitan Community Church of Toronto joined this suit in 2001 when the province refused to register the marriage certificates issued by the church to a lesbian and gay couple after the church and Pastor Brent Hawkes had become licenced to perform banns marriages. (Kevin Bourassa and Joe Varnell, married by the MCCT, are interviewed in Part II.)

British Columbia

The B.C. case was initiated by the provincial government. When Cynthia Callahan and Judy Lightwater were planning their July 2000 wedding, they decided to see if they could obtain a marriage licence toward the end of May. Word of their application reached The Hon. Andrew Petter, then the Attorney General of B.C. Instead of turning them down, the Attorney General called a press conference and issued the following statement: 'In a modern society there is no justification for denying same-sex couples the same option to form marital bonds as are afforded to opposite-sex couples.'

The Attorney General went on to cite the *M.* v. *H.* case, saying that 'the Supreme Court of Canada has held that equality rights under section 15 of the Charter protect against discrimination on the basis of sexual orientation.'

The Attorney General did not think that the issue should be permitted to languish in the courts, but called on the federal government to 'change the federal law to allow for equality for all couples who are in a committed relationship.'

When the federal government refused to respond to this call, the Attorney General initiated the B.C. marriage challenge himself, and joined in that suit B.C. couples who had attempted to marry as early as 1998. These couples included Peter Cook and Murray Warren, Joy Masuhara and Jane Hamilton, and Dawn and Elizabeth Barbeau, all of whom were represented by barbara findlay and Kathleen Lahey. Also included were the five couples represented by Egale and its lawyers Joe Arvay and Cynthia Petersen: David Shortt and Shane McCloskey, Melinda Roy and Tanya Chambers, Lloyd Thornhill and Robert Peacock, Robin Roberts and Diana Denny, and Wendy Young and Mary Theresa Healy.[64] (Peter Cook and Murray Warren,

Robin Roberts and Diana Denny, and Lloyd Thornhill and Robert Peacock are interviewed in Part II.)

Until the NDP government lost the spring election in 2001, the Attorney General of B.C.'s legal staff took the lead in developing expert reports in support of same-sex marriage and in sketching out the legal submissions. After the new Liberal government was elected, the B.C. government then took no position on the merits of the case, and the couples' own petitions were the ones that were eventually heard by the courts.

The Couples' Evidence

The original plan in B.C., which had originally been agreed upon with the Attorney General, was to try to limit the record to a few salient points and to dispense with cross-examination. The goal was to ground the case directly in the realities of the couples' lives. After all, Peter Cook and Murray Warren had been together for over twenty years and had an adopted son; Joy Masuhara and Jane Hamilton had two daughters; Dawn and Elizabeth Barbeau had taken every imaginable legal step to gain access to the rights and responsibilities of marriage, but still faced barriers; and the other couples collectively represented the diversity of hopes and dreams that are well-understood as being typical of those who want to marry.

The expert evidence that was filed by the couples was primarily focused on the changing nature of the family in B.C.; the functioning and needs of same-sex couples and parents; and the needs of children with same-sex parents. When the B.C. Attorney General dropped its active role in the case, and as the federal government and some of the religious interveners kept widening the scope of the evidence by filing more affidavits, the couples' lawyers provided some additional material, but the plan was to place most of the evidentiary emphasis on the needs and lives of contemporary queers and their families themselves.

The evidentiary record in the Ontario case was much larger. This was due in part to the fact that the federal lawyer heading that case insisted on filing a large number of expert reports and conducting extensive cross-examination of the couples' experts. As in B.C., the couples also filed extensive evidence about their own reasons for wanting to marry, and the MCCT filed experts' reports on matters specific to the church's claim. Relatively little expert evidence was filed by the couple in the Quebec case.

The Federal Government's Position

Unlike the City of Toronto or the B.C. government, the federal government was actively hostile to all three of these applications. The lawyers who acted for the federal government obtained and filed expert reports from over twenty academics and professionals who noticeably did not attempt to present any kind of balanced view of changing social realities or the diversity of family life in Canada. Every single expert report was aimed at trying to convince the courts that heterosexual-only marriage was and ought to remain a 'universal norm.' The experts included an employee of the Catholic Archdiocese of Toronto who held a degree in anthropology; a conservative Catholic lawyer from the U.S.; and, experts in comparative religion, U.K. and U.S. family law, linguistics, statistics and ethics. The federal government even submitted opinions by experts in law and economics analysis who predicted that 'the sky will fall' if queer couples are allowed to marry. (The federal government later revealed that it paid experts' fees of some $350, 000.)

The federal government's legal position was simple: prohibiting same-sex marriage cannot be considered to be discriminatory within the meaning of the Charter of Rights because only heterosexual couples can procreate and most children are born of heterosexual marriages. Marriage between two people of the same sex has never been a 'norm' anywhere in recorded history, and conceptually what might look like a 'marriage' between two people of the same sex cannot actually be a marriage because of essential differences relating to biological procreation.

If this seems to be an extreme characterization of the federal government's position, consider how the Ontario trial court in *Halpern; MCCT* summarized the federal government's legal position:

'The AGC submits that the institution of marriage is an historical and universal pre-legal concept of an opposite-sex union that was ultimately adopted by law. It contends that there is—and always has been—three basic universal norms, or "Goods and Goals," that constitutes marriage. They are (i) procreation, (ii) fidelity, and (iii) sacrament. It argues that—while variables may exist within marriage—the universal norms, namely, the Goods and Goals, always remain. Any relationship, it says, that is outside the universal Goods and Goals does not constitute a marriage but rather an alternative to marriage:

"... same-sex marriage is an oxymoron, because it lacks the universal, or *defining* feature of marriage according to religious, historical, and anthropological evidence. Apart from anything else, marriage expresses one fundamental and universal need: a setting for reproduction that recognizes the reciprocity between nature (sexual dimorphism) and cultural (gender complementarity)."[65]

This last passage was a quotation from an affidavit provided by Dr. Katherine Young, a Professor of Comparative Religion at McGill University—one of the experts retained by the federal government. Professor Young was also of the view that extending marriage to same-sex couples could have 'unforeseen unfavourable consequences for society' such as 'increased polarization of men and women and/or to an identity crisis for men.'[66]

Elsewhere the Ontario trial court gave this rendition of the federal government's claim that the legal scope of 'marriage' was outside the reach of *any* government or court:

> 'The argument is that marriage pre-exists the law, and that the common law simply recognizes the institution of marriage (being the union of one man and one woman); it did not create the institution. Accordingly, it should not be changed by the law.'[67]

By the time the first trial of these cases took place, same-sex couples in the Netherlands had been permitted to marry legally for over three months. Nonetheless, the federal government persisted in arguing that those Dutch marriages were not really 'marriages' because same-sex couples could not procreate—they were in some other type of legal relationship that had been inaccurately labelled 'marriage.'

The Trial Court Rulings
In the first round of hearings, the rulings looked like this:

B.C.   No marriage
Ontario   Marriage beginning July 12, 2004
Quebec   Marriage beginning July 12, 2004

The B.C. trial court decision (the *Barbeau; Egale* case) has to be one of the worst same-sex marriage rulings on the books. The court did find that denial of the right to marry violates section 15 of the Charter, but went on to conclude that such a violation did not matter for two reasons: because it is 'demonstrably justifiable' under section 1 of the Charter, and because the meaning of the word 'marriage' as used in the older part of the Canadian constitution (the British North America Act, 1867) independently prohibits same-sex marriage no matter how section 1 is applied.

The B.C. trial court did not bother to address remedy, so convinced was it that same-sex marriage was barred by the words of the constitution itself. As that court stated, the Charter cannot be used to challenge or change the interpretation of another part of the constitution. By ruling that the word 'marriage' in the B.N.A. Act had obviously not contemplated same-sex marriage when the constitution was set up in 1867, the court placed same-sex marriage completely beyond reach of any government in Canada. Indeed, the court suggested that the constitution would have to be amended in order to give some branch of government the constitutional authority to extend marriage to same-sex couples.

The Ontario and Quebec trial court decisions went off on completely different grounds. Both courts held that denying same-sex couples the right to marry unjustifiably violates section 15 of the Charter. Both courts flatly rejected the B.C. trial court's analysis of the constitutional status of the word 'marriage.' Both courts ordered that if the federal government did not enact legislation extending marriage to same-sex couples by July 12, 2004, they could go ahead and get married as of that date by virtue of the courts' orders.

The Appellate Court Decisions

This picture changed radically once the B.C. and Ontario courts issued their rulings in the spring of 2003:

B.C. Court of Appeal	Marriage beginning July 12, 2004
Ontario Court of Appeal	Marriage immediately—on June 10, 2003
Quebec Court of Appeal	Appeal decided March 19, 2004—immediate marriage

The B.C. Court of Appeal reversed the B.C. trial court on every point, and made the same order that the Ontario court had made: same-sex couples can marry as of July 12, 2004, unless the federal government opens marriage to same-sex couples before that. The Ontario Court of Appeal affirmed the Ontario trial court on every point, but took a step that no court had ever taken before—it ordered that same-sex couples be permitted to marry from the moment the decision was issued.

Two couples, including the Michaels, got married in Toronto that same day, on June 10, 2003. On July 8, 2003, the B.C. Court of Appeal followed the Ontario Court of Appeal and lifted its suspension order, effective immediately. Thousands of marriages have now been carried out in these two provinces. The Quebec Court of Appeal finally permitted marriage when it ruled on March 19, 2004. No doubt thousands more marriages will take place there.

The B.C. Court of Appeal Decision

The B.C. Court of Appeal decision was unanimous, written by Justice Jo Ann Prowse, with a separate concurring opinion on the meaning of 'marriage' as used in the B.N.A. Act, 1867, by Justice Mackenzie. This case established two crucial points: courts can look to changing social conditions to adapt the common law concept of marriage to contemporary social needs, and segregated 'alternatives' to marriage such as RDPs or civil unions are not constitutionally acceptable remedies.

On the basis of those two points, and relying on the equality provisions of the Charter, the court ruled that marriage must be opened to same-sex couples as 'the only road to true equality.' The court further ordered that if the federal government did not amend the law to reflect the new definition by July 12, 2004, then its reformulation would take effect on that date. That specific date had been chosen to coordinate with the dates set by the trial courts in Ontario and Quebec.

Evolving Concepts of Marriage: The definition of 'marriage' was an issue in the B.C. appeal in two ways. The court had to decide whether the statement in an 1866 English *Hyde* decision that referred to marriage as the union of 'a man and a woman' still defined capacity to marry in federal law. And the court also had to determine whether the term 'marriage' as used in the B.N.A. Act, 1867, somehow precluded the Canadian government or the courts from extending marriage to same-sex couples in 2003.

With regard to the first aspect of the issue, the court had no difficulty in reformulating 'marriage' in gender-neutral terms as 'the lawful union of two persons to the exclusion of all others.' Strictly speaking, this may not have been necessary, since the federal Marriage Act was already expressed in gender-neutral terms. Strictly speaking, the court did not have to rely on section 15 of the Charter to reach this conclusion. However, it was obvious that all the courts wanted to make sure that their decisions were as appeal-proof as possible.

With regard to the second aspect of the issue, Mr. Justice Mackenzie tackled the core contention, which had been raised by religious interveners, by addressing 'whether the heterosexual element of the common law definition is immutable.' It is significant that he applied the classic common law analysis of the issue that had originally been set out in the *Persons* case[68] to answer this question. The *Persons* case was the famous decision obtained in 1929 by Emily Murphy and the rest of the 'Alberta Five' when they sought to establish that women are 'persons' who are qualified under the B.N.A. Act, 1867, to sit in the Senate. The Privy Council held that stereotypes relating to women had become outmoded by changing social realities. Mr. Justice Mackenzie said:

> 'In my respectful view, the trial judge's reasons [on the meaning of 'marriage' in the constitution] fail to give adequate weight to the evolution of societal views with respect to homosexuality. Until relatively recently, homosexual relations were subject to criminal sanctions and the idea of same-sex marriage was not a possibility that could be seriously considered. Since the de-criminalization of homosexual relationships in Canada in 1969, there has been a steady expansion of the rights of gay, lesbian and bi-sexual persons reflected in human rights legislation and Charter jurisprudence. These developments have substantial public support, although the matter remains controversial. In my view, this evolution cannot be ignored. Civil marriage should adapt to contemporary notions of marriage as an institution in a society which recognizes the rights of homosexual persons to non-discriminatory treatment. In that context, I do not think it can be said that extending the capacity to marry to same-sex couples is so fundamental a change as to exceed Parliament's jurisdiction over marriage under s. 91(26).'[69]

Although Justice Mackenzie did not expressly rely on the *Persons* case, he implicitly reaffirmed the progressive doctrine of interpretation of the Canadian constitution, labelled the 'living tree' doctrine in the *Persons* case. This 'living tree' doctrine looks not to historical practices or assumptions, but to evolving social conditions and the social realities surrounding each specific case that comes before the courts.

'Alternatives' to Marriage Unacceptable: The other critically important aspect of the *Barbeau;Egale* decision is the court's unanimous ruling on remedy. Writing for the Court, Justice Prowse held that the federal government now has only three policy options open to it: 'permit same-sex couples to marry; use its override power under section 33 of the Charter'; or 'abolish marriage altogether.'

The court decisively rejected the remedy proposed by the government—the enactment of some 'alternative' form of relationship recognition such as the Nova Scotia RDPs or the Quebec civil unions. The court emphatically ruled that it would not grant a remedy 'which makes same-sex couples "almost equal,"' nor that it would 'leave it to governments to choose amongst less-than-equal solutions.' The court stated unequivocally that such 'parallel institutions' would 'fall short of true equality.' The court made it crystal clear that only one remedy would be acceptable to it: full civil marriage.

These rulings had been prompted by the federal government's suggestion during oral argument that the Department of Justice Committee on Same-sex Marriage should be given time to complete public consultations that were going on at the time and to make recommendations to Parliament. Relying on a detailed report of the Law Commission of Canada on adult relationships that had been published in 2001 (*Beyond Conjugality*),[70] Justice Prowse concluded that 'further consultation will not change the fact' that even though same-sex marriage is controversial, excluding same-sex couples from marriage is discriminatory.

Justice Prowse further pointed out that the Law Commission of Canada had already carried out exactly the same kind of in-depth consultation. The Law Commission had carried out extensive public consultations; it had engaged a wide-ranging panel of experts to carry out detailed studies on the issue and to advise it; it had carefully considered diverse views on same-sex marriage expressed by religious and secular groups; and, it had reached the very considered conclusion that 'alternatives' such as RDPs were not accept-able, and that only marriage will solve the problem: 'If governments are to continue to maintain an institution called marriage, they cannot do so in a discriminatory fashion.'[71]

This aspect of the B.C. Court of Appeal decision is important because it is now the leading statement in Canadian law that 'separate equality' is constitutionally impermissible. Both the Quebec decision in *Hendricks* and some individual judges in the Ontario *Halpern; MCCT* case had earlier also rejected the notion that queers could somehow be dealt with by enacting a new civil structure. This aspect of the B.C. appellate judgment confirms those two decisions and adds the weight of the B.C. Court of Appeal to those rulings in a way that the Ontario appellate judgment could not—by ordering immediate marriage, the question of 'alternatives' to marriage became irrelevant to that court's analysis.

The Ontario Court of Appeal Decision

The Ontario Court of Appeal decision was released on June 10, 2003. Thus, the Ontario court had the benefit of having read the *Barbeau; Egale* decision of the B.C. Court of Appeal as it prepared its own decision in *Halpern; MCCT*. The two courts reached the same conclusions on all the substantive Charter issues, but the Ontario court did not have to spend time considering the viability of 'alternatives' to marriage: by ordering that marriage be opened to queer couples immediately, there was no space of time in which the federal government could even consider going off to devise some other remedy.

The Ontario Court of Appeal ordered that the old common law definition of marriage be changed immediately from 'a voluntary union for life of one man and one woman, to the exclusion of all others' to 'the voluntary union for life of two persons to the exclusion of all others.' As the Ontario court explained, it was appropriate to make this change effective immediately instead of ordering some period of deferral because of the nature of the common law itself:

> '[B]ecause this appeal involves a Charter challenge to a common law, judge-made rule, the Charter analysis involves somewhat different considerations than would apply to a challenge to a legislative provision. … Given that the common law rule was fashioned by judges and not by Parliament or a legislature, judicial deference to elected bodies is not an issue. If it is possible to reformulate a common law rule so that it will not conflict with the principles of fundamental justice, such a reformulation should be undertaken.'[72]

The Ontario court also concluded that '[a] delayed declaration allows a state of affairs which has been found to violate standards embodied in the Charter to persist for a time despite the violation.' Further, the court determined that no delay was necessary because same-sex marriage would not cause any 'harm to the public, threaten the rule of law, or deny anyone the benefit of legal recognition of their marriage,'[73] nor require the legislature to adjust other areas of law.

The Ontario Court of Appeal gave its adaptation of the common law immediate effect because it felt that it was critical to take immediate steps to 'ensure that opposite-sex couples and same-sex couples immediately receive equal treatment in law in accordance with s. 15(1) of the Charter.'[74]

When the B.C. Court of Appeal adopted the Ontario Court of Appeal's order for immediate marriage less than a month later, both of those appellate decisions became authority for the proposition that governments should not be given *any* time to consider how they will implement such orders—the courts will simply do it for them. It is worth noting that the Massachusetts appellate court relied directly on these Canadian decisions when it ruled in *Goodridge II* in January 2004 that civil union legislation would not be an adequate substitute for marriage. If the Massachusetts government does not enact new inclusive marriage legislation by mid-May 2004, the court's own adaptation of the common law in that state will take effect at that time.

Reactions to the Ontario Decision

The May 1, 2003 decision of the B.C. Court of Appeal created quite a sensation, but it died fairly quickly. When the Ontario Court of Appeal decision was released on June 10, 2003, images of lesbian and gay weddings remained in the media until the end of the summer. By far the most important reaction was that of queers themselves. As soon as word of the decision came out, couples began appearing in growing numbers at the Toronto Clerk's office, and other municipal offices across Ontario began to get inquiries from couples who wanted marriage certificates. The Attorney General of Ontario issued a directive within a few days of the Ontario decision that alleviated residual worries about just which municipalities were bound by the court's order, and marriages began to take place all across Ontario.

However, the celebration of the *Halpern* decision was tinged with fear. Many people simply could not believe that this had happened—that if they and their partner wanted to get married, all they had to do was walk into the nearest Ontario registry office, fill out a one-page form, pay a fee of $100, and find an officiant—or just use the municipal officiant right there in the office. After decades of denial, appeals to religious morality, claims that queer marriage would impair 'the family' and ruin Canadian society, it seemed too simple, too easy.

This fear and sense of urgency to claim a right that had been so difficult to obtain, resulted in a real rush on Ontario registry offices. Couples from all over Ontario, B.C. (which had not yet lifted its suspension), other provinces, the U.S., and even couples from Europe and other continents came to Ontario registry offices in the first month after the *Halpern* decision was issued to seize this opportunity. Some of the couples who had brought the same-sex marriage challenge into the B.C. courts actually came to Ontario as soon as they could get on a plane to get married. It was just too good to be true—and too important to let the opportunity slip by, in case the federal government changed its mind and got the registry offices to turn them away again.

The same pattern was repeated in B.C. when marriage became available there on July 8, 2003. Couples from twenty-two other countries as well as from every province in Canada flooded in to marry in B.C. in just a few months after that decision. For some, their urgency was spurred by threatening illnesses or family crises. For others, it was simply impossible to wait any longer.

The Quebec Court of Appeal did not rule until March 19, 2004. No doubt the same demand will emerge there as soon as banns can be announced.

Hopefully the fear that this newly-won right may yet be snatched away has dissipated by now, and queers can relax and plan their weddings with the same confidence in the law that heterosexual couples have. But for the first few months after these decisions were issued, the speed with which couples from around the world came to Canada to get married revealed more than any study ever could, just how wounding the denial of the right to marry on the basis of sexuality has been. For example, of the 1,466 queers married in B.C. by the end of 2003, 889 came to B.C. from other provinces, from the U.S., from Japan, and from elsewhere around the world.

The lifting of the marriage ban has made it possible for many queers to experience their full humanity as it is defined in this culture for the first time in their lives. No longer forced to be permanent 'cohabitants,' 'boyfriends' or 'partners,' queers can now make all the same choices that have always been available to other adults in Canadian society. Some of us have realized with a jolt that not being permitted to even think about marriage in the past had prevented us from seeing our relationships in that framework. Some queers have reported going through a process of meeting those parts of themselves who are just starting to realize what it might mean to be able to think about getting married.

Of course, not everyone has been thrilled with the Ontario and B.C. decisions. The Catholic Pope spoke out against it, as have George W. Bush, the President of the U.S., spokespersons for conservative social and religious groups and many elected Canadian politicians. The Catholic Church actually announced that it expects Catholic politicians and public officers to exercise their public and elective duties consistent with Catholic doctrine, and politicians in the U.S. have begun to step up efforts to avert the importation of Canadian marriages to their states by strengthening anti-queer-marriage laws.

Although a couple who were refused a marriage licence in Alberta have filed a human rights complaint there, the trend at the moment is for couples in Canada who wish to travel to either Ontario or B.C. to marry. There are no citizenship, residency, or medical conditions that must be fulfilled to marry in any Canadian province, so the biggest source of delay is likely to arise from the complexities of proving up prior divorces, especially foreign divorces. The rest of the country is waiting to see what the federal government does after the Supreme Court of Canada delivers its advisory opinion on the federal government's new marriage law in a legal proceeding known as a Reference. A Supreme Court of Canada Reference is a special legal procedure by which the federal government can refer important legal issues to the Supreme Court for the purpose of requesting an advisory opinion from the Court. Such opinions are not binding on the government or on the Court itself, but, as in the Quebec Secession Reference, the Court's opinion on the issue can provide useful guidance on constitutional issues for the government as it grapples with significant political issues.

The Supreme Court of Canada Marriage Reference

If same-sex couples are now legally permitted to marry, why is there a 'Reference' on same-sex marriage to the Supreme Court of Canada? Any provincial Court of Appeal can rule on the validity of federal law, and with three of the most prestigious appellate courts now having ruled that federal marriage law must be extended to same-sex couples, how can there be anything left to decide? Indeed, if the Ontario appellate court already changed federal law as of June 10, 2003, and if both the B.C. and Quebec appellate courts have now affirmed that change, why does the federal government even need to pass legislation on the issue?

The Reference

The Reference is not legally necessary. Until and unless the Ontario Court of Appeal decision in *Halpern; MCCT* is overturned by invoking the notwithstanding clause of the Charter, nothing can turn the clock back on federal marriage law. The federal Justice Minister said as much in July 2003 when he indicated that the federal government would not oppose the issue of marriage licences in other provinces. As far as the federal government is concerned, the law changed on June 10, 2003.

Then why a new marriage bill? And why a Supreme Court of Canada Reference on top of that?

Ordinary Canadians may never know exactly why the Ontario and B.C. cases were never appealed, or why the federal government felt that it needed to take this route. Part of the answer lies in the well-known split among Liberal MPs themselves; there are some vehement opponents to same-sex marriage in the Liberal government. With a spring 2004 election coming up, staging a Reference on a draft bill is an excellent way to defuse the issue during the election, because the government makes it clear that it intends to listen to what people all across the country have to say. The new bill could even fail when the government puts it to a free vote, and that fact will no doubt have some impact on voting in some closely-contested ridings, such as that of Deputy Prime Minister, the Hon. Anne McLellan of Alberta.

From the point of view of established queer rights to same-sex marriage, the Reference is procedurally not the type of legal process in which the Supreme Court of Canada could actually reverse the Ontario, B.C. or Quebec

Court of Appeal decisions. A reference is *not* an appeal. A reference is an advisory process, not binding on any parties, and is not binding even on the Supreme Court of Canada itself.

The Court is being asked to offer its advisory opinion on four questions submitted by the federal government:

> 1. Is the *Proposal for an Act respecting certain aspects of legal capacity for marriage for civil purposes* within the exclusive legislative authority of the Parliament of Canada?
> 2. If the answer to question 1 is yes, is section 1 of the proposal, which extends capacity to marry to persons of the same sex, consistent with the *Canadian Charter of Rights and Freedoms*?
> 3. Does the freedom of religion guaranteed by paragraph 2(a) of the *Canadian Charter of Rights and Freedoms* protect religious officials from being compelled to perform a marriage between two persons of the same sex that is contrary to their religious beliefs?
> 4. Is the opposite-sex requirement for marriage for civil purposes, as established by the common law and set out for Quebec in s. 5 of the Federal Law-Civil Code Harmonization Act, No. 1, consistent with the *Canadian Charter of Rights and Freedoms*? If not, in what particular or particulars and to what extent?

The first three questions were filed with the Court on July 17, 2003, and the fourth on January 28, 2004. The federal government is taking the position that the first three questions should be answered in the affirmative, and that the fourth question should be answered in the negative.

Many lawyers have found the fourth question to be confusing. This is because the 'common law' referred to in the fourth question has already been changed as of June 10, 2003, by the Ontario Court of Appeal, and the Quebec Court of Appeal has ruled that the Quebec trial court correctly concluded that section 5 of the Harmonization Act is merely an interpretive provision that has no independent legal effect. That artifact of heterosexual-only marriage is also defunct. So some people are having a hard time understanding how there can be a Reference question on the continued constitutional validity of laws that are no longer in effect. It will be interesting to see how the various lawyers approach that question.

The Reference is scheduled to be heard by the Supreme Court of Canada on October 6, 7 and 8, 2004. The original list of twenty-odd interveners will no doubt expand further as additional groups take up the Court's invitation to apply for intervener status.

The Interveners

Because this legal proceeding is a Reference, strictly speaking, there are no parties in the sense of plaintiff, defendant or appellant. The only real 'party' is the federal government, which can shape the questions any way it wants and can make any legal submissions it wants to in support of the way it wants those questions to be answered. Provincial governments are entitled as a matter of right to be heard in these types of proceedings, especially when a constitutional question is involved. And other groups and individuals can apply to the Court for permission to 'intervene' in the reference, which simply means that they can file legal arguments too, and even be allowed some time to address the Court.

By the time any Charter issue gets to the Supreme Court of Canada even through the usual appeal route, the number of governments and intervener groups is usually quite large. For example, in the *M.* v. *H.* appeal, there were a total of ten participants: one government (Ontario, which had received special leave to bring the appeal), two individuals who had been involved in the litigation in the lower courts (M. and H.), and seven intervener groups. In one of the most important constitutional references in recent years, the 1998 Quebec Secession Reference, there were thirteen: four governments, six intervener groups, and three individuals who had been involved in the litigation in the lower courts.

The federal government has invited additional groups and governments to seek leave during the extension period, but as of January 23, 2004, there were already over twenty participants: four governments, fourteen intervener groups, two members of Parliament, as well as the original groups of litigants from the Ontario, Quebec and B.C. cases. The fourteen intervener groups are split somewhat evenly between the two positions, with several human rights commissions and one group of rabbis included in the pro-marriage group, and the U.S.-based *Focus on the Family* joining religious organizations in the anti same-sex marriage group.

The involvement of *Focus on the Family* in this Canadian litigation deserves some comment. Although this Colorado-based group has several overseas branches, its main concern regarding Canadian marriage laws is that it feels that heterosexual-only marriage in the U.S. will be threatened because people living in the U.S. will have easy access to same-sex marriage in Ontario, Quebec or B.C. With openly-held views like 'homosexually active persons [are] less psychologically healthy than the general population'; 'lesbian relationships are equally unhealthy, and just as life-threatening as gay male relationships'; and, 'homosexual male relationships are rarely monogamous and those involved are more at risk for life-threatening ill-nesses,'[75] many of the pro same-sex marriage groups are apprehensive at what types of materials and legal arguments *Focus on the Family* and the other anti same-sex marriage interveners might want to inject into the Reference.

Several of the original petitioners in the lower courts found it painful to sit through discussions of some of the more extreme views of the social conservative and religious interveners. It is not likely to be any easier in the Supreme Court of Canada.

The Path Ahead in Canada
The Ontario, Quebec and B.C. Courts of Appeal will go down in history as having been the courts with the vision and courage to break through the ban on same-sex marriage in North America. Public opinion on same-sex marriage has shifted rapidly in Canada since the summer of 2003, due both to the solemn terms in which the Ontario and B.C. courts recognized the human dignity of queer couples and by the flood of images of ordinary queers, their families, and their friends celebrating their new right to marry. The Quebec Court of Appeal has confirmed that this change affects the whole of Canada, not just the provinces in which these decisions were made.

The federal government in Canada will go down in history as the first North American government to come forward with proposed legislation that confirms that same-sex couples cannot be denied the right to marry. Although the enactment of this draft legislation will depend on how and when the Supreme Court of Canada rules on the Marriage Reference after the hearing in October 2004, the tabling of this draft legislation is by itself a monumental step.

The federal government in Canada will also go down in history as the first government that did *not* attempt to stave off queer marriage by offering segregated alternatives like RDPs or civil union to queers instead of the right to civil marriage. Unlike the Netherlands, Belgium and even Massachusetts, the Canadian government—once the Court of Appeal decisions in Ontario and B.C. were released—did not subject queers in Canada to the indignity of having that form of legislation offered to them. This is undoubtedly due to the fact that the Ontario and B.C. courts expressly followed the Law Commission of Canada report on marriage in rejecting anything but full formal civil marriage.

Until the Supreme Court of Canada rules on the Marriage Reference or the federal government enacts the Marriage Bill, however, the status of marriage for queer couples in Canada will of course remain unsettled in many ways. Provincial and federal courts will have to continue to respond to the remaining issues on a case by case basis during the interim period. The issues that may still have to come before the courts fall into four basic categories: validity of marriages within Canada; recognition outside Canada; passport rules and access to emergency services outside Canada; and immigration status.

The most pressing of these issues is whether every province and territory in Canada will recognize same-sex marriages validly performed and registered in Quebec, Ontario and B.C. Certainly both the B.C. and Quebec Courts of Appeal have decisively ruled that *Halpern* changed the law of marriage for the entire country as of June 10, 2003. Some governments have announced that they will; for example, the government of Nunavut in the northwest announced in 2003 that it would recognize same-sex marriages even though it was not yet performing them. As the number of couples from non-marriage provinces who travel to Ontario, B.C. and, recently, Quebec, to marry continue to grow, the validity of their marriages in their home communities will become more pressing as time passes. Inheritance rights, parent-child relationships, issues surrounding social and employment benefits, even the right to file for divorce, for example, will all require local courts to rule on the validity of the couple's marriage.

Given that the validity of marriage is strictly a question of federal law, and that queer couples who marry will have done so in the three provinces in which the top courts have ruled that federal law permits same-sex couples to marry, it seems unlikely that courts in other provinces will refuse to recognize Ontario, B.C. and Quebec marriages. However, the simple fact that couples or surviving family members may have to turn to the courts for such rulings injects an element of uncertainty into the status of same-sex marriages outside those three provinces.

Travel outside Canada raises similar questions for same-sex spouses and their families. The norm in international and transnational law is that marriages valid where they are performed will be treated as valid in other states. However, given the level of prejudice that exists in other countries, it may well be that Canadian couples will only be fully accepted in the Netherlands, Belgium, and, after mid-May 2004, Massachusetts. Until the courts in California, New Mexico, New York, New Jersey and Oregon clarify the status of marriages performed in 2004 there, those states cannot necessarily be counted on to recognize Canadian marriages. Of particular concern to Canadian queer couples should be the thirty-eight states in the U.S. that have express 'defence of marriage' statutes that prevent them from recognizing same-sex marriages. Depending on the level of legal protection given to people characterized by their sexual orientations in those states, queer spouses could face not only refusal to recognize their marriages but also varying levels of active discrimination. For couples with children, this lack of legal recognition could be particularly concerning.

Problems surrounding travel outside Canada are not necessarily caused by foreign governments alone. Couples and families travelling outside Canada may still face problems with passports and with emergency services from the Canadian government. Married couples living in B.C. are presumptively both legal parents to children born to them (this rule also applies to unmarried cohabiting couples), and the federal government will probably follow the birth certificates of the children when issuing passports. But married or unmarried queer couples living in Ontario are not presumptively both legal parents of their children, and so far the federal government has insisted on sticking to the parent-child relationships set out on the children's birth certificates in issuing their passports. There is also the possibility that if a family were caught in an emergency situation outside Canada, the consular services might not want to process the family as a legal unit but might want to have the flexibility to treat them as unrelated individuals in some circumstances. Federal legislation does not completely clarify these issues.

Immigration problems may also still arise because the right to marry in Ontario, Quebec and B.C. has not clearly led to agreement by the federal government that it will process immigration applications from queer couples on the same basis that it does those from heterosexual couples. A queer fiancé ought to be able to sponsor the immigration of their future spouse on the same basis as heterosexual couples, but this is not what federal immigration law says at this point. Alternative compassionate grounds are available, but they are far more discretionary, require more documentation, and take far longer. Families with same-sex parents ought to be able to immigrate under the family rules, but so far they have not been permitted to do so even when the marriage took place validly in the Netherlands, Belgium, Ontario or B.C.

No doubt these issues will eventually be resolved in Canada. Indeed, it is far more likely that even though Canada is geographically similar in size to both the U.S. and the European Union, the legal status of queer couples across Canada is likely to be accepted far more quickly than it will be in the more politically atomized U.S. states and E.U. Unlike the U.S. states and the E.U. countries, which has jurisdiction over marriage within their boundaries, it is the federal government in Canada that has exclusive legislative jurisdiction over capacity to marry in Canada. Thus, once the status of same-sex marriage is completely confirmed either by the Supreme Court of Canada or by federal legislation in Canada, that will be the end of the matter domestically. In the U.S. and the E.U., however, the status of same-sex marriages will have to worked out state by state as well as at the level of the national U.S. government and the governing council of the E.U. There is the theoretical possibility that some future government may invoke a special constitutional clause called the 'notwithstanding clause' in section 33 of the Canadian Charter of Rights and Freedoms to roll back queer marriage. But even if that did happen, the roll back would only last for five years. And there is every indication that younger Canadians overwhelmingly embrace the validity of same-sex marriage to the extent of at least 75%.

By comparison with the status of married couples in the Netherlands and Belgium, queer couples who marry in Canada still live in a patchwork of inconsistent relationship laws. They also continue to face uncertainty as to when and to exactly what extent their new matrimonial rights will be respected.

But uncertainty about the path ahead can never take away from the absolute awe and joy felt by queers who now know that in at least three provinces in Canada, anyone who can get there can marry. Queer marriage has come to Canada to stay.

Also here to stay is the new presumption arising from the Ontario, B.C. and Quebec Court of Appeal decisions that all laws, practices and programs in Canada are to be considered to *include* queers unless they are expressly excluded. The net effect of the Canadian marriage decisions is that they have essentially just confirmed what queers always knew—that they are 'persons' too. That it has taken three decades of protracted and soul-wrenching litigation to establish the simple proposition that lesbian and gay couples can now be considered to be 'any two persons' for purposes of marriage laws reveals the shocking depths of homophobia that have shaped Canadian and other legal cultures.

Hopefully ours will be the last generations in Canada to be so aware of how far queers in Canada have had to come to become what everyone else has always been—just ordinary people with ordinary hopes and dreams and rights.

Endnotes

Chapter One

1. John Boswell, *Same-Sex Unions in Pre-Modern Europe* (New York: Villard, 1994).

2. The scholarship on same-sex relationships in history is extensive. Some of the leading references include: Rome and Greece: Boswell, *Same-Sex Unions*, generally; Hans Licht, *Sexual Life in Ancient Greece* (London: Routledge and Kegan Paul, 1932); China: Bret Hinsch, *Passions of the Cut Sleeve: The Male Homosexual Tradition in China* (Berkeley and Los Angeles: University of California Press, 1990); Michael Szonyi, "The Cult of Hu Tianbao and the Eighteenth-Century Discourse of Homosexuality," *Late Imperial China* 19:1 (1998), 1; Japan: Ihara Saikaku, *The Great Mirror of Male Love*, translated by Paul Gordon Schalow (Stanford CA: Stanford University Press, 1990); South East Asia: Rakesh Ratti, ed., *A Lotus of Another Color: An Unfolding of the South Asian Gay and Lesbian Experience*, (Boston: Alyson, 1993); Australia: Edward Westermarck, *The Origin and Development of Moral Ideas* (London: Macmillan, 1906), p. 104; India: Anu and Giti, "Inverting Tradition: The Marriage of Lila and Urmila", in Ratti, *Lotus*, pp. 81-84; the Americas: Robert Morris, *"Aikāne*: Accounts of Hawaiian Same-Sex Relationships in the Journals of Captain Cook's Third Voyage (1776-1780)," *Journal of Homosexuality* 19, 4 (1990), pp. 21-54; Westermarck, *Moral Ideas*, pp. 101-103; Will Roscoe, *The Zuni Man-Woman* (Albuquerque: University of New Mexico Press, 1991); medieval and early modern Europe: Boswell, *Same-Sex Unions*; Portugal: Michel de Montaigne, 'A Strange Brotherhood' (Travel Journal, entry of 18 March 1581), in *The Complete Essays of Montaigne,* translated by Donald M. Frame (Stanford, CA, Stanford University Press, 1958); England: Rictor Norton, *Mother Clap's Molly House: The Gay Subculture in England 1700-1830* (Gay Mens Press, 1992); Emma Donahue, *Passions Between Women: British Lesbian Culture 1668-1801* (New York: HarperCollins, 1995, British. ed. 1993), esp. pp. 65-73; Netherlands: Kent Gerard and Gert Kekma, eds., *The Pursuit of Sodomy: Male Homosexuality in Renaissance and Enlightenment Europe* (New York: Harrington Park Press, 1988), esp. pp. 217-218, 263-310; Pirates: B.R. Burg, *Sodomy and the Pirate Tradition: English Sea Rivers in the Seventeenth-Century Caribbean* (New York: New York University Press, 1984), pp. 128-30; Africa: Edward Evans-Pritchard, *The Azande: History*

and Political Institutions (Oxford: Oxford University Press, 1971), pp. 199-200; Ngozi Oti, 'Same-Sex Marriage Among the Ibo and Nuer' (Kingston, Ont.: Queen's University, Faculty of Law, Law and Sexuality Seminar, November 1996) [paper on file with K. Lahey]; Ifi Amadiume, *Male Daughters, Female Husbands: Gender and Sex in an African Society* (London: Zed, 1987).

3. *Brown* v. *Board of Education of Topeka, Kansas*, 347 U.S. 483 (U.S. Supreme Court, 1954).

4. *Loving* v. *Virginia*, 388 U.S. 1 (U.S. Supreme Court, 1967).

5. See generally Mark Thompson, ed., *Long Road to Freedom: The Advocate History of the Gay and Lesbian Movement* (New York: St. Martin's Press, 1994) for a more detailed account of these events.

6. One of the men married in Boulder, Colorado, later tried to sponsor his husband for immigration purposes. The federal immigration department rejected this application on the basis that they were not validly married in the eyes of state law. The couple took the government to court and lost. *Adams* v. *Howerton*, 486 F. Supp. 119, 673 F. 2d 1036 (CCA 9, 1983), *cert. den.* 458 U.S. 111, 102 S. Ct. 3494 (U.S. S.C., 1985).

Chapter Two

7. These events are described in Caroline Forder, 'European Models of Domestic Partnership Laws: the Field of Choice,' *Canadian Journal of Family Law* 2000, pp. 370-452 and Caroline Forder, *Civil Law Aspects of Emerging Forms of Registered Partnerships*, commissioned by the Ministry of Justice of the Netherlands and the Council of Europe for the Fifth Family Law Conference of the Council of Europe (Hague, May 15-16, 1999).

8. Dr. Caroline Forder, *Affidavit* (Supreme Court of Canada, Marriage Reference Case, Court file number 29866, affidavit filed November 26, 2003), para. 35, quoting the Dutch legislative debates (Second Chamber 1999-2000, 26 672, nr. 5, p. 7) [on file with K. Lahey].

9. *Baker* v. *Nelson*, 191 N.W. 2d 185, at 187 (Minnesota Supreme Ct., 1971).

10. *Dean* v. *District of Columbia* (D.C. Superior Court, 1995) (Court File No. 90-13892, 1991).

11. *Singer* v. *Hara*, 11 Washington App. 247, 522 P.2d 1187 (Washington Appeal Ct., 1974).

12. *Jones* v. *Hallahan*, 501 S.W. 2d 588 (Kentucky Ct. of Appeal, 1973).

13. *Bowers* v. *Hardwick*, 478 U.S. 186 (U.S. Supreme Ct., 1986).

14. *Lawrence and Garner* v. *Texas*, Docket No. 02-102 (U.S. Supreme Ct., 2003), *reversing* 41 S.W. 3d 349.

15. *Re North et al. and Matheson* (1974), 52 D.L.R. (3d) 280, at 282 (County Ct. Winnipeg), per Philp, County Ct. J.

16. *Hyde* v. *Hyde and Woodmansee* (1866), L.R. 1 P. & D. 130, at 133, 35 L.J.P. & M. 57, Lord Penzance, Judge Ordinary.

17. *Corbett* v. *Corbett (Ashley) (No. 2)*, [1970] 2 All E.R. 33, Ormrod J.

18. *Sherwood Atkinson (Sheri de Cartier)* (1972), 5 Imm. App. Cases 185 (Imm. App. Bd.).

19. *C.(L.)* v. *C.(C.)* (1992), 10 O.R. (3d) 254 (Ont. Ct. Gen. Div.).

20. *Layland* v. *Ontario (Minister of Consumer & Commercial Relations)* (1993), 14 O.R. (3d) 658 (Ont. Divisional Ct.), Greer J. dissenting.

21. Royal Commission on the Status of Women, *Report* (Ottawa: Information Canada, 1970) [sometimes referred to as the Bird Commission after its Chair, Florence Bird].

22. House of Commons Standing Committee on Veterans Affairs, First Sess., 30th Parl., 1974, 31-10-1974, 3:35 (Mr. Jones).

23. Legislative Assembly of Ontario, 2d Sess., 33rd Parl., 19 January 1987, 4665-6; 25 November 1986, 3622 (The Hon. Mr. Scott, Attorney General of Ontario).

24. Legislative Assemby of Ontario, 2d Sess., 33rd Parl., 2 December 1986, at 3839 (The Hon. Mr. Wrye, Minister Responsible for the Human Rights Code).

25. *Egan and Nesbit* v. *Canada*, [1995] 2. S.C.R. 513 (Supreme Ct. of Canada).

26. *M.* v. *H.*, [1999] 2 S.C.R. 3 (Supreme Ct. of Canada).

27. Arizona Revised Statutes Annotated, section 25-112.

28. Virginia Code Annotated, chapter A7, section 20-57.

29. Forder, note 7 above.

30. For further details on the discriminatory structure and effects of RDPs and other 'alternatives' to marriage, see Kathleen A. Lahey, *Are We 'Persons' Yet? Law and Sexuality in Canada* (Toronto: University of Toronto Press, 1999), chapter 11; Kathleen A. Lahey, *The Impact of Relationship Recognition on Lesbian Women in Canada: Still Separate and Only Somewhat 'Equivalent'* (Ottawa: Status of Women Canada, 2001); Kathleen A. Lahey, 'Becoming "Persons" in Canadian Law: Genuine Equality or "Separate But Equal"?' in Robert Wintemute and M. Andenaes, eds., *Legal Recognition of Same-Sex Relationships in Domestic and International Law: A Study of National, European and International Law* (Oxford: Hart Press, 2001).

Chapter Three

31. This discussion of the Dutch and Belgian marriage reforms draws heavily on Nancy G. Maxwell, 'Opening Civil Marriage to Same-Gender Couples: A Netherlands-United States Comparison,' (2001) *Arizona J. International and Comparative Law* [available online at www.law.kub.nl]; Kees Waaldijk, 'Small Change: How the Road to Same-Sex Marriage Got Paved in the Netherlands,' in Robert Wintemute, ed., *Legal Recognition of Same-Sex Relationships in Domestic and International Law* (Oxford: Hart Press, 2001); and the writings of Caroline Forder listed above in note 7.

32. *K. Boele-Woelki en P.C. Tange*, NJCM-Bulletin 1990, pp. 456-460 (Rb Amsterdam 13 februari 1990).

33. *EAAL en EAA*, NJ 1992, 192 (HR 19 oktober 1990).

34. Translation by Caroline Forder quoted in Maxwell, note 31 above.

35. Forder, *Affidavit*, note 8 above; Maxwell, note 31 above.

36. Maxwell, note 31 above, citing Y. Scherf, *Registered Partnership in the Netherlands: a quick scan* (March 1999), (WODC), The Hague, p. 22.

37. Forder, *Affidavit*, note 8 above; the remainder of the information on the Dutch legislative process surrounding the new marriage law is also based on Forder's account in this document.

38. See MarriageWatch, which summarizes contemporaneous news reports: <http://www.marriagewatch.org/news/020303a.htm> [viewed on March 1, 2004].

Chapter Four

39. *Baehr* v. *Lewin*, 852 P. 2d 44 (Haw. Supreme Ct., 1993).

40. *Baehr* v. *Miike*, 1996 WL 694235 (Haw. Cir. Ct.), Chang J.

41. See Thomas F. Coleman, 'The Hawaii Legislature has Compelling Reasons to Adopt a Comprehensive Domestic Partnership Act,' *Law and Sexuality* (1995) 5: 541-581.

42. *Baehr* v. *Anderson*, Hawaii Supreme Court (December 9, 1999).

43. *Brause* v. *Bureau of Vital Statistics*, 1998 WL 88743 (Alaska Superior Ct., 1998).

44. *Baker* v. *State*, 744 A.2d 864, (Vermont Supreme Ct., 1999).

45. The provisions of the Vermont Civil Union law are found in An Act Relating to Civil Unions, H.847 (signed April 26, 2000), s. 3, amending 15 V.S.A., c. 23, s. 1202(2).

46. *Goodridge* v. *Dept. of Public Health (Massachusetts)*, 798 N.E. 2d 941

(Mass. Supreme Court, 2003).

47. *Opinions of the Justices to the Senate*, 802 N.E. 2d 565 (Mass. Supreme Court, 2004) [referred to here as *Goodridge II*].

48. This account is based on the articles published from February 12, 2004 onward by the *San Francisco Chronicle* and archived in <http://sfgate.com/samesexmarriage/> [viewed March 1, 2004].

49. *Proposition 22 Legal Defense and Education Fund* v. *City and County of San Francisco* (Calif. Superior Court, Feb. 13, 2004), per Warren J.

50. *Thomasson* v. *City and County of San Francisco* (Calif. Superior Court, Feb. 17, 2004), per Quidachay J. The hearings on the merits of these cases were permitted to go ahead a few weeks later, however.

51. At least one other suit has been filed by private citizens opposed to same-sex marriage.

52. *USA Today*, 'Poll on same-sex marriage amendment' (March 1, 2004).

53. Rev. Linda S. Slabon, 'Freedom to love, freedom to marry,' *Sycamore Daily Chronicle*, February 29, 2004 [available on-line at <http://www.daily-chronicle.com/articles/2004/02/28/neighbors/neighbors03.txt>; viewed February 29, 2004].

Chapter Five

54. *Haig and Birch*, (1992), 9 O.R. (3d) 495 (Ont. App. Ct.), per Lacourcière, Krever, and McKinley JJ.A.

55. *Veysey* v. *Correctional Service of Canada*, (1990), 109 N.R. 300 (F.C.A.), per Iacobucci, C.J., Urie and Decary JJ., *affirmed* (1989), 29 F.T.R. 74.

56. *Vriend* v. *Alberta,* [1994] 6 W.W.R. 414 (Alta. Q.B.), per Russell J., reversed (1996), 132 D.L.R. (4th) 595 (Alta. C.A.), per McClung, O'Leary, JJ.A., Hunt JJ.A. dissenting, *reinstated* (1998), 156 D.L.R. (4th) 385 (S.C.C.), per Cory and Iacobucci JJ.

57. *M.*v. *H.*, note 26 above.

58. *Layland and Beaulne*, note 20 above.

59. These cases are discussed in Lahey, *'Persons,'* Chapter One.

60. *Attorney General of Canada* v. *Mossop*, [1993] 1 S.C.R. 554, L'Heureux-Dubé, Cory and McLachlin JJ. dissenting (1990), 71 D.L.R. (4th) 661 (F.C.A.), *affirming* [1991] 1 F.C. 18, 71 D.L.R. (4th) 661 (F.C.A.), *reversing* (1989), 10 C.H.R.R. D/6064 (Can. H.R. Trib.).

61. *Law* v. *Canada*, [1999] 1 S.C.R. 497.

62. *Hendricks and Leboeuf* v. *Attorney General of Quebec and Attorney General of Canada*, [2002] J.Q. No. 3816, per Lemelin J., *affirmed* Quebec Court of Appeal (March 19, 2004) (File no. 500-09-012719-027). [available

on-line at <http://www.jugements.qc.ca/primeur/documents/ligue-catholique-19032004.doc>].

63. *Halpern et al.* v. *Attorney General of Canada* (2003), 172 Ont. App. Cases 276, 60 O.R. 3d 321 (Ont. App. Ct., 2003), per McMurtry C.J.O., Macpherson and Gillese JJ.A., *affirming* [2002] O.J. No. 2714 (Nos. 684/00, 39/2001, July 12, 2002) (Ont. Ct. Div. Ct.) but vacating the period of suspension ordered by the Divisional Court. [The Court of Appeal decision is available on-line at <http://www.ontariocourts.on.ca/decisions/2003/june/halpernC39172.htm>].

64. *Barbeau et al* v. *Canada (Attorney General)*, [2003] BCCA 251 (B.C. App. Ct.) (*sub nom Egale Canada, Shortt et al.*), period of suspension vacated [2003] BCCA 406 [decisions available online at <http://www.courts.gov.bc.ca/jdb-txt/ca/03/02/2003bcca0251.htm> and <http://www.courts.gov.bc.ca/jdb-txt/ca/03/04/2003bcca0406.htm>].

65. *Halpern.* [2002] O.J. No. 2714, paragraph 315.

66. *Halpern*, paragraph 145.

67. *Halpern*, paragraph 97.

68. *Edwards* v. *Attorney General of Canada*, [1930] A.C. 124. This is the Privy Council case that established that women could be considered to be 'persons' for purposes of sitting in the Senate under the constitution of Canada. Justice Mackenzie relied on the doctrine it established, although he did not cite the case by name.

69. *Barbeau*, [2003] BCCA 251, paragraph 178.

70. Law Commission of Canada, *Beyond Conjugality: Recognizing and supporting close personal adult relationships* (Ottawa: Law Commission of Canada, 2001).

71. *Barbeau*, [2003] BCCA 251, paragraph 154.

72. *Halpern* (2003), 60 O.R. 3d paragraph 149.

73. *Halpern* (2003), 60 O.R. 3d paragraphs 142, 152, quoting Chief Justice Lamer of the Supreme Court of Canada, and paragraph 153.

74. *Halpern*, paragraph 153.

75. Focus on the Family webpage: http://www.family.org/cforum/fosi/homosexuality/maf/a0028248.cfm

PART II
The Personal—Interviews

Pattie LaCroix and Terrah Keener
photo by Kevin Midbo

Breathing Ocean Air
Pattie LaCroix and Terrah Keener

Date: August 8, 2003
Time: 3:30 pm
Place: Vancouver, British Columbia

While entering the Calgary International Airport on August 8, 2003, en route to my first interview with Pattie LaCroix and Terrah Keener in Vancouver, my partner, Kevin, invited me to join him in the Maple Leaf Lounge. I had been with Kevin three times before, and he always introduced me as his same-sex partner. Each time I entered for free. This time, the attendant wanted $20. Kevin reiterated, "This is my same-sex partner." The attendant replied, "Like I said, that will be $20. Only spouses and immediate family are provided complimentary admission." Maintaining his calm, Kevin retorted, "This has never been an issue before now." The attendant perused his procedures manual for the exact stated policy. After a minute or two, he looked up and said, "The manual is clear on this point—only spouses and immediate family."

Both of us stood there in shock. We've been together eight years, so we often feel like we're married. Once I regained my composure, I paid the money, we entered, and I started writing notes describing the experience. I felt hurt. The old scripts of "I'm not good enough" and "Gays are second-class citizens" began playing in my head. As I sat there and worked through my feelings, the attendant approached me and returned the $20. The caring in his expression was mixed with angst at policies that are only inclusive of heterosexuality. This event sets the tone for my first interview; it reminds me why this book is so important.

I've named Pattie and Terrah's story *Breathing Ocean Air* because it's been a year since I was on the Canadian coast, and I've missed it. More importantly, *Breathing Ocean Air* has important resonance for Pattie and Terrah.

Pattie and Terrah have been together for eight years, just like Kevin and I. They are articulate and easy to listen to, easy to be with. Their son, Ellis, is two years old. He will grow up in a whole different world than you and I—one that is more tolerant, more accepting, more loving. A boy couldn't have asked for better parents.

[Each interview begins with the same initial question, which I indicate here but not in future chapters:]

K: *I want to understand your experience of being in a same-sex marriage. I am looking for a rich and detailed exploration of what this has been like for the two of you.*

P: We've been together for eight years and lived together for six of them. In 1998 we had a commitment ceremony in which we rented a big yacht and had seventy-five to eighty people attend. We had a minister do the ceremony and it was a big, big deal—a fabulous party, a great celebration. At that point, we would have legally married had it been available, but it wasn't. Now that we can, we will marry on October 10, 2003. That date is also our commitment ceremony anniversary.

Now that's a logistical overview, but your question was a little more personal—I think we've considered ourselves married for many years. And what has it been like? I don't think it's any different from any other relationship in many ways. We have our joys and we have our sorrows and we have things to work through. We are two people in a marriage. When you start engaging in a larger world, that's when the same-sexness of it becomes an issue sometimes, or you become more conscious of it because you're engaging in the outside [world] which doesn't always recognize you as a couple. I don't really think of myself as different from any two people that would come together.

T: I think there's a huge difference with how we present ourselves to the outside world. Right now we pick and choose who we tell that we're in a "same-sex" relationship. With certain people, especially in a work situation, or people that I don't know very well, when they ask, "Are you married?", and depending on how comfortable I am with outing myself, I may reply "No." Although I feel it is deceitful and I'm not respectfully honouring my relationship with Pattie, I feel I can get away with it because our relationship is not legally recognized. But once we get legally married, I can't lie, and I need to rethink that. I don't want to have to "lie" to people, but sometimes I just don't have the energy or the desire to come out to people who are only casually in my life. It's a matter of safety.

P: We wear rings, though, on our wedding fingers, so many times it's an issue of safety, which perhaps women are more aware of than men. In environments where people notice your ring, they think you're married and then, of course, they assume you're married to a man. Sometimes, depending on your feeling of safety in the moment, you will decide to correct them or [else] decide to go with their assumption. Once we're legally married, however, if somebody says, "Are you married?", I'm going to say, "Yes, I am."

K: *You had your commitment ceremony in 1998, but is there for the two of you a qualitative difference between the fact that now this is "marriage" you're embarking on and not simply a commitment ceremony? Does that create something different for either of you?*

T: Yes it does, and that surprises me. When I think about it, I'm a little nervous because it feels more legally binding, obviously, even though we're considered common-law, which means that in this province (i.e., British Columbia) if we were to split up, our property would already be divided between the two of us.

Not that I want to focus on the negative, like splitting up. But this does feel bigger than the ceremony and I'm not sure why. Our ceremony was, and is, very important to us. We publicly in front of friends and family pledged our love to each other and our commitment to being life partners. It doesn't get much bigger than that. But a marriage that is legally recognized just feels different, bigger. I never thought I would have this in my life.

K: *What does marriage mean to you, Pattie?*

P: Well, there are two things. I think it's different now than before we had Ellis, our son. I'm not sure there would have been such a push for me to get married before having him. There are probably three levels of motivation. One is about coming out in the world on an individual, personal level. The second level for me would be to have external recognition by society as an equal to heterosexual couples, which acknowledges that this relationship is as valuable as theirs and that it contributes to society in the same way. Thirdly, and probably most important, is I want to do this for Ellis because I want every mechanism and every…document that I [can] possibly get for him so that he has as many choices in his life as any other person would have. I want him to be able to speak about his family as married, if he chooses to.

I want to enrich and enlarge his vocabulary so he can discuss, describe and talk about his own experience. That's really important to me. I want to provide him with as much choice as possible. I think the thing that I get particularly emotional around, when I'm reflecting on it, is how it changes my perception of myself. When [you are] recognized externally, it changes the perception that you have of yourself: all of a sudden you belong. Within gay culture there's a lot of discussion and talk about, "We don't really want to belong to the status quo: instead, we want to create out own identity," and that's where our freedom rests, actually, as outside of the status quo, as not belonging to the status quo. But I don't think gay men and lesbians have to get married. However, I want to have the choice. That's what motivates me. When and if you want to exercise the choice to get married, go ahead. If you don't, don't—just like any other member of society.

...

K: *Is there a spiritual component to your marriage?*

P: ... Yes there is although...I've never felt that because when we brought a child into the world, we were making a statement for a certain kind of society. I felt more that, on a spiritual level, it was something that I would naturally do as a human being in the world, that I would go through the spiritual journey of creating a family—which is, especially when you have a young child, a spiritual journey. As soon as you put language to the experience of being a same-sex family, while also experiencing that journey of parenthood, you can't represent the essence of it. That's the spirituality part that I'm talking about—the part that is indescribable. It's very powerful to be recognized. We don't need organized religion to recognize us or a particular church for that matter.

T: I didn't grow up with religion, although Pattie did. Pattie grew up in a very devout Catholic family. When we decided to have a ceremony, we both leaned towards incorporating familiar rituals we have experienced at heterosexual weddings. We wanted someone to officiate, so we invited a gay United Church minister to lead the ceremony. We wanted our ceremony to incorporate the larger global issues of spirituality. It was interesting that we both thought a minister could do that. He spoke eloquently about bringing people together in the spirit of family, friends and love. For me family is about community and I wanted to be sure to incorporate that sentiment into the ceremony, which our minister did beautifully.

I think one of the reasons it's so important for the gay community to have the right to marry is because by bringing people together to witness and in a sense "bless" your union you are creating a community of people who care about you and your relationship, which I think is very powerful.

P: For me, I just see these rituals as natural, social reference points. Regardless of our sexuality, we all have the same kind of social icons that we turn to at certain times in our lives, and that doesn't make us or more or less religious. I'd have to say I have a very healthy separation between secular and non-secular, which some of our friends to the south could maybe look at from time to time. I don't need the state to define my spirituality. What external forces can do, such as state laws, is recognize people and validate their existence, or not, if they're excluded.

K: *Is it okay if I ask you how Ellis came to be in your relationship?*

...

P: Ellis is almost two and a half, and we are a two-parent family, so the donor is known but is not an active parent. He's a known donor to us but not to Ellis. ... If he wishes to know who the donor was, we will tell him. I have legally adopted Ellis, so the donor has legally recanted all of his natural rights that come by being a biological donor, which you can do in this province. He is a total joy and having him is a great source of spirituality in our family. We want another child and we're planning to have one.

We're in the process of trying with the same donor, but this time I would like to be the birth mother. ...

...

We're very excited about [Ellis] being able to share the experience with a sibling—you know, when he becomes a sullen teenage boy and goes to the basement and listens to music because he hates us. It will be nice for him to have somebody to share that experience with!

K: *Tell me about the quality of your relationship.*

P: Our relationship is very much a partnership. We're both very creative individuals, and we're both equally and actively involved in parenting. We both share the same fundamental values and we have a very strong level of communication. We have a low tolerance for being out of sync with each other. Being in this relationship is a very fundamental spiritual journey.

T: Partnership is the operative word, we talk about things and help each other grow and move forward. We'd both love to be leading totally creative lives, but we can't, not full-time, [although] we really encourage each other to do that, and our goal is someday we can. Right now we both work, but we support each other to carve out time to write and do film work and pursue the different creative paths that we want to follow. It's very enriching. I would say we don't go stale, which is really nice, we each always have some sort of project percolating or on the go.

P: We have a passionate aversion for the mundane, and that's something we share. We almost have a passionate aversion to being totally comfortable, because from that modicum of discomfort comes the edge of creativity that we both thrive in.

T: I'm a writer and Pattie is a filmmaker, and pushing our passions forward is how we avoid the mundane.

...

K: *What sort of films and writing are you into?*

T: Well, I don't make a living as a writer! I do some fiction and non-fiction work and I write children's stories. I've been working in adult education for a long time. My job title is Instructional Designer, and I design curriculum and training for the high tech sector mostly. I just finished my masters in education and I would like to pursue my PhD. I would love to focus my research on the experience of gay and lesbian parents, and their children, in the education system.

P: One of [Terrah's] non-fiction pieces is being published in a journal this month. I always have about three or four writing projects on the go. You can find out about me at www.tenacityproductions.com. That's where you'll find all my work.

...

As a documentary filmmaker, I did a lot of work overseas. I did a documentary in Ethiopia. I started out in International Development so I looked at global issues. From there, I did a music video and some educational videos, but I would have to say in the last three years, I have focused on my own voice. I produced a short film in the gay and lesbian film festival here last year, which was great. It was about motherhood, actually, about becoming a mother for the first time.

...

The whole idea was about what we bring into our experiences in the world, specifically focussing on parenting. This was before I had any idea what parenting was really about. It made it into the film festival after Ellis was born, which was kind of neat.

K: *Has the quality of your relationship fluctuated over time? If "yes," what accounts for this?*

P: Yeah. I think the quality of all my relationships has fluctuated over time. I don't think this relationship is anything different. We went through a period of time of having to deal with issues around my family and coming out to my family. I was in this relationship with Terrah when I came out to my family. That has been really intense for most of our relationship.

...

Having a child together has to be one of the most intense things you can do with another person, and it changes your relationship. You think you know a person and then it goes to a far deeper and more intimate level.

T: If you've had a busy week you can catch up on Friday night and the weekend, but with a young child you realize that you're never catching up.

P: ... The highlight of our relationship right now is sleep. We're okay with that right now.

...

K: *This might be a good time to talk about your parents because they had a problem with you being lesbian, right?*

P: That's an understatement.

...

K: *Will they be coming to your wedding?*

P: ... Oh, my goodness, no. They're very orthodox Catholic. I don't think they would ever look at my relationship with Terrah as remotely equal to the relationships my brother and my sister have with their wife and husband, respectively. For many years, we spoke on an irregular basis, but we stopped that last summer at my request. We exchange letters and stuff, but when you have a child and you're building a family of your own, you really need to focus on that. To be the kind of parent that I want to be, I can't have my entire family saying that I'm a horrible person, or who I am is wrong, or, you can come home but Terrah and Ellis can't come with you. I would never do that to my family, nor would I permit anyone else to do that and that's exactly what they would like to do. They would like it if they could just pretend I wasn't gay.

...

None of my siblings are accepting of me. They follow what my parents dictate. My family experience is the antithesis—you couldn't get two groups of people more different from Terrah's family and my family when it comes to this issue. For example, Terrah's parents were divorced when she was quite young. Her father has remarried and he's been married for twenty-five or twenty-six years. They're Catholic and they cannot figure out my family's take on this, so I don't necessarily think it's just about being Catholic: I think it's one's interpretation of Catholicism as well. I don't want to say all Catholics are non-accepting because Terrah's father and his wife are fabu-lously accepting. They're wonderful people.

T: My mother is very supportive, she has actually became involved politically. I'm from Connecticut. Connecticut is considering passing common-law same-sex unions legislation. A senator from Connecticut wanted to hear from people regarding this issue, and my mother went and sat with the senator and brought pictures of Pattie and me—and Ellis. She's been an environmental activist all her life. She's a real believer in "You write your congressman when you have a problem," and she does!

…

K: *What do you most value about your partner?*

P: That's easy. What attracted me to her initially was her total genuineness of spirit and generosity of heart. It's who Terrah is, and I think she has a deep faith in the spirituality of relationships and friendships. She has a lot of faith in other people and cuts them a lot of slack. She works on friendships, she enjoys friendships, and consequently she is the beneficiary of many lifelong friends. Terrah's default is to give. She has a spectacularly beautiful smile, which I think reflects her very giving heart.

T: Oh, my God, how do I top that? Well, what I still value in Pattie is also what I first saw in her—she's very open about life. She has the attitude, "Well, we can do anything we want until we can't." There's nothing that we can't do, and I really value that because I have a tendency to think the other way. Pattie has a way of embracing life in a very big way: sometimes I just feel like I'm holding on. She's also very open. She can speak from the heart and she has a way of making people feel very important. She does that with me all the time, which has been wonderful. She also has a sense of fun, and we like to laugh and have fun with life. I've always been very impressed that she would go off to Africa and India and do things like that. There is so much adventure inside her. I can imagine her as an eighty-year-old, "Out of my way! You're slowing me down!" She doesn't let much get in her way, and I like that. I like that edge that she has, but she is also very genuine and open. When I think of what we've done together, it's no easy feat, you know, for two women to come together and carve out a living, buy a home, and have a child.

P: We share a lot of fundamental values and perspectives, and not to sound morbid or anything but Terrah and I are really aware that life is short, so have fun—enjoy yourself. You know, get out of your own way. I think whether you are in a gay relationship, a lesbian relationship or a heterosexual relationship, the best gift that you can give each other is the permission to be yourself, and if you can keep doing that, things are going to be okay in your relationship.

Same-Sex Marriage

K: *We've talked about some of the struggles the two of you have faced, especially regarding family of origin. What other issues have the two of you had to face, as a couple?*

P: Fertility has been a big issue for us. I tried to get pregnant for a year and didn't, and then Terrah had Ellis. I tried to get pregnant again, and did, but miscarried. I was thirteen weeks along—it was quite horrifying on many levels. …I'm trying to get pregnant again, but now I'm forty-one.

…

K: *In what ways do you believe your relationship is different from heterosexual married couples?*

P: I think two women together probably talk more than other couples, although these are generalizations.

You don't have the gender gap in a same-sex relationship, right? In the case of two women getting together, I think you discuss your feelings a lot more. This could be a female thing or a same-sex thing. In other words, I don't know if that's exclusive to just lesbian relationships.

T: What was interesting was that when I was pregnant, a lot of my straight women friends said, "I would have loved to have shared my pregnancy with another woman." And they all had kids. They all loved their husbands but they admitted that their husbands just didn't really understand the magnitude of what they were experiencing during pregnancy.

…

K: *How did your friends react when you told them you were planning to have a commitment ceremony?*

T: Interestingly enough, my het friends were far more into it than our gay and lesbian friends. I guess they could relate to marriage. With our gay and lesbian friends, it was mixed. There were some people that thought it was an excellent thing to do, but saw it as a political statement. I didn't look at it as a political statement. Other people said, "It's the kiss of death for your relationship!" You know, that just appalled me because they would never say that to a heterosexual couple who were getting married.

...

Usually it was the people who were in healthy relationships that were happy for us. Those who were not in good relationships, or had just left a relationship, were quite cynical.

K: *How have others responded to you as a same-sex couple? And I mean outside of family and friends, so strangers on the street, bankers, proprietors, others who are not part of your more intimate circle. How have they responded when they recognize that you're most likely a same-sex couple?*

T: It's hard to know now, because with Ellis, you're very out, so they're not only reacting to you as a couple but also as parents, which are two separate issues in some people's minds. It's fine that you're gay, but, oh my God! Should you be having children? Some people are not quite sure, and that goes for both heterosexuals and gay lesbians. In Vancouver, the reactions have been mostly okay. Once we had to whisk Ellis off to the hospital because he had a high fever. No one batted an eye that we were both his parents. I have not seen any outward hostility or experienced any homophobic behaviour. But I'm sure it's out there. I have also developed a bit of a blind eye towards homophobic behaviour. If I actually took in all the "hate" that can surround homosexuality I would be suicidal.

P: I think it really depends on where you live in a lot of the cases. We live in the gay community, in the west end of Vancouver, and it's one of the most densely populated gay areas.

T: We wondered what it was going to be like in our apartment complex when Ellis was born, to see what the reaction would be. My God, since he's been born, we're like the favourite couple in the building.

...

K: *What do you think is the societal impact of same-sex marriage?*

T: I think it's going to take many years to see a real change, but it will help to push that change. My dream is to see the end of the term "alternative lifestyle." I get tired of being told that I live an alternative lifestyle—I just hate that language. Some people may embrace it, but not me. This is simply my life, it's just who I am. I don't need a label on it! For example, I don't want the way my life is structured with Pattie and Ellis to always be considered a special topic in a high-school sex education class.

P: You look at the civil rights movement in the States, and even still language is evolving around that. We don't use derogatory language to identify African-Americans and we don't talk about integration as some sort of upheaval in our social strata anymore, but there are still a lot of realities about being an African-American that are unique to being part of that group in society. I suspect that will always be the case. I would challenge anyone to look at our struggle for human rights as any different from the civil rights movement or the women's movement. It is the same opposition. Paying women the same. Giving women the vote. Allowing women access to education, to jobs—that's been part of history.

I think it's a big step that we now recognize same-sex families, and it's a big step in eventually changing the language [that] powers people's perceptions, which will eventually change the language around human sexuality. It doesn't fit into a little heterosexual box for all people because there is a breadth of human sexuality.... Changing the language around this may take generations.

...

K: *What advice would you give to gays and lesbians thinking of getting married?*

P: Try to catch yourself when you're taking the other person for granted. The other day I was leaving the house and while locking the door, I began having really wonderful thoughts about Terrah and I thought, "I should really leave Terrah a really nice note," but I was outside and I thought, "No, don't take Terrah for granted. Take the effort, go back in the house and leave her the nice note you're thinking about and then go to work." In any way you can, express the good thoughts and feelings that you may be having about one another. Don't assume that the other person knows, and even if they know, who doesn't like to hear it over and over again?

Remember this is the most special person in your life. I remember Terrah telling me that gay and lesbian people are probably the most courageous people we will ever know because we've all had our own journey of being who we are in our life and to being out in our life, which is a celebration. Coming out is the result of a long journey, and it deserves to be celebrated. If you finally meet someone you want to spend the rest of your life with, celebrate that as much as you can, and don't take the other person for granted. I would recommend that for anybody who went into a relationship.

T: And also, allow each other to be who they are. The relationships, gay or straight that I see work, that's one of the big components. They're not trying to change who the other one is.

P: When Terrah and I get into a rut, we realize that we haven't had a good laugh together. You've got to have fun. Enjoy every joyful moment that comes your way with abandon.

K: *Upon reflection, is there a metaphor, image, movie or piece of music that really speaks to your feelings or thoughts about same-sex marriage?*

P: I'd have to say the image for me would be the ocean…. My relationship is as easy as breathing, much like the tide going in and out—it's effortless, it's just there. It's as scary and as deep. And it's as crashing and as loud and it's as constant and it's soothing and it's an unending source of inspiration to me. It's a lot like the ocean.

T: That was good! I don't think I want to compete with that.

…

K: *What would you put in a "hope box" for gay people? What needs to happen within the gay community?*

T: We have to stop hating ourselves. That's a big one. There's so much self-loathing and I think that's the big killer in relationships.
Not only accept who you are, but also accept others in the community. Let's be supportive of people who are choosing to get married, and those who are choosing to have children. For some in the gay community, if anything starts to "smell" of heterosexuality, it's seen as a bad thing. We have to stop the "us" and "them" mindset and be supportive of people's choices.

…

P: Put in a nice dance tape and a mirror in the hope box. Gay people need to celebrate who they are.
[Besides this], I think we need to work on being out in certain professions, whether that be the police force, the fire department, the military, whatever. People need to stop being afraid to be out in male-dominated sectors of

society. I think that's really hard for gay men actually. The big thing for me that I would put in that box is a sense of safety. I don't want people to walk down the street and be afraid of being beaten up because they are perceived to be gay or lesbian.

K: *Excellent. We've come to the end of the questions. Thank you both.*

Peter Cook and Murray Warren
photo by Kevin Midbo

Still Sailing

Murray Warren and Peter Cook

Date: August 9, 2003
Time: 10:00 am
Place: Vancouver, British Columbia

I enter one of the most elegant condominiums I have seen, nestled in a neighbourhood that strikes me as far less impressive. I am greeted at the door and led outside to an amazing sundeck, an area reminiscent of a magical garden paradise with trickling water and carefully managed greenery. A lot of care has gone into this. Soon I am transfixed and spellbound by listening to Murray and Peter. A lot more has gone into their thirty-two-year relationship. My seven-and-a-half year relationship leaves me feeling like a neophyte in comparison Their story humbles me as they have had a profound influence in the gay rights movement in British Columbia. Strong activists, they have pushed for adoption rights, removal of school censorship of same-sex educational material, and of course, same-sex marriage.

When I leave their home, I don't know how to feel. I am awestruck, bewildered and hypnotized. Now I know what it's like to walk amongst angels for a while.

P: We met on Sunday, July 11, 1971, in London, England, and we are planning to wed on Sunday, July 11, 2004, which will be our thirty-third anniversary. We are going to run the whole event as a fundraiser, complete with dinner and entertainment. Our host for the evening will be Bill Richardson and our witnesses for the marriage will be Svend Robinson and Barbara Findlay. An openly gay judge will marry us and we have a gay and lesbian youth choir that will sing at the event. We've also asked a number of well-known entertainers to perform, Mary Walsh to speak at our wedding, and we have approached Diana Krall to see if she'll perform. The proceeds from the evening, including the donations that we've asked for in place of wedding presents, will all go to queer youth in British Columbia.

M: When I think back to when we met, homosexuality had not been decriminalized in Britain for that long. The thought that we would someday get legally married was nowhere on the horizon: the word "marriage" did not exist in our vernacular because there was no prospect that this day would ever come. Looking back to where we started and to what our lives were like at the very beginning, we have come light years ahead. It has been an extraordinary journey.

K: *It is absolutely unbelievable. It was only in 1973 that the American Psychiatric Association declassified homosexuality as a mental disorder in the United States.*

M: Exactly.

P: At the time we met, Murray was doing research at the British Museum and I was working for IBM. We got involved in floristry and other businesses in Britain. We later sold these and moved to South Africa for five years between 1983 and 1988. We were right in the middle of the state of emergency.

M: That was quite an experience and it probably began the dawning of our consciousness around oppression of minorities. We'd never led closeted lives in England, but we weren't very active either. The culture in South Africa was very oppressive then toward both the blacks, who were the majority, and toward whites like ourselves, who were the minority. We didn't have the right to travel, live or associate with whom we wanted. There were many restrictions on our personal freedom that, over a period of five years, raised our consciousness about minorities and oppression.

P: I would include government manipulation as well. You were never sure of what was going on, which made me very critical of the press and news items. We lost so much of our base there that we bought a short wave radio and listened to the BBC World Service in South Africa to find out what was going on not only in this country, but also in the rest of the world. That provided us the balanced reporting that we sought. Now when we read things, we read between the lines and we don't just accept what is provided to us, the public. We have far less propaganda in Canada compared to South Africa.

...

M: Due to the political situation in South Africa, our consciousness expanded. Following our five years there, we returned to Canada. I had been away from Canada for eighteen years and the country had changed so much in my absence. I grew up in Newfoundland and then moved to Vancouver, so we're talking two different sides of the country. The experiences I had as a child were completely different from the experiences we had when we returned in 1988. It took us a while to get established. It wasn't until the early 1990s that we began to think that we could make our family complete if we adopted a child.

P: We've had many experiences in our lives, and we felt that in some ways, it would be meaningless if we did not have someone to pass on our accumulated wisdom.

M: I don't think that was the primary reason, however. I believe our ultimate motive was that we have enjoyed a good standard of living and we knew from our time in South Africa that there are many children in this world who need a home. We could have had a child conceived for us in fact, but we weren't prepared to do that. We didn't want to bring another child into the world when there were so many who are already in need. That is when we started to talk about adoption. It was 1993, and we first went to the Ministry of Social Services in British Columbia and I picked up the appropriate application form. The first thing they ask on the form is the father's name and the mother's name, so we were confronted with it immediately. I crossed this off and substituted *partner's* name and *partner's* name. Well, we were basically told by adoption services that if we wanted to adopt a child, one of us would have to be the legal parent and the other would have to be a legal guardian. We would also need to keep our relationship hidden from the authorities. In effect, one of us would be the adoptive parent and the other person would be somebody who lived in the household. We were not prepared to accept that. To help facilitate this, I became elected to the British Columbia Adoptive Parents Association Board of Directors. This was the beginning of our activism.

P: The form was one of the easiest things to change. Then Murray got appointed to the Law Reform Committee. The disaster in Ontario soon followed when the omnibus bill was defeated, which ended Bob Rae's stint as premier. This bill would have protected many gay and lesbian rights.

The approach here in British Columbia was softer. We went to Victoria for the introduction of the bill because they thought there was going to be a huge outcry about it. The government, however, put into wording that any two *persons* could adopt. That opened it up for gay and lesbian adoptions. As it turned out, the press [was] far more interested in the issue of opening up adoption rights than [it was] in the same-sex marriage issue. So British Columbia became a leader in the world for adoption rights.

M: Yes. British Columbia became the first jurisdiction in the world where same-sex couples could jointly and legally adopt.

K: *And this was largely due to your activism.*

P: Yes, through Murray working on the committee, going to meetings, and presenting our case. The new adoption act came into effect in 1994.

M: Then we went through a whole process with the Ministry of Children and Families, or Social Services. We decided to request adoption of a special needs child. The definition of special needs is very broad, and the Ministry requires applicants to go through nine, four-hour weekly sessions on adoption of special-needs children, which we completed. In fact, of that entire intake of applicants, we were the only couple who completed it.

P: We even attended the session on infertility. Now we realized why we weren't able to have our own biological child! Much of that course was rewritten after we completed every part of it.

M: Eventually the Ministry began to present us with possible adoptive children, including a ten-month old severely physically and mentally disabled child. Peter himself is disabled and he requires crutches to walk. I asked the social worker, "What do you think will be the situation if I was away from home so Peter was left to tend to the child?" We actually hadn't thought of that at first. The other special-needs children who were possibilities would have created similar unreasonable challenges to us. We basically dropped our plans to adopt.

Eventually we did end up fostering our now adoptive son, Brent, who was seventeen years old at the time. He was in voluntary Ministry care. Brent is gay and was going through a lot of difficulties in his life.

P: We were actually able to do an adult adoption, because he had been in our care prior to turning nineteen, which is the age of majority in British Columbia. Brent is now twenty-two. He lived with us for almost three years, off and on.

K: *Can you also adopt a child that's not the biological child of either parent?*

P: Absolutely.

K: *Good. How did you sustain your relationship, given that when it began, homosexuality was considered a mental disorder and a criminal act in Britain?*

M: No, actually the law changed in Britain in 1967, so when we met in 1971, homosexuality was no longer considered illegal there. However, the gay environment was definitely "underground" to some extent. In London, given the city that it is, you could have a very active gay lifestyle without much impediment. Nonetheless, when we left London in 1976 to move to a little hamlet in West Yorkshire, the environment was very different.

P: It wasn't hostile, though.

M: We were obviously two men living together in the same house. People didn't seem to have a problem with us, however.

P: We were quite well accepted, in fact. We threw community parties in our large garden and all the community would turn out, so there was never an issue.

K: *By 1976, you already had a five-year relationship. Was this common in the gay community for men to be in sustainable relationships then?*

M: Interestingly, there were another two couples who met within months of when we met. Unfortunately, four or five years ago, one of the partners in one of the couples passed away, but they'd been together then well over twenty-five years. We are still in regular contact with the other couple.

K: *But was it remarkably uncommon?*

P: I don't think it was as uncommon as you might think, but it certainly wasn't as open. There were so many people, including famous actors and other people of notoriety, who were in long-term gay relationships, but they were very quiet and discreet about it. Now it's much safer to say, "We are a couple and we've been together for X number of years." In the past, most who knew us as gay would have known that through our private social circle. It was mostly mutual support among friends.

M: Let's take a look at what happened subsequent to the whole adoption issue. I am an elementary school teacher in Coquitlam, a suburb of Vancouver, teaching grades two and three. In December 1996, Peter and I started talking about the queer youth in our schools and we knew that their experiences at school were not positive or happy. I called together a meeting of representatives from the various constituent groups: parents, principals, school board officials, the teachers' union and local youth. I said, "You will hear from the experiences of two queer youth who we found who will speak to this issue. As you will hear, they have had less than positive experiences at school. I want to ask the school board to establish an ad hoc committee to look into this. I want your support." We also invited a member of the local press to this meeting. I naively assumed that all I had to do was bring up the question and people would say, "Of course."

P: There was a lot of humming and hawing, and then we decided that Murray would make the presentation at the Board meeting regardless. We got supporters out and filled the boardroom, so many in fact that they were trailing down the stairs. There were media everywhere too. The school board trustees must have thought, "What on earth has happened?"

M: They were totally taken by surprise. A number of people made presentations saying, "It's time that you recognized you have these youth in the school system and that you did something to ensure that their experiences are safe and positive." That's when the Christian right really kicked in and organized [itself]. Two weeks later, the board was to give me a response to my request. They moved the board meeting from the office to a nearby school gymnasium.

P: Several hundred church supporters came out, and there we were with our little group of queer kids.

M: The board turned down my request. [It] passed a personal discriminatory and sexual harassment policy and then turned to me and said, "Now that we have this policy, we don't need to have this committee because the kids are protected."

P: The queer kids with us were verbally attacked by teachers who said, "You're only gay because you were sexually abused as children." They were verbally harassed by the people in the audience—it was terrible. We had kids running out, screaming and crying, because of it.

M: Oh, it was really ugly.

P: Then in 1997, Murray and a group of other queer teachers brought a motion to the British Columbia Teachers' Federation requesting a program to eliminate homophobia and heterosexism from the BC public school system. The motion was passed, in a modified form, after much debate. The Federation then established an ad hoc committee to examine how it could address the issue. The motion involved educating teachers about the issue and coming up with initiatives to help make schools safer for kids. Then the Surrey school board became involved because there was a teacher there that had applied to use three children's books to meet certain sections of the curriculum. The books were banned because they contained same-gender family content—they were not about sex.

M: Essentially they were little children's books about somebody having two moms or two dads.

P: Exactly. I started negotiating with the Attorney General's office, the Civil Liberties Association, the Ministry of Education and the Teachers' Federation. Nobody was going to do anything, despite being appalled by the book banning. After all was said and done, I started talking to Joe Arvay, a famous lawyer here. He had earlier dealt with the Egan and Ethan Nesbitt case and the censorship challenge against Little Sister's Book Store, which is our city's large gay bookstore. He said, "Okay, Peter. We reckon we could do this case this way and that way," so I came back and spoke to Murray about it. I said, "They're going to get away with it, but Joe's prepared to work with us." Murray agreed, so we employed Joe Arvay on the understanding that it would cost us about $50,000. By the time our case was heard by the Supreme Court of Canada, the cost was over $400,000. The school board spent nearly a million dollars fighting us.

Luckily, we got costs at the Supreme Court because we won substantially there. Joe has now settled costs with the Surrey school board. We also had fundraised about $160,000 to help offset the costs, most of it from the Teachers' Federation.

K: *So what was actually won at the Supreme Court?*

M: What we won is that school boards cannot deny access to learning resources based on the religious views of some parents in the community in the public school system. In our school act, there is a restriction that schools much be conducted in a strictly non-sectarian, secular manner. Consequently, the school board acted illegally in allowing the religious views of some parents to prevent the use of these books.

K: *I see. The ruling only applies to the public school system?*

M: Yes, but what was said there was highly significant. For instance, one of the school board's arguments was that children in kindergarten and grade one couldn't possibly understand same-sex couples, or that they would be frightened by the prospect. They argued that it was age inappropriate to bring up this issue with such young children. The Chief Justice of the Supreme Court, Beverly McLaughlin, said in one of her statements, "Tolerance is always age appropriate."

P: This really connects in with the same-sex marriage issue because if they'd got away with banning those books because of same-sex couples, how [would] they handle books that portray same-sex weddings? There is already a book out that deals with this one.

M: This children's book is available at Little Sister's and it is called *King and King*. It's the story of a prince and his mother, the queen. She decides he has to get married so she calls for princesses from around the country to come meet her son. He refuses to choose a new bride and decides instead that he wants to marry another prince. He finds one, they get married, and eventually they become king and king.

Now I would like to go back again because…around 1994, the Ministry of Education here was bringing out a new series of curriculum documents. Each of those curriculum documents had appendices, and Appendix C is called Cross-Curricular Interests. Appendix C gives direction to teachers…to take into account issues around gender, equity, racism, multiculturalism, First Nations students, special-needs students, and so on. Of course, what was glaringly missing from this were issues around sexual orientation. In August 1996, I wrote to the then Minister of Education and said, "Can you tell me why sexual orientation is not included in this appendix, and what are you going to do about it?" The minister delayed doing anything about my request.

After we were granted costs and won at the Supreme Court, the Surrey school board appealed to the British Columbia Court of Appeals. During the sixty-day appeal period, I met with the Minister of Education and said to him, "Look, all you have to do is approve these three books and this whole court case goes away—it's solved." He refused to do that. My point is that over the whole period of the appeal, I kept on at the Ministry of Education about making the curriculum inclusive of issues around sexual orientation, and [got] nowhere. When the Surrey school board decided to appeal, Peter and I said, "Enough is enough." We filed a British Columbia human rights complaint against the Ministry of Education based on the exclusion of sexual orientation from this appendix. We're now at the stage where they've gone through their third lawyer.

P: The Ministry keeps on changing [its] position and trying to get out of it with technicalities. We naturally keep them on course. They're trying to wear us down, but that strategy doesn't work with us. It is now a seven-year fight.

M: What happened in the course of all of this was that one of the ministry's responses to the Human Rights Commission was to suggest that the whole appendix be deleted in the next revision of the curriculum documents. Instead of fighting for the very principles upon which the curriculum was developed, they would remove [them] altogether rather than include sexual orientation. Then they wrote to the commission and said, "Now that we're taking the appendix out altogether, there's no complaint to answer." The commission replied, "Sorry—discrimination has already occurred. This is now going to a tribunal."

All we've been asking for this whole time is that the Ministry of Education restore this appendix to the curriculum, inclusive of sexual orientation and gender identity as issues to be considered in the curriculum. There is already a policy that parents can opt their children out of any classes that have to do with a particular curriculum called personal planning, or career and personal planning. Parents already have the option of taking their kids out of classes that deal with family life, sex education, drugs and alcohol abuse, and that kind of thing.

We have asked the Ministry of Education to change three things, none of which cost money. They have steadfastly refused to do any of them. Consequently, we're headed towards a human rights tribunal that may occur in the spring. Our issues relate directly to same-sex partners, sexual orientation, gender identity and same-sex families. As far as we're concerned, who we are and what our family is is not a sensitive issue. Like the Surrey school board, they would like to keep us invisible and oppressed.

I can't wait until next summer when Peter and I get married. I look forward to the day when I can walk into my classroom and have a picture of Peter, Brent and me on my desk. When the kids ask me, "Who's that in the picture?", I will be able to say, "That is my husband and my son." What are parents going to do about that? I'm not going to hide who I am.

K: *It's going to be a very proud moment when you can say, "This is my husband." After all, you have been with him for more than thirty-two years!*

P: I think one of the things that has always been difficult in a gay relationship is explaining to others what your relationship means—in a meaningful way that people can understand.

M: You know, you say, "He's my partner," and they either ask or wonder, "What kind of partner? Business partners?"

P: Some people have assumed that because I'm disabled, Murray is my caregiver. Some have developed all kinds of interpretations to avoid thinking that Murray is my life partner. People know what the words "spouse" or "husband" means. They won't need to develop alternate explanations of our relationship. One story I would like to tell you is about going over the U.S. border from the Vancouver airport. It's happened to us twice. I usually carry the passports and the immigration officer asked, "What is your relationship?" I say, "This is my partner, we live together." Then he sends Murray back with his passport and says, "You stand back behind the line while I deal with this person." Now I ask…would they do that to a married couple?

K: *You mentioned earlier about how some of the events already described have contributed to the passing of same-sex marriage in British Columbia.*

M: That's right. It was near the end of 1998 when Peter and I decided that we would apply for a marriage licence with a Notary Public. I met him one lunch time over the Christmas holiday. At his office, I asked, "Could we have an application for a marriage licence?" The woman handed us an application and of course it asked for the groom's name and the bride's name. We crossed that out again, completed the application, and took it back to the desk. She looked at it and retorted, "Oh, this is for you two." We replied, "Yes." Then she said, "I was wondering when we were going to get one of these! I'm going to make some phone calls." She went off straightaway, made phone calls, and came back and showed us the policy. The policy specifically states that a marriage licence cannot be issued to same-sex couples.

P: So I said, "You cannot deny us something based simply on policy, it has to be denied under law. Can you tell me what law you're using to deny us the marriage licence?" She replied, "I think you should deal with this person," and she gave me the name of the head of vital statistics. I began a correspondence and was getting nowhere—I was getting the runaround. They were essentially saying that this was the common law. However, we had the Marriage Prohibited Degrees Act, an act passed by the federal government sometime earlier in the 1990s. It basically states who may and may not marry, including people who are related by adoption or by blood—that's it. So my argument with them was that the common law of England, which exists under our constitution, applies unless Canada passes its own law. Since gay people weren't explicitly named in the Marriage Prohibited Degrees Act included in our own federal law, I argued that they couldn't deny us a marriage licence. Their response was, "Well, the list isn't exhaustive," and I replied, "You can't have a list that isn't." Anyway, I ended up talking to the Attorney General of British Columbia. He wrote back and said, "No, this is squarely in the realm of federal legislation. We have no say in it and if you have an issue, you should take it up with the federal government."

One day we were discussing matters with barbara findlay, who is one of our lawyers. She is also well known. She received a Queen's Council for her activism work regarding sexual orientation and gender identity. She does a lot of volunteer work for the community. She has done all of our work pro bono, for example. As we were walking out of our meeting, she said, "Oh, about the marriage issue (I had been copying her with my correspondence)," she said, "Why don't you issue a human rights complaint against the provincial government?" We said, "Fine." We left her office and walked in and filed a human rights complaint.

The human rights people were all for it and thought it was a good idea. We found out that somebody else in Victoria tried to get a marriage licence, accompanied by some press. Then the Attorney General got involved in that and decided to apply to the Supreme Court of British Columbia to get clarification as to whether [the Minister] could deny a marriage licence to this other same-sex couple.

Our lawyer rang the Attorney General's office and said, "You're already on the record regarding this," and they said, "What?" And we said, "I've got a letter here signed by the Attorney General." Then they started negotiating with our lawyer, Murray and me. barbara findlay then suggested to us that we should have more people included in the human rights complaint. She got two more couples involved—Jane [Hamilton] and Joy [Masuhara], and Dawn and Elizabeth [Barbeau]. Soon after, we realized that the provincial government would likely change in British Columbia, and it did: the NDP were out and the Liberals were in. We were concerned that the Liberals would drop the case, so we launched our own case with the other two couples. Collectively we then became known as the *British Columbia partners*.

After we launched our own case, Egale wanted us to be part of [its] upcoming class action suit. We declined this invitation. Egale soon began [its] own case with five same-sex couples, including Diana [Denny] and Robin [Roberts], Lloyd [Thornhill] and Bob [Peacock], Tanya and Melinda [Chambers-Roy], and two other couples. These five couples, all from British Columbia as well, became known as the *Egale partners*. Because Egale...actually issued the writ, the couples who joined [its] fight basically signed all their rights away to Egale. Consequently, they don't have any say on what goes on legally and they have to answer to press via Egale.

After the NDP lost the election, the British Columbia government withdrew [its] case because [it] said [it] didn't want to be taking the federal government to court. [B.C.] remained as an interested party, however, instead of as a litigant because [it was] worried that [it might] be accused of denying us the licence if there weren't any grounds. If the courts said, "There isn't any federal law that prohibits it," then the British Columbia government would have been liable for refusing us a licence.

...

It finally went before the British Columbia court and all litigants banded together. The judge rendered a terrible decision. He said, "Yes it's unconstitutional, but it's justified according to the common law definition of marriage." In effect, he agreed that it was against our Charter of Rights, but that the government was allowed to do that.

M: His reasoning was that because marriage is an institution, it is not re-definable. This is a prime example of the kind of decision that a judge of the Supreme Court should never make. Subsequently, we decided to appeal to the Appeal Court of British Columbia.

P: After that, our lawyer, barbara findlay, was replaced by Kathy Lahey. ... [Kathy became] our co-counsel at the lower court and she became our lead counsel at the appeal court. It was then that the British Columbia Appeal Court rendered [its] decision that re-defined the definition of a common-law marriage as a marriage between two *persons*. However, the decision was suspended until July 12, 2004. That will be the day after our anniversary date. That date was fixed and came out of the lower courts in Quebec and [Ontario]. The intent was to harmonize the date so we weren't all over the place in Canada.

M: While we were waiting for the Ontario Appeal Court decision, Peter and I started making plans. We decided that we would go back to Newfoundland, where I am from, to be married on July 11, 2004, at midnight. The mayor of St. John's had agreed to marry us, and it would have made us the first "legally married same-sex couple in the Americas" at one minute after midnight with the anticipated change of the law.

P: And, of course, Newfoundland's half an hour ahead of everybody else, and the mayor was right up to it. CBC radio had got the mayor live on radio with Murray and he said, "Have you got something to ask the mayor, Murray?" Murray answered, "Yeah. Mayor, will you marry us?" The mayor replied, "Sure, boy." After organizing a big party, the Ontario Court of Appeal came down with [its] decision that agreed with the earlier British Columbia Court of Appeal decision (that the common law definition of marriage be changed from the union of one man and one woman to two persons), but Ontario removed the dates. [It] said, "There's no reason to have this prohibition, so people can get married immediately." That's when Michael and Michael rushed off and became the first [male couple] to legally marry in Canada. Before that, people had been married in the Metropolitan Community Church (MCC), but their marriages were not legally recognized at the time they married.

M: There is also the couple in Manitoba, but I can't remember their names [NOTE: Murray is referring to Chris Vogel and Rich North, who are included in this book].

P: That was many years ago, but then there were all these people that married by Proclaiming the Banns in Ontario. The MCC church reckoned that they legally married them, but the government refused to register their marriage. Part of the decision in Ontario was that those marriages would have to be registered. That meant that all of the marriages conducted by the MCC church were automatically registered, and these all occurred prior to Michael and Michael's wedding. That means there is a technicality regarding who was really the first to legally marry in Canada.

To finish off the story, we then went back to the Appeal Court here and said, "Now that they removed this date in Ontario, there's no need to have the date here any longer." We then applied for this to happen. Egale nearly messed the whole thing up by interfering, but despite [it], we got the date changed.

M: Before getting the date changed, Peter and I said, "Well, we really ought to have a couple ready to get married immediately after it changes." We ourselves could have been the couple…but we decided to wait because we still wanted to organize our wedding as a fundraiser. We wouldn't have had enough time to do this following the decision by the British Columbia Appeal Court on July 11, 2003, to make same-sex marriage effective here immediately. We then arranged for Tom Graff and Antony Porcino to be the first same-sex couple to marry in British Columbia, and they agreed.

P: Murray went down and walked Tom and Antony through the whole process of where they'd have to go for the licence and where they were going to get married. We arranged for Tim Stevenson, the first openly gay ordained minister in the United Church of Canada, to marry them.

M: At 8:30 am on the day the decision was coming down, I took Tom and Antony for coffee after we'd done our little jaunt around. Then we went to the Appeal Court Registry and there were loads of media because we had earlier sent out press releases to all of them. As soon as the decision came down to remove the date restriction of July 12, 2004, all hell broke loose.

P: Murray phoned me on his cell and said, "Go," and I clicked "send" on the e-mail message and the press release announcing the lifting of the restriction and the first same-sex marriage in B.C. went out to thousands of people throughout North America almost instantly.

M: We came downstairs through the main doors of the appeal court and Tom and Antony were absolutely mobbed by media. I stood behind Tom and I had warned him before this that it would be easy to get bogged down with all the media. As this was actually happening, I tapped Tom on the shoulder and said, "Come on, Tom, we have to go and get a marriage licence." We had to go about two blocks from the Appeal Court Registry to get the marriage licence. The entire way there's this mob of media cameras and television cameras. The press are all walking backwards, filming them as they proceed to get their marriage licence. Then we went to the Vital Statistics office. We had forewarned the office that this would likely happen and that there would be some media attention. The mob of media followed Tom and Antony up to the desk and when one of them asked, "Can we have a marriage licence?", the poor lady was just shaking! Now all the cameras are on her, and her boss is in the background keeping a very close eye on what was going on! They got the marriage licence and then walked back the two-and-a half blocks to the courtroom steps. Outside the Statue of Justice is where the wedding took place. That was history in the making.

P: It was just amazing. I was here dealing with the press and getting things out on the fax machine and Murray kept on saying, "You know, they got the licence," and I'm saying, "Well, I'll get there as soon as I can." "They've started the marriage." "I'll get there as soon as I can." By the time I got there, it was finished! After Tom and Antony, there were quite a few others that married that first day.

K: *Let me now take you back into your own long-standing relationship with each other. What do you value about Murray, Peter?*

P: Our relationship is [at] the stage where there are so many things that we don't need to discuss because we're so much in tune. We support each other, he's always there for me, and he looks out for me. There are no put-downs. Murray knows my limitations, whether it's physical, educational, or whatever. The best times of my life have been with him. For twelve years, we had a business together and we were together 24-7. It was the best time of our relationship: we always knew what each other's day was like because we totally shared them. I can't imagine my life without him now. We can achieve so much more together than apart. There are so many facets to our relationship.

M: It is difficult to define what those elements are that comprise our rela-tionship. It has become so much of what defines us, both individually and as a couple. Peter talks about my supporting him, but he does exactly the same for me. There are so many things that I couldn't possibly begin to do if it were not for his capabilities and talents. We complement each other really well. Even in our floristry business that we had, I was inclined towards the creative side, while Peter dealt with the business side of it. With our activism,

I'm often the one in front of the camera, while Peter works diligently in the background organizing and making the media connections.

I'm only scratching the surface because we have a lot more than that. It has to do with being completely honest with one another and being committed to one another. When you make a commitment, you keep it. There's also a huge thing called love in all of this that you can't define. What makes you love somebody to the extent that we love each other? I can't imagine what it would be like to not have Peter in my life—I can't even conceive of it.

I think having common goals that you work towards together [is] really important. Our goal of bringing about equality for gays, lesbians and especially youth, is an important part of our lives.

P: A lot of what we do, I think, is based around making the world a better place for youth.

M: For instance, look at the marriage issue. We've been together for over thirty-two years now. Although there are aspects of having a marriage certificate that are important, such as the legal and social aspects, we've lived without it for thirty-two years. We could go on living without it. But our son now lives in a world where if he chooses, he can marry his life partner. That was never available to us, but now it's available to him.

P: The recognition of a relationship is tremendously important, and so much of life revolves around that rite of passage. You see the impact and promotion of marriage in publications, in songs, in films, and throughout society. Now those things are available to gays and lesbians. They no longer need to hide their partners in the closet—they can proudly introduce them as…spouses. The queer kid in the class can say, "When we get married."

M: Those kids could never say that before. It is light years away from where we started.

K: *What do you guys still struggle with in your relationship?*

P: We're getting to the stage now where we are thinking about early retirement. We would like the freedom to do more of what we really want to do rather than be constrained by work.

M: Peter gets less satisfaction from his career than I do from mine because I really do love teaching. If we retired, however, we could again have more time together, and that would be great.

P: One of the biggest problems that we have is time. Much of what we get involved in requires that we be available during the day, to meet people and respond. Right now it is really difficult.

K: *Do you still face struggles between the two of you in the interpersonal sense?*

M: Of course—every couple has differences of opinion at times. Nothing, however, that's worth worrying about. We live in a completely interdependent relationship. All of our finances are shared.

P: The bank manager rings up and he discusses the mortgage with me. He knows it's a joint mortgage. He never turns around and says, "Oh, does Murray agree with that?"

M: There is nothing about our lives that is separate. Even in our careers, there's overlapping. There's nothing that I can think of in our lives where it's, "That's mine. That's yours." Nothing.

P: We share our house, our friends, everything. You know, we sail together— even our pastimes are shared.

M: Another thing that Brent struggled with when he first moved in was that every evening, we would sit down together at dinner to discuss the day. The television would be turned off and the telephone would be left unanswered while we sat down to eat. I think this is quite uncommon in North American society today. This coming together as a family every day is really important to the cohesiveness and the coherence of what it is that makes a family.

P: If Murray is going to be late, I wait and have dinner with him.

M: Or vice versa. At one point Brent lived with us, we would regularly turn the television off in the evening after dinner and I'd read novels aloud to Peter and Brent. I still read aloud to Peter when we're out sailing. It's those kinds of rituals, habits and observances that cement the family relationship. They are extremely important.

K: *Precisely. Do you find a way to celebrate your anniversary every year?*

P: We usually just acknowledge it. Sometimes I get it right and sometimes I get it wrong—I'm not very good with dates. I wished him a happy anniversary a month early one year.

K: *That always wins points.*

P: I think that's one reason why we'd like to get married.

M: We did have a special celebration on our thirtieth anniversary. Peter, Brent and I went to San Francisco and we had a fabulous time with our friends there. We went for a beautiful meal in a lovely restaurant in the Napa Valley. All of our friends joined us. These friends are coming to our wedding. Two of the couples are going to get married here the day before our wedding.

Our own marriage will have special significance to us—symbolically, it will tie together so much of what we have fought for for so many years. Everybody knows what marriage is, and the social approbation that comes with the term is huge. Marriage is so pervasive an idea that it is woven throughout society. To give it any other name would just not cut it. I wouldn't settle for anything less.

Marriage puts an imprimatur on the relationship that's so socially significant, it's hard to put into words. It says to society that this enduring, loving, supportive relationship is equal to, but not better than, other relationships. It represents two people coming together before society and declaring, "This is who we are as a couple and we are prepared to take on the rights and responsibilities of the institution of marriage." That approbation is something that cannot be underestimated.

Marriage is something that needs to be freely chosen, so it is also great for those couples who choose not to participate in the institution of marriage. There has been debate and controversy in the queer community regarding same-sex marriage, particularly here in Vancouver.

I'm going to tell you a story about [the editor of a gay tabloid]. We've had a lot of contact with him about the issues we have fought for over the past few years. He found out that we have a sailboat and he asked us if we would take him out sailing one day. We said, "Of course we'll take you out." We sailed and spent a lot of time talking to him about the work that we've been doing. We also told him a lot of personal things about ourselves, such as being together for thirty years. When the whole question of whether queers should marry came up, he took the approach that gays should be using their sexual liberty to keep pushing the boundaries, not for public acceptance, but to confront the heterosexual world regarding homosexuality.

Then he wrote in his tabloid that, in his view, the vast majority of the queer community is against marriage, and in his view, by buying into this oppressive misogynist institution, those gays who wanted to do so were endangering, and putting at risk, queer culture. He never produced any evidence to back up his claim that the vast majority of the queer community is against gay marriage, but he wrote an editorial in which he said that a thirty-year relationship was of no more value than a twenty-minute blow job in Stanley Park. He can publish all the views he wishes because this is a free country, but to have attacked us in such a personal way was unconscionable.

K: *Did he mention your names?*

M: No, he didn't need to. We made the connection and other people did as well.

K: *Same-sex marriage is a human rights issue, regardless of what people think about same-sex marriage itself. You know, Kathy and I hope that this book will be read by gays, lesbians and heterosexuals. I also hope that many gays and lesbians will read the book because they are thinking about same-sex marriage. What advice would you give to same-sex couples who are considering getting married?*

P: I don't think marriage in itself is going to solve any problems. Unless your relationship is well-founded to start with, don't use marriage as a way of trying to hold your relationship together.

M: Don't do it unless you're prepared to live up to the commitments that it brings. Some heterosexual couples have married because their relationship is rocky and they think by getting married that it's going to solve everything. That's like having a child if your relationship is shaky. I'm afraid it doesn't work that way.

K: *Tell me more about how the two of you met.*

P: We met quite late on a very hot Sunday night at a gay bar in London, England. Murray had actually left the bar, and as he walked out, he offered me a drink. I said, "No," and he walked out. He had forgotten his coat so when he returned for it, I chatted him up and here we are thirty-two years later. We went for coffee, I took him home, dropped him off, kissed him goodnight and that was it. It's funny because I can't tell you what we talked about, but we seemed to have no end to our conversation. I couldn't wait to see him again. It wasn't a sexual thing or anything like that.

M: From the beginning of that conversation to when he dropped me off at home, I could already sense a bond forming. Since then, it has only deepened and matured. It was like discovering your soul-mate. He was so easy to communicate with. It was love at first sight.

P: I took the Wednesday following our meeting off work and we spent the day together. I happened to casually mention, "Well, why don't you move in?" I came home on Thursday and he was on the doorstep with his suitcase.

K: *That's hilarious!*

P: And that's it. This is horrific to our son, Brent, who thinks that the whole business of courtship, wooing and dating should be really prolonged with great long poems going back and forth, all of that stuff. We had communication that was so meaningful right from the beginning—we didn't begin with any nonsense talk. We were talking about issues, politics and positions. It was such fun! I always had the issue of my disability to deal with, and that was obviously not an issue for Murray. There were a lot of issues that I had to deal with regarding being gay and being disabled. You know, Murray's got a wonderful way with language, which I appreciated, and a sense of humour. We even laugh about the same things!

M: I think that's what I was talking about when I spoke earlier about commitment. It's having common goals and being committed to them and being prepared to work through whatever is necessary to reach those goals.

P: We've had some really hard times. We moved continents, from England to South Africa to here. We arrived here almost penniless. Both Murray and I have been out of work at times, but you support each other and you work through those things. That's what it's all about. In the end you know that you're there for each other.

K: *I just have one more question I want to ask. Is there a metaphor, image, movie or piece of music that really speaks to your feelings or thoughts about same-sex marriage?*

P: Let me begin with a sideline. I participated in a phone-in program with a representative from *Focus on the Family*. This was the Canadian version of the American organization based in Vancouver. One of their hosts was going on about the heterosexual married family and how that is the best situation. His argument was that heterosexual marriage is the most supportive and constructive of all relationships. So I said, "Well, what are you comparing it to? How can you say that it's the best if all we have is heterosexual marriage?"

...

He didn't like that argument at all. I said, "You know, you can't make statements like that and not have a comparison to make them to." Same-sex marriage is so new that there isn't any statistical information yet about separation and divorce.

M: I've come up with a metaphor that should have come to me straightaway. About a year after we met, we moved into a house in London and we became involved in gardening. Gardening is such an important aspect of our lives—we've always gardened. If I were to compare marriage to anything, it would be to a garden. A garden is something that has to be created and it will only thrive and mature if you're prepared to put into it what's necessary for that to happen. A garden left neglected will no longer be a garden. A marriage left neglected will fall apart. That's my metaphor.

K: *That's beautiful. Do you think we've dealt with this topic thoroughly?*

P: I just wish everybody the best. You know, if people could have anywhere near the relationship that I've had with my Murray over these years, and now having the opportunity to publicly acknowledge that relationship under the definition of marriage, they're going to have a wonderful life.

M: I agree.

K: *Thank you.*

Robin Roberts and Diana Denny
photo by Kevin Midbo

The Arbutus Tree
Robin Roberts and Diana Denny

Date: August 9, 2003
Time: 3:00 pm
Place: Vancouver, British Columbia

I get the sense right away that Robin and Diana are a warm, hospitable couple. The coffee is waiting, and their story begins before the tape starts recording. Moments like this are precious. Soon the tape catches up, and so does the record of their twenty-year relationship.

R: Well, it's been fantastic, hasn't it?

D: Yeah. We've always looked at each other in wonder as the years have passed. We have been amazed at how wonderfully happy, supportive of each other, and compatible we are.

R: We have many things in common, including our backgrounds, which makes it easy to understand one another. Diana taught me co-counselling theory, which has been extremely useful in improving our communication with each other. It has also helped me to work with kids and teach English as a second language. I came from a family that repressed [its] emotions, whereas Diana came from a family where emotions were expressed all over the place.

K: *What do you value about your partner?*

D: From time to time, we ask each other if we want to hear how we feel about each other.

R: One of us will say, "I love you," and the other might be in that certain state where you want to say, "Why? What do you love about me? I want to hear it." Some of what I love about Diana is the way she looks at me. I love her curves and her soft sensual skin. I love her round, strong fingers and how she can use them. I love her sparkling smile, her beautiful teeth, and her hands. She's got a wonderful touch. I love her beautiful musical voice—it's full of fun and mischief. I love her creativity, her sensitivity, and her insight. I love her quick spontaneity, which makes life fun and interesting. I love her honesty. I love that she's relaxed with herself and extremely self-confident. If there's an area where she doesn't feel self-confident, she's completely open and honest about it, and it's usually in an area where I am confident, so we balance each other that way. She's got a neat energy about her.

Diana helps me see a different view and way of life. Diana enriches my life. We can be walking along or doing something and all of a sudden she will say, "Oh, look at that!" I'm always delighted with that. She is interested in a lot of the things that we like to do together. We like travelling and exploring and she researches things in a different way than I do. Together, we make each other's life fuller. I always know where I stand with her. That is comforting, even if she's feeling crappy, annoyed and pissed off. There is nothing I need to wonder about—except the awe I have for our love. I love waking up every morning and knowing she's there. I love to touch her, hug her, and kiss her when I whisper in her ear, "Good morning."

K: *I think I'm falling in love with you! Those are the loveliest, most poetic words I have heard. Diana, what do you value in Robin?*

D: Oh, my God—you expect me to follow after that? Well, I admired Robin from afar for a long time, but not realizing why. She has so many talents. She's very musical. I knew Robin from her writing initially because she wrote in boating magazines. When I was still with my husband, he and I got into sailing. I was introduced to yachting magazines and I had been reading Robin's articles for a long time. I was actually very close to meeting her in person one day, but I was too shy. Sometimes I'm a real extrovert, but then I have these shy moments. If not for that, I would have met her sooner. I have always enjoyed her writing, but aside from that, I fell in love with her the minute we met, and we have had an incredible connection ever since. After we met, there was going to be no separating us, despite all the complications and difficulties.

K: *Were you both married at the time?*

D: Yes. When we met, we didn't know what it was, but we just kept looking into each other's eyes as we stood there talking. I love her gorgeous lips, with the beautiful line at the edges. I love her hair and the colour of it. It's matured from blonde to almost white while we've been together. Snow never looked brighter as it continues to melt in my hand and in my heart.

K: *You two are going to make me cry—stop it right now. Where did the two of you meet?*

D: At my house. My ex and I were building a wooden sailboat and her ex is a yacht designer. We wrote to them to inquire about plans. We started writing back and forth and while we were in the midst of building our boat, Robin and her ex came up from the San Juan Islands in their sailboat to Victoria. They rented a car and came out to our house. I have this memory of Robin standing on the patio and me standing on the kitchen floor. There was a small drop between us, and because Robin is a little taller than I am, we were literally eye-to-eye. I don't know what we talked about, but we were glued to each other. At one point, we looked down and one of us said, "Oh, you're wearing my other pair of shoes!" The other one of us said, "Well, you have on my only other pair of shoes!" It was rather funny that we had the same taste in shoes. That was in April 1982, and by August 1983, we were living together. Before then, I was living in Victoria, Robin was living in the States on San Juan Island, and we had two husbands and four children between us. Somehow we managed to extricate ourselves and get together. We ended up together in my home with my ex still living there! We managed to get free of him after eight months.

That was difficult, because my ex-husband, Rob, is a very sweet man, but I knew that I needed to be with Robin, so that was the end of it. I felt fantastic with her. She brought out the joy in me, whereas he was a damper on my enthusiasm. He was attracted to me because I am so bumptious, whereas he is a very quiet person. He dragged me down and I didn't realize it until I was semi-free of his oppression.

K: *Did you know before you met Robin that you were attracted to women?*

D: No, that was interesting. In retrospect, I realize that I had some feeling for women, but I didn't identify them as sexual feelings. It was just that I enjoyed being with certain people. Falling in love with Robin was a shock to me—I was so homophobic about our getting together. It was really scary for me, and I did lose family. I lost all my in-laws for a long time except for my father-in-law. He stuck around and remained friends with us. However, my ninety-three-year old mother-in-law hasn't spoken to me in all these years, except once when my eldest son was critically ill and she wanted to know the medical perspective from the family nurse.

K: *What about yourself, Robin? Did you already know you had an attraction to women when you two met?*

R: No, I never even thought about it. I grew up in a more open-minded family than Diana. My parents' best friends were involved in the theatre and we had lots of gay people at our house. My dad always made a point of saying homosexuality is completely normal and fine. I had my own homosexual friends, but I never identified it within myself. When I realized what my heart and my body were telling me, I thought, "My God, it's one thing to have homosexual friends, but it's another to be one." I was really frightened that we would be targeted. I didn't know how to deal with it.

D: Things were different twenty years ago.

R: Exactly. I realized the richness of my feelings for Diana, and in hindsight, if society had been totally free and accepting, I would have been happily involved with women a lot sooner.

D: For the first ten months of our relationship, we couldn't call ourselves lesbians. I said, "I don't want to even say that word!" The word sounds scary.

R: I love the word "gay." I just wish we could have something comparable to that. I think *gay* is a good umbrella term for all of us, although I understand lesbians who want to have their own identity.

K: *What struggles are the two of you currently facing as a couple?*

D: I don't know if we have any struggles, do we? I'd like a bit more money.

R: I think in a relationship, you're always working at making sure you clarify misunderstandings or miscommunications. You have to constantly work at making sure that your partner understands the thoughts you have. I think there's always work involved in a relationship if you choose to grow and build with it. In that sense, yes, we have that struggle.

K: *Was there a time when the two of you really did struggle as a couple?*

R: I think more around parenting and at the very beginning. I didn't know if I could express anger and tears that I had bottled up for years. I remember one time I ran out of the house and drove down to the beach and cooled off before coming back: I couldn't face anger or expression.

D: She didn't know what was going to happen after I exploded. It wasn't easy raising four children who were four, five, thirteen and sixteen years old. Our household was very busy.

R: We also had our homophobia to contend with, and so did the kids. We also had Diana's friends, some of whom decided to support us and others who said, "Forget this." We had a tremendous amount to deal with. My husband was also trying to find out if we were in a lesbian relationship. If he knew, I felt his innuendos suggested that he would take Josh from me if he found out. I didn't want that to happen because he had moved to the east coast of the United States and that was just too far away.

K: *How did the children eventually cope with living with the two of you?*

D: They were comfortable from the very beginning. My eldest was sixteen and he already adored Robin. She's very good with young people, and she appreciated each one of them individually. Her ability to parent was one of the first things I told her that I admired about her. I loved the way she parented Josh as we got to know each other. Before we lived together, we spent time together as families. I loved the way she was so calm. She was able to direct Josh in a way that left him feeling it was his idea all along. Robin is absolutely a natural teacher, and she can teach anybody anything.

R: Unfortunately, poor Angus struggled and cried occasionally because he got teased about the fact that he had two moms, but even during that period, we kept communicating with him. When he was having difficulty, he let us know and we would listen.

D: He knew he would be listened to because of our training in co-counselling. He could have his temper tantrum and cry as a thirteen-, fourteen-, fifteen-, and sixteen-year-old adolescent. That allowed him a wonderful discharge.

R: Once he calmed down, we could talk rationally to him and tell him, "I'm really sorry that you're having to go through this. Your mom and I are not going to stop loving each other. You shouldn't be teased the way you are and I'm sorry society is like that. I think it will be different in another ten to twenty years, but right now, you're a teenager and you're getting it, and that's not fair." That's the way we'd handle it.

D: [What's] lovely is that our children are adults now, and they are really supportive and loving of us. They come and visit us and they enjoy our company.

K: *How have your family and friends responded to you through all of your changes?*

R: My family has been wonderfully supportive, although my sister had a rougher time at first. I think she had a hard time seeing me as a lesbian. I also have an older brother, and he was immediately supportive of our relationship. I was born and raised in Canada, but I spent my thirteen heterosexually married years in the United States. I have good friends there and they're totally behind me. When Diana and I got together, I moved to Victoria, and my brother was already living there.

K: *What was your experience, Diana?*

D: Well, my brothers- and sisters-in-law completely divorced me. I went with my children to their grandfather's funeral, who I was really close to, a few years ago. Their grandfather had always supported my youngest, my daughter. When he died, I was terrified to go to the funeral because of the outlaw clan. My brother-in-law, who's rather scary, approached me with open arms and said, "Diana! How wonderful to see you," and then gave me a big hug. My two sisters-in-law were next and they both gave me big hugs and greeted me. I was taken aback by their friendliness and acceptance of me.

On the other hand, I've had a lot of difficulty with my side of the family. Most of my siblings were horrified when I left Rob to be with Robin, and when the marriage thing came up, the only person who talked to us about it was my nephew from my eldest brother. The day before the court case, we were with Peter, Murray and a few others. The press came and took many pictures of us, so we were on the front page of the *Province* the next morning, which was the beginning of the court case. That was in July 2001. A few weeks later, this same nephew wrote and said, "I was camping and I picked up a paper, a Sunday paper and, oh, my God! There's my aunt on the front page regarding the same-sex marriage case."

I have three siblings and my mother and nobody has ever said boo. Nobody has asked us anything about it or commented on any of the press, until July 2003 when the B.C. court said, "Yes, go ahead." That evening, my younger brother phoned and said, "Congratulations," and I said, "Oh, what for?" As far as I knew, nobody knew anything about it, right? He said, "Well, for what you and Robin have been doing in this marriage thing," he said, "I've been following the whole thing and I think it's wonderful." I said, "Thank you. But where have you been for the last three years? Why haven't you said anything about it?" He said, "I didn't know what to say. We thought you were still married to Rob and so we thought, how can she be doing this when she's still married to Rob?" I said, "What? What are you talking about? I've been legally separated since 1984 and divorced since 1998!"

We talked for a couple of hours actually. The next day, I got a phone call from my sister and, my God, she was very interested too. They both said they wanted to come to the wedding and my instant thought was, "No bloody way! I'm not having them at my wedding. They haven't been supportive of us at all." We didn't know what to do, so we asked over a listserv to find out how others thought we should proceed. The consensus was now that the siblings have opened the door, we should let them in and begin to break down barriers, and that is what we've started doing.

R: It's sort of ironic because we set out to do this, not thinking of ourselves so much, but thinking more of the future generation. We've had older people who are complete strangers to us phone and leave messages on our tape machine when we're not home, telling us that what we are doing is very helpful and wonderful. We've come full circle: Diana's family is now opening up to us, except for her eldest brother.

I don't know if her ninety-year-old mother could ever bring herself to talk about it either. She lets us sleep in the same bed in the guest bedroom, nonetheless, and she says she loves me. I have to accept that because I think she means it from her heart.

Our son, Josh, has been our staunchest ally as a kid. He used to wear a pink pin on his baseball cap that said, "My mom's a lesbian," with a pink heart underneath it. He wore it continually for three years, and he was a skateboarder.

K: *I learned from Peter and Murray that the two of you have also been part of the legal challenges in British Columbia, but through a national organization.*

They are part of the B.C. Partners, and your involvement is through Egale. Is that correct?

D: That's right—we volunteered from a listserv. Egale was looking for volunteers who were involved in long-term committed relationships to help push this challenge. Two representatives of Egale then interviewed us. I think they interviewed seventeen couples and they selected five from British Columbia. There's a couple in Prince George, us in Victoria, and three couples that live in Vancouver. The B.C. Partners had already started their own litigation.

R: I think the difference between the two groups is that the B.C. Partners were funding themselves while Egale was funding us. I think having two groups challenge the laws made it more powerful.

D: We were the only couple on the island that was taking the government to court, and we didn't realize how much media attention that would create for us. We were often telephoned and television crews showing up at our door became a common occurrence. The media were all really nice people—we really enjoyed them.

R: We never felt harassed.

D: People are starting to recognize us now. We've had strangers come up to us and introduce themselves. After one of our interviews, we were having coffee and a croissant and this beaming woman in her forties came up to us and said, "Congratulations you two, and blah, blah, blah. I've been watching the whole thing, and it's just wonderful," and we were astounded.

K: *I suspect some readers are going to wonder how gay marriages and gay relationships are different from heterosexual marriages and relationships. You have both been heterosexually married in the past, so you have that base of experience too. How would you compare and contrast straight versus gay relationships?*

R: Well, having lived thirteen years in a heterosexual relationship and twenty years in a homosexual relationship, I would have to say that a homosexual relationship is so much better, for me. I found myself and it's wonderful. Honouring who I am as a homosexual woman is fantastic. Therefore, the loving relationship that I have is vastly superior to the heterosexual relationship that I ever could have had.

The roles are not as clearly defined in a gay relationship as they are in a heterosexual relationship. You know, the husband is expected to do X and the wife is expected to do Y. Although the roles do overlap, it can cause stress because it creates confusion when roles overlap or are questioned. In our relationship, roles are not clearly defined. There were things that we both wanted to do that were defined as tasks for our husbands only. Now if we need to do some hammering, for example, one will say, "Okay. I'll hammer the first two nails and you hammer the next two." On the other hand, I hate ironing and Diana enjoys the meditation of ironing. She hates working with numbers but I'm good at it. We make a number of great trade-offs. I think because we're the same gender and the roles aren't clearly defined, it opens up a whole lot more possibilities for supporting each other in creative ways.

D: Another thing is that as women, we see things the same way rather than the contrast created when a man and a woman are in a relationship. We don't have to have the same opinion or anything, but there is a type of understanding that is always there. We've talked about it with other women too, and it's definitely easier. We have several friends who have done what we've done. They've been married and had children and then got together with another woman. I can't put my finger on it, but it's something about not having to explain where you're coming from.

R: When I think of the book, *Men Are From Mars: Women Are From Venus,* it is much easier when you are both of the same gender. Let's use the example of making love. You know what your body feels like as a woman and you know what feels pleasurable to you. You also know what the other person is thinking and feeling inside because you've experienced it. Mind you, you've got different bodies, but when your partner tells you what makes her feel good, [you] can readily understand and be empathic. In a way, that can also be a turn on. You know, we have both had caesarean births, and we know what nursing a baby is like. Unfortunately men can't have that experience. Although my ex husband was extremely attentive during my caesarean and very helpful in the hospital, I could also feel how perplexed, fearful and concerned he was with the amount of bleeding. A woman would not be so fearful because it's a normal thing that we do every month. We bleed a lot, so it's not such a big deal to us.

K: *I never thought about that.*

R: Consequently, homosexual relationships have quite a few benefits. Sometimes I think we're cheating because it's so easy: it's a lazy route to communication.

K: *That is one way in which lesbian relationships are different from heterosexual relationships. In what ways do you see them as the same?*

R: We both cook, we both clean, and we have to raise money and pay bills like everyone else. If Diana is out working and I'm working at home, I need to get up from writing and exercise my body occasionally. It's great to do some housework.

If you look at the sexual arena, you still have to communicate what feels good for you and what doesn't. You want to make sure you're loving and attentive to each other.

D: I think it is like any real partnership between two people.

K: *Right. What advice would you give to gay couples that are contemplating marriage?*

D: Learn to really communicate with each other. There needs to be sharing, listening and honesty.

R: Don't shove your feelings down. That was the second biggest mistake I made in my first marriage: the first was not being aware of my homosexuality. I shoved my feelings down in subjugation of what I thought was the fantasy of marriage and societal expectations. Learn to express your feelings and honour your partner's need to express his or her feelings. Check in with each other if it's okay to express your feelings or thoughts right now, remembering that we are not always ready or able to listen carefully and nondefensively.

If you need to cry, ask for your partner's support. First check and see if she's in a space where she can listen. If she can, just say "Please hold me and listen to me. I'll be able to talk in a few minutes." Have an agreement with your partner that you'll each listen with a deeply open, loving heart at these times, giving full attention, looking at your partner with compassion and respect, in the knowledge that after the tears are shed, your partner will feel clear enough to move forward in a full, rational, loving manner. You don't need to say anything, nor does your partner need to have any particular information other than that you need to cry. It's helpful to give each other equal time for tears, trading back and forth. If your partner is too distressed to listen, seek out other friends who can, and with whom you are willing to give equal listening/crying time—but get rid of those tears so that they don't bottleneck and come out inappropriately in a rage, or swell up inside until they make you sick or kill you.

Give each other space: the silent moments are healing and wonderful as well. You need time to do your Tai Chi, or walk your dog, or whatever. You don't always have to do things together. There's one plus one, and a third one makes three. The third one is the relationship. Laugh together, cry together, and be open. The most important ingredient is honest communication, and not just of the verbal stuff, but also of the heart stuff.

D: I used to run away from a situation when I was upset. Eventually Robin asked me, "What do you need from me when you feel like this?" I told her, "Don't let me run away, but hold me, because nobody has ever done that for me when I needed it." I needed to learn to stay and feel the feelings I was having.

K: *I find that fascinating because with your partner, you were able to finish a piece of business that you could never deal with in childhood.*

D: Exactly—it's all old stuff. Think about your childhood and how you felt when whatever happened? It's really amazing what we have stored in our brains and the slightest thing will trigger it. See if you can go back there, and with a loving partner, you can change the old pattern. Here I am talking to a psychologist!

K: *What you've said makes perfect sense to me. Is there a metaphor, an image, a movie or a piece of music that really speaks to your feelings or thoughts about same-sex marriage?*

R: Not many people in Canada know about the Arbutus tree. These trees are all around here. They are so sensual; so similar, yet so different.

D: The skin on the trunk of the tree is smooth and rusty red and as the summer advances, that skin splits and peels off—in a similar way to birch bark. Unlike birch bark, however, the peeling occurs in vertical curls rather than going around the tree.

R: There are many different colours in that new bark underneath the skin: sort of red and green. The bark is silky but firm.

D: The trees grow in beautiful curves and where branches have come off, there are scars that themselves are beautiful, and they are round like a body.

R: It's an evergreen, yet it sheds its leaves. It has white blossoms in the spring and red berries in the fall.

D: In July, the leaves dry and drop all over the ground.

R: The Arbutus tree is very productive, sensual and creative. I think it's really a good image for same-sex marriage. It's a tree you can't resist photographing. Another good part of the image is that the Arbutus [are] protected trees. They're known as heritage trees, and it's illegal to cut them down unless they're diseased. Even then, they have to be certified as diseased.

K: *That is a beautiful metaphor. Do you think that we've dealt with this topic thoroughly, or is there something else that you think would be really important to get out there?*

R: Yes, I think so.

D: I agree.

K: *Thank you very much for the interview today.*

Lloyd Thornhill and Robert Peacock
photo by Kevin Midbo

Where the Mustard Seed Grows

Bob Peacock and Lloyd Thornhill

Date: August 10, 2003
Time: 11:00 am
Place: Vancouver, British Columbia

I knew that God would eventually enter a conversation about same-sex marriage. Together for thirty-five years, Bob and Lloyd are born-again Christians with a take on God that I can understand. These people, like the rest of us, are God's children, and they have an interesting message to share.

L: Ours is a thirty-five-year story because we met in 1968, which was at about the same time that Pierre Trudeau said that the government has no business in the bedrooms of the nation. Here we are, thirty-five years later, still trying to keep the government out of our bedrooms and out of our lives. It's been a long road with many mountains and valleys along the way. Bob and I have had some wonderful times together. We've also shared grief, we've lost family members, and there was a time when we dealt with alcoholism. In 1988, we became born-again Christians, and our lives changed from that moment onward.

Speaking about the marriage challenge, we saw an ad on the Egale Web site when they were looking for volunteers to take on the federal government regarding same-sex marriage. Bob and I talked about it, and we decided to become involved. We thought it could help young gay and lesbian people who are coming out, and that it might reduce the homophobia that we've had to face throughout our relationship. We were selected by Egale as one of the couples to take on the case. It's been an incredibly fulfilling experience—we feel honoured and proud to be part of that decision.

It's had its valleys, however, like the first decision by Justice Pitfield who denied us that right. He admitted that the decision was discriminatory to us, but he believed it was okay to do that. I felt totally devastated when I read that decision, but after that, the skies opened and the stars began to shine. Things began to fall into place. Here we are preparing for our wedding next year, along with the other couples.

K: *What have you set as the date for your marriage?*

L: It will be July 17, 2004, just two days short of our thirty-sixth anniversary. We plan on having the wedding at the Ryerson United Church, which has a gay minister. A good friend of ours, who is also a gay minister, will perform the service. Our reception will be at the Supreme Court buildings in downtown Vancouver where we obtained our marriage rights. That will make a statement.

K: *That is wonderful. What is your perspective, Bob?*

B: My perspective is different from Lloyd's. From the first day we met, I felt we were destined to be together. The marriage thing didn't come into my mind because who would have believed that there would be same-sex marriage in our lifetime? I'm fifty-six years old, and I figured I would die before same-sex marriage would ever happen. It is really exciting. For me, I was already committed to Lloyd—we made that commitment back in 1968. I never wavered from it because I truly believed that we were destined by God to be together. I think the longest we've been apart, if you combine it all, would be about a month.

I was his boss at one time and he was my boss. We worked together, so we were together 24-7. We have much happiness between us. There has also been sadness and alcoholism. There have been family tragedies too, but we dealt with them. By the time Egale was beginning its same-sex marriage campaign, I was tired of being an activist. We had fought within the trade union movement to have same-sex benefits instilled in constitutions and in contracts. That struggle could have ended in us getting beaten or killed, but we stuck through it. I thought, "Do I want to go through this again? Do I really want to have my skin come off my hands and go through that incredible stress again?" I was also thinking about my church upbringing and the messages…instilled within me. Then I thought, "It's worth it." It was John Fisher from Egale who really convinced me that we should do it. You know, Lloyd has strength beyond belief and he has lots of grace. I knew, as a couple, we could get through this and that the stories had to be told. People had to know that there are people like us out there.

I am concerned because of what's happening now with the Vatican, the fundamentalist church groups in this country, and our federal government. I know that if they try to block same-sex marriage nationally, they will have a real battle on their hands.

K: *Absolutely. Tell me about where you guys first met and how your relationship developed.*

L: I can't lie to you, so I've got to tell you exactly what happened. My wife and I had lived together for five years and she had a son from a previous relationship. Together [we] had a daughter, despite the fact that I was struggling with my sexuality. I was working on the railway at the time and travelling to Montreal a lot. I basically ended up living two lives. It was really hard on me because I loved my wife as a person, but I couldn't love her the way that I needed to to fulfil my needs. One day, I told her that I am gay. She started to blame herself. "What have I not given you for you to be like that?" She offered to free me for a few days a week, but I thought, "No." I needed to be free: I needed to be me.

When we broke up, I was totally lost. I didn't know where to go. I was drinking in those days and there was a tavern in Halifax, Nova Scotia called the *Piccadilly*. It was a straight tavern by day and the gay people went there at night. I was hanging around with a couple of guys. I was a bit of a punk and a rebel.

B: You were a punk?

L: A very good-looking punk. So I went inside the bar and sat with a couple of buddies. The only time I had the courage to talk was after a few beers, and along came this young man. I thought, "Gee, this guy's really attractive," but I didn't know how to start up a conversation with him. So I just looked at him for a moment and said, "How would you like to have a baby by me?" And he said, "Not particularly," and away he went.

B: He was disgusting.

L: But within a few minutes he returned for the baby.

B: Oh, what a lie! (*Laughter.*)

L: I think he had a test tube in his pocket. Anyway, we got talking. A couple of days later, we met again in the same pub, and we've never been apart since.

K: *Did you start living together immediately?*

L: Uh-huh.

B: Maybe I'll pick it up from there. I had just married Diane on June 15 of that year. I was twenty years old, but soon to turn twenty-one. Diane and I already had a child, Denise, who was nearly a year old. I was in the navy at the time, and Diane wanted me to leave the navy. I had a platonic friendship with Hugh, a doctor who wanted more, but I wasn't ready to give him anything at all. He professed that he loved me, but he was the one who pushed Diane and me together. I ended up getting married for the sake of our child. I wanted to run out of the church on our wedding day, but I couldn't.

Even the Anglican minister who was marrying us felt something, and he asked me, "Robert, do you really want to do this?" My half-brother also came up to me and said, "Bobby, I just don't know." I said, "I can't. I've got to do it." I really tried to convince myself and talk myself into loving this woman unconditionally. I thought I could suppress my homosexuality. Within a matter of a week I knew it wasn't going to work.

There were also some mitigating circumstances. Her parents moved in with us at the same time and that was adding to the stress. She was driving me nuts, telling me that she knew I was gay. She knew it instinctively, even though we never talked about it. If I wasn't home from work by 4:30, there was hell to pay. I had lots of gay friends and her quote was, "Never will a fruit step a foot in the doorway of this house," and I said, "That's what you think." So I set up a party with all my gay friends and non-gay friends. I told her, "Okay—they really haven't met you, so now they're going to meet you." My mother-in-law thought this was terrific: she actually helped me set up this big party. Diane was not so supportive. The afternoon of the party, my friends came to the door and Diane said, "Sorry, there is no party."

We got into a big argument about it and I walked out. The only place I could think of going was to the Piccadilly. So I went there with some buddies. Several of my friends there had attended my wedding, and someone said, "Oh my gosh! Is it over already?" I said, "It's not over. I'm just here to see everybody." I lied about that because I really believed it was over that day. I didn't even want to ever go back.

There were a bunch of punks or greasers at a nearby table. My friend said, "Let's go over and talk to Patty." I said, "I don't want to go over and talk to Patty: he's a punk. I think he's a murderer!" I didn't know what he was, but I didn't want to talk to him. My friend insisted, so I went over and we sat down. I looked over at the person next to me and I thought I was going to die. He was the most handsome person I had seen in my life. He was a little drunk though, so I thought, "Can I handle a drunk?" So I didn't speak to him, but I thought eventually, he'll speak to me. Then this guy leaned over and said, "Would you like to have a baby by me?" I thought, "Oh, my God. What a pig!" And I just said, "Not particularly would I want to have a baby by you," and I walked out.

I talked to my friend Jackie about it, and thought, "Oh my God, will I ever see him again?" I didn't know at the time that I already knew his brother. I never told my wife that I had Wednesday afternoons off, so I went back to Piccadilly's. When I entered, who should be in there but him? Then Hugh came in and I decided that the only way I would get together with Lloyd would be to have a party. I had a place out on a lake, so I said to Hugh, "Why don't we invite everybody out for a big party?" So we did, and I never went home for the three days the party continued. My aunt knew where I was and she was phoning me. She would then phone Diane and say, "He's okay, he's on a toot. He's really pissed off and he's on a binge. He's mad at you and that's it." Then I called my mother-in-law and talked to her. She knew Diane and I had had a fight, so she told me it was okay and that I should just let it all out and come home when I felt better.

The only way I decided I would go home was for it to end. I went home and said, "You know, it's not going to work. I met Lloyd, I'm in love with him, and we're going to be together." There was some other stuff in between there as well. Diane caught Lloyd and me together at an apartment we had in town. Lloyd thought it was the housekeeper entering.

We were sitting on the chesterfield in towels, so she put two and two together and threw a big bottle of pennies at me, trying to kill me, but it didn't obviously work. But it was devastating. To this day, she thinks that she is the woman that could change me. She knew that I liked guys, but she thought she could change that. I have to give her credit where credit is due. She was prepared to allow me to be with Lloyd for a few days a week, and then come home to her. But what would I be coming home to? To be celibate with Diane? I told her I'm not going to do it. She went nuts and destroyed everything that meant something to me: my record collection, my photos from when I was in the navy, everything. She came out to the car and pulled a long nail file out from her skirt. She tried to stab Lloyd in the jugular vein with it.

K: *My gosh. It sounds like she really lost it over this.*

B: She did, and then she proceeded to harass us for the next seventeen years. She wouldn't allow me to divorce her either. We had to leave the city.

L: We moved to Montreal where Bob's parents were living because we just couldn't survive in a small town with two wives running around.

K: *Bob, when did you come out to yourself?*

B: I was seven years old.

K: *Seven years old— wow! How about you, Lloyd?*

L: I had thought it over many times, but I think I was in my early teens when I realized that there was something different about me. In those days, the word used to describe us was usually *fruit*, so when I heard the word homosexual, I had to find out what it was all about. When I started looking the word up, I thought, "Gee, this could be me." I was having dreams about boys. I knew that this wasn't what I was supposed to be, so I struggled with it. I thought that if I met the right woman, everything would be fine. When I met Lynn, I did fall in love with her, but I think we rushed it. When I said to her, "Someday I'm going to marry you," she said, "How about November 15?" Like Bob, I wanted to run. I got totally drunk the night before the wedding because I couldn't deal with it, but I went through with it. I was twenty-one years old then, and I met Bob when I was twenty-six.

K: *Was Bob the first guy that you felt that strong connection to?*

L: Yes, he was the first man I fell in love with. I felt sexual attractions to other guys, even throughout my marriage, but I didn't want to spend my life with any of them. It was different with Bob.

K: *Were you both raised in religious households?*

L: Not in my case. My mother used to attend the Salvation Army and she loved singing. My grandmother always read the Bible too, right up until she died. When I was nine years old, I went to the Mercy Seat of the Salvation Army: it's a type of vow. I believe that I made a commitment to the Lord at that time, but because I was so young, I didn't realize what I was doing.

But after what happened to Bob and me in Arizona, I thought God had always watched over me since I accepted him into my life. I was in a really bad car accident and they thought I was dead. I felt that God didn't let me die because there was work for us to do. But let me start from the beginning of that story. We gave up drinking a few months before that and we were struggling with that. We decided to take a trip to Arizona.

B: Lloyd wanted to go on a trip. I don't mind the cold climates, but Lloyd hates cold weather. He wanted to go somewhere it was sunny: we were thinking about riverboat cruises and such. I wanted to go someplace different from Palm Springs because we had already been there a few times. Out of the blue, Lloyd said, "Why don't we go to Phoenix?" I said, "Why the hell would you want to go to Phoenix? There's nothing there but desert." I wasn't really that enthusiastic.

We arrived in Phoenix in March 1988, and then out of the blue, Lloyd picks up a newspaper and begins reading about a gay church where they perform holy unions. He asked me to read the article, and then he said, "I think we should go to that church." I reluctantly agreed. We headed for the church the next morning, but we got lost. As we were driving down a street, Lloyd heard music and said, "Maybe that's it."

L: We didn't want to go in because we were scared to death. We hadn't been inside of a church for years.

B: Yeah, and as it turned out, we missed the 9:30 am service. A woman at the door asked us to return for the next service, so we left and went for coffee. We later returned and the same woman greeted us. We walked in, and the music was beyond belief: it reminded me of my Baptist upbringing. This was a little church filled with gay and lesbian people. We thought we had arrived there by accident, but we soon realized it was no accident—we were led there. After the service was over, the pastor, Fred Pattison, came and spoke to us. He invited us back for the evening service.

We returned for the less formal evening service. The congregation began singing, "We are Standing on Holy Ground," and as they sang, I was thinking, "Lord, I don't know if I can take much more of this. You've got to take me— I'm yours." It was that simple. I give my life over to you and whatever it is you want me to do, I will do it. Unbeknown to both of us, Lloyd was accepting the Lord as his saviour at the same time as me. It gives me goose bumps to think about it.

We started attending that church for a while, and I still think of it as our home church. If we could afford it, we would love to get married there and transport all of our friends to witness it.

L: Fred Pattison told us one of my favourite sayings. His saying was, "I'm a Christian in spite of Christians." I loved that phrase because Christians can really turn you off!

I soon realized that God had a reason for bringing us together. After that, we quit our jobs, sold everything, cashed in our pension funds, bought an old van, and took to the road. Bob has a beautiful singing voice, so we went to hospitals and nursing homes singing Christian songs and preaching. It was quite an experience. We eventually ended up on welfare because we had no money, but we continued to put our faith in God.

B: Some people recommitted their lives to Christ while we involved ourselves in evangelism. They would raise their hands to the Lord in singing praises—until they found out we are gay. The venom that came out of their mouths was beyond belief: from Christ to hell in a minute.

K: *Our silence has been overwhelming, even to us. Where are the gay people when you need them to have voice? So many live in closets of hell, and it's so tragic. Let me come back to 1968, the year you met. It was illegal to be gay in Canada until 1969, and the American Psychiatric Association classified homosexuality as a mental illness until 1973. Before these changes occurred, did the two of you live secretively for fear that you could have been institutionalized or jailed?*

L: Do you know what, Kevin? We never thought of it that way. We weren't concerned. I have a favourite saying, "We were out before it was in to be out." That's the way we were.

B: To add perspective to this, we lived in Halifax before we moved to Montreal. In those days, the term "homophobic" was never used. I don't think people knew how to respond to gay individuals. People were getting gay bashed constantly, however, because they were stupid. It was foolish to go by yourself to the outdoor cruising areas because the punks would be out there, "wanting to kick some fruit's ass"—that's what they would say.

Halifax was a heavy military city then, both with Canadian and American forces. The different navies wanted to kick some fag's ass, so they would go fag bashing. But you know what? There [was] a high percentage of gay police officers in Halifax at that time. Consequently, they would be fairly protective of the gay community. We knew many of the gay cops and they didn't want us to spill the beans on them, so they provided us some protection. There were also some well-known gay activists in Halifax.

L: Most of the gay people we saw or knew were stereotypical in their mannerisms—very flamboyant types. We used to have midnight shows at a theatre called the Garrick Repetory Theatre, and the place was packed with young people. They would come into the theatre wearing Humphrey Bogart or George Raft type raincoats. Then they would pull them down around their waists and flaunt themselves to everybody. We would all jeer and cheer them on! Those were the type of gay people we knew.

B: I called them the "pretenders" because they were all in the closet. Most of the radio talk-show hosts and television anchors were gay in Halifax back then, and we'd go to parties and I'd freak when I met them because you would never know they were gay. I was one of the flamboyant ones—I didn't mind walking down the streets wiggling my ass because I couldn't have cared less. The American sailors who saw my friends and me would say, "Hey, girls," and they'd be singing "Where the Boys Are." It's true.

There was a huge black community in Nova Scotia, and there were many black homosexuals. We would watch out for each other and be protective of each other. I would hang out with the black gay groups because some of them were bootleggers. There was only one gay bar, so mostly we went to bootleggers. I remember going to bootleggers when I was sixteen years old. Some of the punks that Lloyd associated with went to see bootleggers and they would all pretend they weren't gay, but the next thing you'd know, they'd be running around with one of the boys.

Let me now change gears and talk about our upcoming marriage in July 2004. The enthusiasm from other gay people is just not there. The heterosexual community where I work is more excited than the gays! They want to be involved and want to help plan it. It's like, "Oh, Bob, can we do this? I want to do that." The heterosexuals are behind us while the gay people give the attitude of, "I don't really know if I want to be a part of this."

L: It's quite a divisive issue in our community—it really is.

B: Totally.

K: *What do you think is the fear that some gay people have about same-sex marriages?*

L: Some gay people are concerned that we are stepping into an area, traditional marriage, where we become too much like heterosexuals, and consequently taking away the uniqueness of being gay and our freedom to be who we are. I don't see that at all.

I've talked to many people and I've said, "Look, we're not forcing you to marry. You have your choice. We just want that option…for [ourselves]. We want to marry and others like us want to marry. No one else is expected to marry." It was like someone wrote in the paper the other day, "What is the big deal?", and this guy was himself heterosexual.

B: I think the other thing, too, is the big "commitment" word. I truly believe that there are a lot of gay people that really want to commit.

L: We've ended up broke because of my bad money management, but we've always acted like a married couple. We share everything.

B: I remember the day I gave you my first paycheque—I've never seen another one!

L: And your wallet. There was nothing in it, but it's a nice wallet.

K: *So, tell me, were either one of you concerned that you might be incarcerated or put into a psych ward?*

B: I was once when I was in the navy, which I joined in 1964. They never asked the question, which I thought was stupid, but I don't know why I joined either. When I went into the barracks, I was setting up and there was nobody in the next bunk. I was flitting around like a little queen. I mean, if you look at me, people can say, "There's one," and I was even more animated then. So I flitted around all over the place, dusting and tidying up. I'm putting my stuff away and the next thing I know, this huge native man comes traipsing in and throws his knapsack on the bunk and says, "What the fuck!" I said, "Excuse me?" He said, "I hope there aren't any faggots around this fucking place!" I replied, "Just me—I'm the only one." Well, you know what? He just laughed his head off, and that broke the ice. Then he said, "No fucking way." That's exactly what he said.

A few days later, I was scrubbing the floors and waxing them. One of the punks from Ontario said, "You need some wax? The fruit down there has it." So I start saying, "Fruit? Is there a fruit in here?" Of course, he was talking about me. So he then said, "Just pass me the fucking wax." I thought, "Here we go—my first fight. I just know it." I was so frightened that I thought I was going to piss myself. I kept waxing, and he said, "I guess you didn't hear me, you fucking fruit." I retorted, "Yeah. I heard you. You want the wax, here," and I heaved it and hit him hard with it. He came after me. I tell you, I don't even remember him coming, but all I know is I beat the shit out of him. I was so frightened I didn't know what I was doing.

L: What a woman!

B: It's true! I didn't know what I was doing. I was so scared that he was going to get the upper hand on me that for some reason, I just beat the shit out of him, and he was a scary guy. After that day, not one person ever called me a fruit again, unless we were playfully joking or something like that. I think they were terrified of me.

K: *You went a bit psycho.*

B: Totally. I was "psycho homo." You know, I used to hang around with the women in the barracks. I'd go out with the Wrens on Friday night and we'd dance and carry on. There were also guys I hung out with, and we would do weird things like kiss each other on the cheek and dance together. The guys would all dance together. Nobody hid themselves at the barracks either. We'd all walk around with hard-ons as we made our way to the showers.

L: Don't forget about that can of wax for Saturday morning.

B: But it's true. They never thought anything about it. We knew who was banging whom and you were supposed to report it if you caught anybody having sex. Well, of course, I was going to protect everybody because I didn't care what they did. Others knew which nights I was on watch duty and they knew on those nights, they could crawl in the bunk with somebody else. They knew they could trust me. There were guys that went to cells for blowing another guy.

K: *How long would they be kept in the cell?*

B: They would be in there until they were thrown out. It was cause for immediate dismissal with a dishonourable discharge. Someone would pack your bags and take your belongings to your cell.

K: *Now tell me about the alcoholism. When did that come into your lives?*

L: We drank from the day we met, and before that. We drank heavily for our first twenty years together.

B: In the navy, you could only drink on weekends. Unless you were on duty, you went out and got soused. When I got out of the navy, I just continued on drinking. I think alcoholism took over later in our lives: after we joined the B.C. Ferries. Can you imagine us being B.C. Ferries? (*Laughter.*)

L: We always drank after work. All the people we hung out with were drinkers. Once we quit drinking, all of our friends disappeared. Our worst drinking years were 1986 and 1987. I think one of the reasons I drank heavily was because I was still dealing with my sexuality. There were a lot of things going through my head. Bob and I used to watch people like Jimmy Swaggart. Jimmy would get up on stage, walk back and forth and say, "Those homosexuals are going to burn in Hell," and that kind of stuff. Those messages were really affecting me. I got to a point where I thought, "I'm not acceptable to God or anybody else," and it was really destroying my life. Once we stopped and we went to Phoenix, that issue became resolved because there was no question in my mind that God created us as we were.

B: We would also watch Oral Roberts. We'd be sitting at the table just bawling as we listened to this man's ministry. Then he would start gay bashing, and so would Swaggart. It made us think, "Am I really that unacceptable? Am I really that abominable? Are we really in a sin[ful] relationship? Are we really going to go to Hell? Are we destroying each other by being in this relationship?" It made us wonder, "If I left him, would he be okay? Am I making him gay by keeping him in this relationship?"

L: But I really think that God gives us inner strength to take us through really rough periods and become stronger from it. My experiences have strengthened me.

K: *Were either of you ever gay-bashed?*

L: We've been taunted with remarks. One night after Bob and I had been together seventeen years, there was a pub near where we lived in Horseshoe Bay. That's where the ferry terminal is. The pub is built like a ship inside, and this means that large groups of people sit together despite not knowing each other. Bob and I were sitting with some friends and this man sitting next to us nudged me on the knee and said, "Faggot," referring to Bob. I said, "Not faggots, fairies. Where?" He said, "The guy over there." I said, "Well, I don't know. I've lived with him for seventeen years and I didn't know he was." He replied, "Oops, I'm sorry." My humour usually took away the sting and people, like him, felt embarrassed.

Another time, I was running for president of our union and this friend of ours came from an area where they were all macho types. He said, "Lloyd, I think you're a great guy, but how do I go back to my delegates and tell them that the ferries are being run by a fairy." We were attempting to change the union constitution to make it an offence to discriminate based on sexual orientation. It became a battle of words on the convention floor, but it passed through. Bob and I worked together and we were always open. That garnered us a lot of respect with the other employees and members of our union.

B: I don't know how familiar you are with unions, but I was at a winter school for trade unionists up in Harrison Hot Springs. The president of the woodworkers' union, the IWA, would always want to tell gay jokes. All the loggers were up there, these big macho assholes as I used to call them. At the plenary session, the president of the IWA made a derogatory comment about lesbians.

Everybody just sat there. I said, "This is bullshit. I'm not standing here and taking that crap. I'm telling you right now that as a gay man, your comments are unacceptable." One of the lesbians then stood up and said, "My brother over there is right. We're not going to take this crap from you or anybody else." That created quite a furore, and they had to shut down the plenary. The president then filed a charge against me, [saying] stuff like, "You put this fruit in my room and he could have attacked me." I'm thinking, "Please, go take a look in the mirror. Get over yourself!" We would say that to the guys, and they would get upset! One guy said, "How dare you?" I responded, "You're not my cup of tea. You think we want you guys?" They would freak, "How can this gay guy reject us? How dare he?" In response, they set up a plenary session on the subject of homosexuality. It turned into a panel on gay rights and on homosexuality, and through that, we changed the federation.

The straight men were in tears. A lot of them didn't know what was going on, and they didn't realize how offensive their jokes were. They thought it was okay because no gay person ever went up to them and said, "It's unacceptable. You're not going to say this." Jerry Stoney who was at that time one of the vice-presidents within the federation, came up to me and said, "Bob, my brother, I give you all the accolades. Nobody in this place would have had the guts to stand up and say anything against Jack." He said, "Weren't you the least bit scared?" I said, "I was terrified, but it had to be said." He said, "Look at what you guys have done, and the changes that are going to occur."

K: *That is profound. With my next question, I want you to be completely honest. Thirty-five years later, can you honestly say your relationship is better than it was five, ten, fifteen, or twenty years ago? Did it keep getting better for the two of you?*

L: I think there are different challenges as the years go by. I don't think it gets any easier by a long shot. Every day we have to work on our relationship because we're two different personalities. Bob has more of an "A" type personality, and I'm more laid-back. Every day we have our spats, and that's been there since day one. I think that just firms up and strengthens our relationship: it gets rid of all the frustrations we have. In our thirty-five years, there have been challenges. When I was younger, I made some mistakes and I'm not proud of it. The important thing is—don't lie to one another: be honest, and admit your mistakes.

...

We're reaching a time in our lives where we're thinking about retirement and issues like that. We don't see a lot around for our community, like retirement villages and things like that, unless you have lots of money to go to Florida or Palm Springs. I'm not sure if Bob is having similar thoughts, but I am.

B: In the early beginnings of our relationship, I thought to myself, "Do I really want to put myself through this shit?", referring to the drinking. I came from a family of drunks. Then I thought about how much I love him. Sometimes it was the movements he made or his gestures, our little talks, or his funny jokes—they just thrilled me to death. Sometimes all he has to do is touch me, after thirty-five years, and I still get a hard-on. Sexually, it's still like day one. In some cases, depending on the day, it's better than before.

L: Especially if he can wake me up.

B: Especially if he's not comatose! You know, I'm an old hag because I nitpick at the smallest of things. I'm a perfectionist and a neat freak. Lloyd is not.

L: That's the navy background.

B: I was so glad when I saw that iron and ironing board when I walked into your hotel room.

L: Bob, you haven't seen Kevin and Kevin's washroom yet—believe me, get on the counter and straighten it up.

B: I'm like that, you know, and there are little things I expect done. If they're not done, I go ballistic. I have a temper, but he can crack a joke or just sit there and smile—that's enough for me. God has given me the capacity to know when to back off when he gets angry and when to be totally loving and committed, and that's what I am. The commitment and the relationship that we have is more than sex, and that's what the public needs to know, but I don't think they know that. I think the public only looks at our bedroom— they never look at who we are as people and how our minds and souls have connected.

L: Sex is only a small part of a relationship. Our sexuality is us, is our inner being, and we can't change that. We're about as ordinary as people get. Really, we're quite boring. We watch too much television and we don't exercise enough.

B: If somebody had to come in and live with us for a month, they'd probably get totally bored. Before Lloyd's accident, we golfed and we played tennis, but now he's limited in some of that stuff.

L: But, we feel we've contributed to our society. We are activists and we believe in advocacy for people. We help whoever we can, and right now, we're trying to do some work for our community.

K: *Do you think there's any difference between your relationship and that which is typical of heterosexual marriages?*

B: So what are the differences? All couples have spats, they have to wash, they have to do dishes, and they have to clean. Do they have gender roles? Well, we all have to sort these out in one way or another. I think in most gay relationships, there is more of an equal sharing of household duties and chores.

L: For example, I don't allow him to fill up with gas—it would end up in the radiator.

B: Well, I can't stand the smell of it. The car would be without gas if I had to fill it up, let me tell you.

K: *What advice would you give to gay couples that are thinking about marriage?*

L: Think carefully about it before you do it. Think about whether the person you're talking about marrying is the person you want to be committed to for the rest of your life. We truly believe that marriage is a lifelong commitment because we don't believe in divorce.

B: I'm sure there are a number of heterosexual people out there, particularly the politicians and church groups, who want to see same-sex marriage fail, and of course, some marriages will fail—that's human nature. Coming back to advice, realize that no relationship is easy, but if it's worth having, it's worth fighting for. It's a daily battle. You just don't toss somebody aside because they sneeze the wrong way, or they've put on an extra few pounds, or whatever. We don't want the heterosexual community to continue to think that we're all just pretty boys that have moustaches and T-shirts who run around in white shorts with our butts hanging out. We're just as plain and as ordinary as everybody else. We put on weight and grow older too. You have to learn to take the good with the bad. When I first met Lloyd, for example, he was twenty-six years old with a body like Arnold Schwarzenegger.

We all go through a metamorphosis. If you think for one minute that your partner is going to stay the same, or that you're going to mould them into what you want, think again. The person has to be who they are. Realize that you're going to take the person with all his or her warts and farts, like everybody else. They sneeze and they get sick, and you've got to be prepared to take care of that. It's amazing how some gay people go on, "Oh, my God! Did you know Johnny just farted in front of me? I'm getting rid of him and going after Donald instead." I've heard that with young people. Some gay people don't want to work at anything, but you have to work at a relationship—you have to place value on that person. Don't just toss them out because there's something you don't like about them.

L: There are very few people that I've met in our community that don't want a long-term relationship. Most people are searching. If you walk into any bar, which we rarely enter these days, it's almost like you never left from years ago. There are almost the same people sitting at every second bar stool, waiting for Mr. Right or Ms. Right to come along, and they never seem to appear. Well, there is no Mr. or Ms. Right because nobody is perfect. Get used to the fact that you will have to settle for less than perfection. But you also need to ask yourself, "Do you want to die old and lonely with nobody to share your love with?"

B: I believe that God has destined somebody for everybody, but you don't have to go through nine thousand people to say, "Oh, there's the one!" I think that most heterosexual people have a belief that for gay people, it's about sex. Many gay people have lived up to their expectations, albeit, but those same souls are looking for a deeper connection with somebody. Many simply don't know how to establish it.

K: *Is there a piece of music, an image, a metaphor or a movie that really speaks to your feeling about same-sex marriage?*

L: Yes, there's a song by Vince Gill called, "Look at Us." We're going to play it at our wedding. It's our story. The words are absolutely beautiful.

K: *Just one more question. What would you put in a "hope box" for gay people? What still needs to happen in the gay community?*

B: There's a T-shirt that I love that says, *I am what I am*. If only gay people could truly believe it—if they could only believe that God truly loves them as they are. There's a song that I sing off and on called, "Since God Is For Us, Who Can Be Against Us?"

L: That seems to be the major problem of our community: self-acceptance. Once you've accepted yourself, it doesn't matter what other people think. We get angry when people judge us, but it really doesn't matter. It's not going to hurt us because we know who we are and we love ourselves. That's the thing I'd like to put in the hope chest is that people believe in themselves and love themselves. It doesn't matter what other people feel because other people can change.

B: Lloyd and I were invited to minister in a Lutheran church. I was singing a song called, "Since God Is For Us," and there was a young teenager, not more than fourteen years old, sitting in the third pew back. He was just bawling his eyes out. I instinctively knew that he was gay, but I couldn't get to him because he left almost immediately afterwards.

I talked to the pastor afterwards, and he also thought this boy is gay, but he didn't know how to reach him either. That was sad. At the reception line, parents came up to us and said, "Gosh, I wish we could have brought our children. If only we had known you were coming." Lutherans don't typically have a Pentecostal, evangelistic concert in their churches. The parents weren't told what type of concert it was going to be, so they didn't bring their kids, but they wished they had. Soon after that, the pastor came out to his congregation, and they decided to keep him as their pastor. There was some controversy around this, however, but not because he is gay. He was also working with the MCC church at the time.

L: We've also attended some *Parents, Families and Friends of Lesbians and Gays* (PFLAG) meetings, and people have been positively affected by the length of time we have been together. When we shared our story with mothers and fathers who were dealing with the sexuality of their children, I remember a young couple of guys there one night and we went out for a cigarette together. This was ten years ago, and these guys looked at me and said, "Twenty-five years—wow, man, how do you do that?" Maybe our relationship does mean something to younger people because particularly in our community, it seems that there are so few relationships that last a long time. It's really important that young gay people have role models of healthy, long-term relationships.

K: *Well, the two of you really break every stereotype that people have of gay relationships because your lives are a testimonial of the fact that it's really about connection, hard work and commitment. These are the same things that heterosexuals pride themselves on. You've done that without the blessing of a Christian ceremony, which is about to unfold for the two of you in July 2004. I want to thank you both for taking part in this interview.*

Tom Graff and Antony Porcino
photo by Kevin Midbo

From Picasso to Armstrong
Tom Graff and Antony Porcino

Date: August 11, 2003
Time: 7:00 pm
Place: Vancouver, British Columbia

Few people are as articulate and wise as Tom, and few are as understated, yet profound, as Antony. On July 8, 2003, in the hour of exuberance that immediately followed the Appeals Court decision, Antony and Tom were the first gay people in British Columbia to perform a rite of passage that the entire world understands: they married.

A: There is a lot in that first question. When we first came together, there was the question of what does this mean to be in a relationship. It was my first real relationship at the time. Learning to live with another person and adapting to that—understand that I was also dealing with coming out issues when our relationship began. When Tom asked me if I'd marry him, I put off answering him for almost a year because I really had to think about it. It seemed like such a big commitment [on] many levels: physical, mental and emotional. There is an age difference between us and I had to reflect on what this means as we get older. What if something happens? There are a lot of factors to consider if you decide to devote yourself to someone. It wasn't until Tom was going away on a trip that I suddenly realized I'd be devastated if something happened to him: the hole in my life would remain forever. I was obviously more committed to him than I had realized because of how I was reacting.

...

Tom and I had a commitment ceremony in 1996. You'll probably notice that Tom is much more free with his vocal expression than I am. One of the big things I worked on as part of that commitment was to begin to speak my own truths, my own honesty. I needed to learn to share what's going on inside of me and to become 100% open and honest with Tom. I knew I could not run away from any aspect of intimacy, and I wanted to be completely present in the relationship. I think I've done well with that for the past seven years. When we legally married, it had a different effect on me. It hasn't changed my relationship with Tom or made it any deeper, but it's different. Now I appreciate the external validity of our relationship. I no longer feel like I need to defend my relationship or explain it. Marriage is an institution that is well recognized by people around the world.

K: *Tom, can you give me your initial response to the question?*

T: Well, we're lucky that we got to get married more than once to each other, which is a luxury that most people don't experience. Some people said that we solved the seven-year itch problem by getting married, but we were not having that problem. We were able to have a sincere wedding of hearts seven years ago. So this time around, in thirty seconds we decided, "Sure, we'll get married *legally*," but I want you to understand Kevin, that our initial commitment ceremony was very real too. This legal marriage was a technicality for us personally.

For the first ceremony Antony was working at the time for a federal agency that allows marriage leave. Marriage leave was in the union book so he went and applied for it. They said to him, "Bring your marriage licence," and he said, "I can't." They replied, "Why?" He said, "Because I'm gay."

A: It was a shock. Everyone else in the station knew except for the manager.

T: Yeah, his boss didn't know, but Canada Post offered Antony a free week of pay to get married to a man.

...

We had an "underground" wedding in an Anglican church. It was such a secret that it couldn't be printed up anywhere, despite the fact that 150 people attended! Some people actually approached us and begged us, including strangers in stores, "Can I come to your wedding?" I guess the "secret" was out.

Eventually we ended up having to have two weddings, one day apart. The one we worked really hard on was the one with all of the witnesses. The one the day before, to satisfy the need of a certificate for Canada Post, was so sincere, so small, and with so few people in attendance, it was like the Haiku version that had all the truth in it. Tim Stevenson performed that marriage, and he said weeks before the event, "Sure. I'll marry you and you'll have a certificate from the United Church." At that first intimate wedding service I started crying and I realized that it can happen: you can find a person that you are meant to be with. We're really fortunate.

The differences between us, and not the similarities, are probably one of the reasons we have an interesting life together. I had really shunned people who just wanted sex. I felt there was something weak with that approach, and I'm talking as well about the period before we had a word for AIDS. I have also lived in places where it was illegal to be gay. I know that type of oppression. Antony, on the other hand, didn't experience that form of oppression, but he certainly knew the form where he grew up hating himself for his sexual feelings.

When I met Antony, it was very corny: love at first sight. I never believed in that before. Our lives keep getting richer and richer, our relationship changes, and by doing so becomes deeper and deeper. ...

In this third marriage ceremony, the legal one, we didn't know we would have a national or international audience that would sit down and have dinner with us while we got married. Hundreds of strangers phoned us and apologized for looking us up on the net or in the phone book, and surprisingly none of them had anything negative to say to us. The people who called attended church, some of them felt, they said, "like refugees in church," and others were non-church goers. Very affirming, those phone calls. Community is built up of affirmations, and we also affirm with our relationship. ...

A: I think that others also see either the fantasy or the reality of what people want marriage to be. In America, television shows like *Who Wants to Marry a Mulit-Millionaire*, or the drive-throughs in Las Vegas—these represent the throwaway marriages that people create all the time. It becomes common entertainment, but I think some people are missing that sincere core of what they think marriage should be.

...

T: I think that marriage has throughout history been transmogrified and changed. We know that historically, women didn't have as many rights in marriage as they do to a greater degree now. Even in Canada we needed a constitutional change at the draft stage and female lawyers in our country had to rewrite some passages that Mr. Trudeau let go by that were not exactly equal rights for everyone. Our current government, noting the growing climate of fairness, realized that gay marriage was a matter of dignity and not just a matter of rights. That is a turning point in modern thinking. It's easy to dismiss the argument of human rights when you're in a religious camp, for example, but it is not so easy to dismiss human dignity. I think also on the matter of enhancement of marriage in general, that same-sex marriage helps remove the stigma that some opposite-sex couples feel when they cannot bear children, or that some people feel regarding not being able to bear offspring. As well, transsexuals have phoned us, declaring tearfully, "Thank you for saying you did it for everyone." There is a profoundly serious, deep malaise in society about coupling. People are having a hard time doing it very well. Relationships are redeemed when it's difficult to have that relationship, and then you fight for it because it's what you believe in, what you know works for you. No one should have the right to declare it second-class.

All the litigants are blessed beyond belief to have sat there and listened to the hogwash that lawyers, some even themselves obviously not believing their own words, had to say because they represented the opposing points of view that marriage is only for procreation, or somehow a God-given institution, sanctioned only by religion. Not long ago, similar lawyers had to argue that marriage should only be allowed between two white people, or between two black people. We've heard these arguments for years, but where is the credibility when such words are now so obviously devoid of truth? We've even heard crazy arguments that say the next step is that we're going to have sex with or marry our horse or house pets! These bogus arguments attempt to reduce relationships to sex and sex alone. It is such a low definition of relationship. …

A: To me, it's an odd reduction of a relationship down to merely a sexual act after you've made marriage vows. How many heterosexually married couples would be asked to do such a thing? Marriage vows are not, "I, John Smith, take you, of female characteristics, to be my wife and procreate," followed by, "I, Jane Doe, take you, John Smith, of male characteristics, to father my children," and that's the end of the ceremony.

…

K: *I would like to know the story of how you guys came to know each other. Where did you meet and how did it take off from there?*

…

A: I had just come out. This was a week before Christmas in 1991. I was living in Victoria for four months, which is a moderate-sized city, but there is little gay community to speak of. I was in university at the time in a coop-erative education program. This meant I did four months of school, followed by four months of work placement, and so forth. One of my work terms was to be in Vancouver, which was great because I knew they had a gay commu-nity here. I arrived here in late April and I wanted to start meeting people. I didn't know anyone in Vancouver whatsoever. I called up the Rainbow Band because I play an instrument, and I thought this was a safe community thing to do. The contact person said, "Well, I don't know if you can just come in for four months. You'd better call up the director, the conductor of the band and ask him about it." So I did, and the director was Tom. We covered that in probably the first couple of minutes and then we talked for at least one and a half hours. I remember we talked about vegetarianism because I was brought up vegetarian.

T: I knew he was the one. I don't know why. It was like a vibration came over the telephone. I thought, "Oh, my gosh! He must be, like—he hasn't even graduated from university. What am I doing? I've got to stop myself here!" Then when I met him, it was again like, "Oh, my gosh!" It was love at first sight, and I never believed that could happen. It didn't happen for Antony that way, but it sure happened for me.

...

I had been out already for some time, even on television, in front of a band, performing and talking. Our biggest concert was called, *Safe Sex, the Concert.* We said it was for the heterosexual public, teens and their families. For publicity appearances I was apprehensive, but not until after the first televi-sion program was taped. I suddenly realized that my name was on the monitor, which meant I could be looked up easily in the phone book. So I thought, "Okay, this is it. Bricks or not, through the window." Nothing happened, and nothing happened with our marriage either. I was inspired by others to be out. The other day Bill Richardson said, "It's a natural thing to be out." He said, "The difficult thing is to do things like go to the gym, or stop eating bad food." Bill is being very clever. It is a natural thing to be out, but often the most difficult thing, [is] to be oneself. And it's totally liberating when you're on television or radio being yourself. ...

…

I was born in San Francisco and I attended university in Los Angeles. I worked for black rights as much as I could back then. I had Black people filling my home when the Watts Riots occurred, people I worked with at the university cafeteria and restaurant. Life is much richer after helping them.

In the 1960s and 1970s, the hippies were the worst enemy of gay people. The hippie movement was such a strong heterosexual movement that if you didn't freely participate, you just weren't a hippie. I didn't join because I thought it was a quick way to illness. In my academic training, I was in a very conservative setting, singing with Igor Stravinsky and working with people from the very high echelon of the performing arts. I chose that intellectual life. …

After a couple of years in university, it was terrible to realize that I was unconsciously contemplating moving to Canada because I didn't like what the Vietnam War was doing, or what it was about in terms of the whole culture. I drove across parts of Canada in 1967 after being at the spectacular Expo 67 in Montreal, and decided that after I graduated from university I was going to move here—and did.

K: *You've been here ever since?*

T: Oh, yeah. I would never go back. I had to become Canadian. If Canada were to lose its sovereign status in relation to the States, I would choose another place to live on this earth, and I hope Antony would go with me! We're personally becoming less and less like Americans each day, and more and more like ourselves. Look at the level of fairness Canadians are willing to afford gays, just with the marriage issues.

K: *Antony, your response to Tom was more gradual than his toward you. Tell me more about that.*

A: I had to deal with my own issues of developing as a gay person. Tom was very much a mentor as well as a partner to me. I had been extremely introverted and a lot of that had to do with the fact that I was gay and I didn't accept myself. Even after I came out, I needed to help my family process this, which slowed down my own process. I needed space to do that and Tom really gave me that space. Despite the process I needed to go through, I have a fairly strong personality. I may be quiet but I can be stubborn, I'm strong, and I'm also quite intellectual. There was also a transition from seeing Tom as a support and mentor to becoming an equal within our relationship. He always had that space open for me to be equal, but I needed to find that space within myself. I came into our relationship when I was twenty-four, and I had missed out on a lot of things as a teenager. I hadn't had the opportunities to experience developing a relationship like many do in their teens and early twenties. I lacked that experience. When we first met, I was also looking at someone almost twice my age! Now we tend to say that I'm a little bit more mature than my age and he's a little younger than his chronological age, so we meet in the middle.

Our psychological ages are probably close in many ways, but I needed to discover what that meant and that physical age didn't necessarily mean a lot. When you are twenty-four and looking at this and new to a relationship, however, some of the issues can seem daunting. It took me a while to realize that they really weren't an issue.

K: *What do you really value about Tom and your relationship with him?*

A: The first thing that comes to mind is his sense of play and his sense of humour. He's much more vocally open and out. He is a lot of fun to be around and he brings me out of my quietness. He has integrity, honesty, enthusiasm, and he is very creative. I also have these within myself, but I don't freely open or share them. Tom does so automatically. He is also very generous and supportive. What you see is what you get completely.

K: *Tom, what have you come to really value in Antony and your relationship?*

T: So much. You know, I'm the one who cries. I cry in all situations and one of the reasons is because he loves me and he doesn't judge me. He says I'm ethical, but he is Mr. Ethics to a fault. I mean he writes ethics for organizations! He is totally reliable. To be loved by a person like that is astounding. He is also a mentor to me, so we mentor each other. He remains calm in a situation that's so crazy. We actually do some work together, we travel together, and we don't even argue. I should say we do argue sometimes, but either we'll have fun doing it or we get over it very quickly. We argued just before you came tonight, over your questions. Yeah! He's the guy who will totally take me on—nobody else does that. Some people tell me I'm scary, but he never says that. I'm scary because I can argue anything. Antony is a match, intellectually as well, and I think that's one of the vital things in a marriage. That's why I cry. This person is my soulmate, and he lives with me—he is my spouse.

K: *How did you guys come to be the first couple to marry in British Columbia?*

T: Antony got a phone call from Jane Hamilton.

A: Yes, that's right. Jane had called me several times previously to encourage me in my minor activist actions, such as going down to the local marriage licence issuer and trying to get marriage licences and do those kinds of actions. Jane called me on a Thursday night and said, "It looks like there might be a change. The judges might be giving a ruling tomorrow that would eliminate the time restriction on gay marriages in British Columbia. Would you and Tom be available to go right away when that's done and get a licence, get married, and be the public face on the issue?" I said, "Well, of course, but I have to talk to Tom first." So I called Tom at work in the late afternoon. I said, "We're doing it, aren't we?" We were both laughing because we didn't think it was going to be a big deal.

T: There was a delay of a few days because the court and the government got together and secretly made it all work within the system and to prepare their statements…for the press. A couple of days after Antony talked to Jane, Peter [Cook] and Murray [Warren] called to say, "There might be a couple of cameras."

A: We were on standby all day that Friday, waiting at work to hear something. We were simply prepared to get up, go down to the courts as soon as the reading came through, and get married. No one really knew if the Court would remove the postponement of government compliance, whether it was going to happen. We still hadn't heard anything by 4:20 pm. We heard from Jane and Joy's lawyer who said, "This isn't going to happen today, there's not enough time to actually process it so you won't be able to get married until first thing Monday." At about 4:45 pm, I got a call from Jane saying, "The Court has stated it will present its decision on Tuesday morning."

T: On Monday night, Antony said, "This is what we're going to practice now for twenty minutes."

A: I said, "Here are the five things that have come up," because by Monday afternoon, a couple of people had called us and asked us to do things. There had been a few interviews on Monday after work with the two of us, and there had been a few questions asked in preparation for what they would ask the next day, so I thought we should discuss our answers to these pre-interview questions. I said to Tom, "I think we'd better go over some of these points so that we know what to say. We want to have a clear idea of how to present ourselves, and why we're doing it."

T: By then we realized it was a big responsibility. We weren't just going to be pictured getting married. We had also decided over the weekend that we really wanted the man who married us originally, Tim Stevenson, the United church minister, to be present. He used to be a member of the NDP government in the province and he is presently a member of city council. We knew it wouldn't hurt his career at all, but we didn't know a picture of our marriage would appear on the front page of newspapers everywhere. I guess we were naive.

A: Afterward, Peter and Murray told us that they had no idea that it would be so big either, and I trust that.

T: Before the wedding, Peter and Murray were overjoyed, and they said, "Go for it. You're doing it so well. We're so happy we chose you." You know, they are two of the litigants and they're the ones who went through all the hard work, not us. I was so happy that they were pleased with how we were representing this monumental moment. That was probably the biggest reward. On the Tuesday morning, we walked through the city after having a 6:00 am interview with *CBC Newsworld*. We rehearsed what we were going to do if it went through, if it passed or if it failed.

A: We thought Citytv and probably CBC radio would be there, and maybe someone from one of the newspapers.

K: *You were thinking there would only be a handful of people there?*

A: Yeah. We didn't think it would be any different from the response the press showed throughout the case. You can imagine the shock when the press corps started building up to a lot more than that.

K: *How many would you estimate were there that day?*

T: Probably about forty-seven people. It was funny too because we would be approached like, "Meet me on this corner so I can do a streeter with you." Then someone else would phone and say, "Now bring photos of your whole courtship and pictures of your life together. I want to do that on CTV."

They all had different ideas, and they were thoughtful ones. July 8 also turned out to be one of those summer days when there was little news in the world that was political enough, so it went to front pages throughout the world. We were shocked. My sister kept finding country after country on the Internet where it was on front page, all continents, many languages.

A: A few days later I thought, "Well, where did this get to?" I went on-line and started downloading the different reports and most of them were based on [the] Canadian Press' report and the Associated Press. It was even translated into numerous languages. Off the top of my head I remember that I found it in Italian, French, Spanish, Portuguese, German and Dutch. There were articles from Argentina, Chile, Australia, and Japan, the UK, all over Europe, New Zealand, [the] Philippines. A friend wrote saying, "We just saw you on the 'Beeb,' as in the BBC!" Lots of media.

T: We were such idiots, spending all of our time giving interviews—we forgot to go to a store to buy Canadian and foreign newspapers. We were exhausted that week and we never thought of it.

...

K: *What did you say when you got to the counter, and who spoke first?*

T: The person who was at the counter spoke first, Harbinder, a wonderful Indo-Canadian woman. She could look us in the eye—everyone was staring at her. She asked, "What can I do for you gentlemen?" Antony replied, "We're here to get a marriage licence." Then the computer form printed out and it had room for a bride and groom. We crossed it off and said, "Can we put what we want?" She said, "Yes, we'll get that fixed later." Then I said, "Harbinder, thank you very much for everything you're doing for us." The $100 fee was some of the nicest money we ever gave to the government. Then she said, "I hope you have a wonderful wedding and I hope you have a wonderful marriage." She said it with such sincerity and she actually looked at us at that moment! The cameras swooped in on her because they could see the emotion in that. We were happy as larks! This must have seemed strange to her to see two guys getting married, and there she is, a person from a country that hasn't even heard of this. She's come to a liberated country. That was a rich, Canadian experience for both of us. I was really glad we didn't have a blonde or a brunette. We had a nice Indo-Canadian woman.

K: *That added to the symbolism of it and what this great country represents. What were the feelings the two of you had during this day? Was it euphoria, was it fear— how would you describe it?*

T: We see the pictures now that they're on-line. Some people send me e-mails and they send them to other people. "See that short guy who's just so happy he's jumping with joy?", and we were. I was shocked and I started crying when the judgment first came down. I just couldn't believe that I had been allowed to be equal to everybody in the country [*at this point in the interview, the three of us cried together, and it became difficult for Tom to continue speaking without his voice breaking*]. I just couldn't believe it, that I had come to this country to escape the Vietnam War, and was now being treated like I had never been treated in my country of origin.

...

K: *How did you feel the day of your marriage, Antony?*

A: I was very elated. I also felt very relieved and confirmed as a full person, absolutely. It was hard not to be buoyed along by the enthusiasm of the people there. It also seemed very odd because I had experienced years of denial and self-hatred, and now I was being accepted by one of the world's oldest institutions, the institution of marriage. I had a couple of gay-bashing incidents when I was in grade five or six. I was completely ostracized all the way through grade seven to the point where I became suicidal. I was so depressed and I managed to shut myself down emotionally. I wasn't even aware of how depressed I remained for the next eleven or twelve years. For me, coming out was a huge liberation. So at our marriage, I stood there and thought, "Look at how things have changed in ten years for me, personally."

I wasn't just thinking about what was happening in society. Knowing also that there is support for gay people now in a way that I never had support— I can't blame my parents or my family in that at all. It's a much greater societal matter, this being gay within the greater community. To be standing there with all the press, going through this so publicly, to be doing it with pride, and knowing that I am a face to a huge issue that is going to have societal ramifications around the world—it's amazing how that felt. A whole other layer of internal hurt was peeled off that day.

K: *What advice would you give to gay couples who are thinking about getting married?*

...

T: Remember that you are committing to becoming more involved with that person. I would urge people to really think deeply about the commitment they're making. We didn't do this, but possibly consider having a prenuptial agreement so that they can remain friends if anything goes wrong. We don't have to get married either. We aren't being pushed by mom and dad and we're not being pushed to procreate. We're not being pushed into anything, so take that extra exhale and look at your relationship, talk about it. Some people don't want to go to the word "marriage" because it has been abused so much, especially against women.

The word "marriage" has a lot of bad baggage. We know that we're changing it. We're counselling men who have had their wives divorce them, and women whose husbands just up and left them. I've lost count of all the people I deal with in my daily life who have gone through a crisis because the other person has left because of a mid-life crisis, leaving the other person bereft. Many of the men especially feel that no one will understand that they're depressed or even hurt, because they're men. They're supposed to be brave.

It's us they can ask those things about or hint at because I suspect they believe that maybe a gay guy will understand being hurt. We also know that both genders get hurt, sometimes deeply, profoundly and disastrously. By getting married, I think that you have to realize that you may be taking on something for your community as well as yourself. You might also be affected by other people's homophobia because people will notice you more. Getting married makes you more visible as a gay couple—it outs you to others. At work it means you sign up your spouse for benefits, stuff like that. You are taking on a wider commitment as to who you are when you marry another person.

Our legal marriage was way more deep and profound than we thought it would be. We thought it was going to be a bit technical. We were already committed to each other, and they chose us on purpose because we can comfortably represent the ideas of gay people in Canadian society. But it was indeed more than that.

A: We've been involved, at least peripherally, since the beginning with the whole legal proceedings here in British Columbia.

K: *How do you think same-sex marriage will be different from heterosexual marriage?*

T: Well, there can always be children, so that isn't different. I don't think bringing them up would be any different except for the social pressures around you. But gay marriage will be different in that it will probably renew the positive parts of marriage for everyone. We put value back into the institution. Gays and lesbians might be redefining relationship all around.

A: I want to approach your question by asking, "What are the things that are going to be the same?" From that you might be able to tell some of the differences. I get about thirty different images when I approach it from this angle. At least currently, marriage is more of a conscious decision for everyone, because it's not something that you're expected to do or that you think is the natural progression of a relationship. Heterosexual couples in larger urban centres might think, "Well, we could get married, or we could live common law." That's still not as common in smaller communities, however, where the norm is still to get married. There are still gay people who have grown up in those communities. Often, they are closeted or in denial and are still entering into heterosexual marriages because it's expected by family and society. The biggest difference to me as a gay man is that marriage is a very conscious decision, saying, "This is an important and significant milestone within our relationship that matters a lot to us." A hundred years from now the significance of a gay couple getting married will probably be very different.

K: *I suspect so, and that's why capturing history right now is so important. It will not stay the same. This is only the first step.*

A: We decided early on that legal recognition of gay relationships as married partnerships could bring about the revitalization of marriage. I would love to be able to look back fifty years from now and see how it really has developed and changed. Already it is changing people's perception of what our relationships look like, of who we are as people and of our dignity as people. It is forcing other countries to talk about it as well. Many countries have reciprocity agreements regarding marriages. It suddenly forces other countries to look at it, countries that normally recognize marriages from another country. We have several of those agreements with countries around the world. Our picture is called the "Canada kiss" in other countries.

There will be teachings and discussions against it probably in very conservative cultures for many years, but the fact is, it actually has happened. It was represented on front pages, television screens, or on radio in those cultures. The concept of gay equality is unfolding into a new dynamic of understanding in human relationships. Gay equality helps all societies enter into places where it's never gone before, and the conservative ones are going to have to begin dealing with it on some level. That's why I say that a hundred years from now it's going to be fascinating to look back and see the world ramifications of what has happened. It matters that we were willing to be on the front pages. These steps in Canada will help the world grow.

T: The profound things that we went through affirm that it isn't only political. Our neighbourhood's not political, for example. They dropped in messages and searched high and low for wedding cards that weren't of two opposite genders. They are hard to find! We probably got all of the ones that exist, and they didn't seem to duplicate each other either. One guy called and couldn't stop saying, "You're getting married! You're getting married!" He just said it over and over on the phone. Our neighbour might appear to be a typical macho construction guy, but he phoned up and said, "Good on you guys! Really, this is so good!" He and his wife are thinking about real-life issues, and they're totally heterosexual and enjoying their lives with their son. They have said to us, "You guys would make great dads." They've seen us interact with their child—they are not afraid of that. They're a beautiful family, just average Canucks, and they were at our first ceremony seven years ago. You don't usually invite your neighbours, but I suggest gay and lesbian people could also invite their neighbours, at least the ones with whom they have a nodding acquaintance. Profound things happen.

Now coming back to your question, "What will be different?" That's like the question they used to ask—when they were close enough to you to say— "What do you do for sex?" My reply would be, "Just the same things you do." It's almost the same. Ninety-nine percent of it is the same. We have the same patterns of arguing as heterosexuals, the same patterns of making up, the same patterns of putting together a home, and the same patterns of role-playing. We all know that wise heterosexual people have broken those roles down too. Now women can repair the plumbing and men can do the cooking. Some men are staying home to take care of the children while after giving birth the women go back to work because they like work. Women are admitting that they aren't "mommy" all the time. This is all okay, and partly gay people helped make it okay. That's how similar it is and different it is.

One of the gay male stereotypes is that we are all promiscuous, that all we do is fuck. Mosquitoes are born, they fuck, and they die. I think we could do it too. But humans have decided to have the brain intervene because it's a really good sex organ. People do other things in life besides have sex. People who have a rich family life know that children are another dimension of yourself and cats and dogs are too. It's just a sad thing that we've taken the detractors and the hater's definition of ourselves and made that into some kind of freedom march. We don't want our only definition of ourselves as crazy people who just go for sex. Many gay people don't find any joy in that anymore. I know they come to you and they say, "Help!"

K: *You're right, you know. They're looking for the kind of connection that marriage represents. It's an interesting social statement that some of the people who are most opposed to same-sex marriage are the very people that have been throwing around for centuries the idea that we're not capable of relationships, yet they're the first to say, "Well, we won't let you either, at least not in any recognized sense because we want to keep the image of you guys as perverts."*

A: It's much more comfortable for them that way.

T: It's a profound masking of what they're really doing—they are not living their own relationships well at all.

A: I remember when we had out commitment ceremony, we particularly had support from women. It was because we were coming together as equals. Neither of us was property of the other nor lesser than the other. Neither was being given away to the other. Neither of us was taking on a traditional role within an institution where one person, classically, has had more control or power than the other.

K: *Do you think that is why some churches are so afraid of same-sex marriage? They're afraid that by redefining marriage, women will no longer be subjugated to men?*

A: I think that's part of it in the really fundamentalist religions.

T: Well, they teach subjugation! If you were to go in there to the "family" workshops with a microphone you would hear it. I miked a sociology professor in Saskatchewan to go into those workshops and she got the goods. She attended a week-long convention about how to keep women in their place. They teach women to adjust to every whim of unreasonable husbands. It is very *Stepford Wives*. The professor still has all the transcripts and tapes. The course is still being taught by Evangelicals and it is about women being second in line. The dog is on the bottom and the kids are in-between, under the woman. Guess who's on top? It's a hierarchy designed to support weak men. They are afraid that being religious and having a faith makes them into a weak man. So, they have to put their women down in order to feel strong. This ancient set-up is being revived as a reaction to feminism, a prop for a contemporary weak fascist male population.

A: It shows up in a lot of ways. When my parents were going through marital troubles, part of it was about differences in ideology and approach to life. My mother was becoming actualised and she was going back to university. She wanted to learn how to drive and it didn't matter that some of my father's sisters had gotten careers or could drive. The fact that my mother now wanted to do this, the whole family came down on her. Our Catholic priest actually gave my father a book about how women were supposed to behave. That was in 1980. "A good wife will do this," and I remember laughing with my mother about this stuff. She was so upset when she saw it, she just had to laugh. According to the book, the "good" wife will actually drop everything else when the man gets home and bring him his slippers and make sure he's comfortable. She will make sure that his dinner is done when he needs it and wants it and it was all outlined very clearly in there.

...

In the relationship, people assume that because I am younger and quieter, I play the role of "wife" in our relationship. Some of the responses we've had [are] from people...innocently trying to understand how a gay relationship works. They naturally try to fit it in with their own classic images of a man and wife.

K: *I think it will be reassuring to the reader that what the two of you are doing, and many other gay couples, is forging a relationship that is not that much different from what they've had to forge, but without the hierarchies of class and structure.*

T: As you were talking, I was thinking about Antony, and what would happen if he was a transsexual. You know, I would go with him on his path. I don't know what I'd do sexually, but I don't think it would bother me. I would try to stay with Antony because I love him, who he is. That's the next step for society—they have to see that one too.

...

A: … I won't mention names, but I am reminded of our lesbian friend who stayed with her lover all the way through her transformation to a male. Our friend said, "Well, it's a non-issue for me because I've always loved the person. The physical appendages are secondary."

T: We've been learning a lot from the transsexual community.

· · ·

K: *Is there a metaphor, an image, a piece of music, a song, something that speaks to your feeling about same-sex marriage?*

· · ·

T: Oh, I had one, but it's very funny. On the one hand, it's like *Guernica*, the painting by Picasso. Guernica was bombed. It was the first big bombing when Hitler tried all his airplanes out to assist Franco to put down the rebels. So Picasso painted this black and white and grey painting: it's vast and it is about the torture of oppression and war. You know, life without full citizenship rights is like living in a bombed-out village. Because gay and lesbian people have been "bombed" for so long, we've lived in a kind of Guernica for ages. And then suddenly, Guernica turns into Louis Armstrong, a man oppressed because of race, but unwilling to be downcast, singing "What a Wonderful World." When a Court of Appeals dares to see human dignity as part of the law, it's like a moment of bliss you thought never possible. It's so corny—and human. I cried when the ruling was read out.

A: I go along with this "corny" metaphor. It's very odd that you bring that up because it was just a day or two after the wedding, and I don't know where I heard it, but the song came on. It was playing and I just burst into tears.

T: Yeah, and Antony doesn't cry easily.

· · ·

K: *Do you think we've dealt with this topic—I can't say thoroughly because I think to be thorough with the two of you, I would need a lot more time.*

A: A lot more time!

T: You have to get to that part about, you know, is there anything destructive about being in a marriage? I think all people need to ask that question, no matter what their sexual proclivities or abilities. We all have the little niggling things in our brains, "Could I have done better?" or, "Maybe I shouldn't have done this because I'm not free while I am in a marriage." That aspect must get in this book. You know, "is this better than being free?" We say, "Yes." I know freedom, but I prefer this.

A: I've not been free, you know, because Tom was my first relationship.

T: That was a tough issue for us. I encouraged him to have a boyfriend in England when he went to school there. He had thought of leaving me and his schoolmates encouraged it.

K: *Was that based on the age difference?*

T: Mostly, and they didn't know me.

A: Mostly. They also knew that Tom was my first relationship and it's a little bit like the couples that get married under eighteen and after a few years, they're trapped and they think, "Well, I can't get out of this" because of social programming or whatever. There were discussions like that.

T: We were very aware of this politically. Yet, you know, I have all my hair and he doesn't, so people look at him with his serious and thoughtful demeanour and think that he's older than he is, and they look at me with my jokes and my full head of hair and think I'm younger than I am.

    Before I met him, I was resigned that I would never have anybody as fun or as interesting as Antony. We know that people crash when they try to look for an ideal person, so there are no ideals. You think about the guy with big muscles, but he was always getting into trouble with the police. Obviously he's not the one. Then there was the guy who really wasn't out, and I had to drop that because it just didn't work. He still isn't out. Then there's the guy who's married that wants me to be his what—his "fuck buddy"? Forget that. Then there was a guy who wasn't my intellectual equal and was always running around, which I found out later. He's still a friend, but I'm not there. The community was just too wound up in its sexual self, you know? There's that huge sexual titillation around being in the closet.

Well, they say the same thing about so-called limits of marriage! It's like, "Oh my God, that's turning myself inside out—I can't be married and stay in the closet!" Antony and I can't be in the closet to each other about anything either, thank God. I think the one nagging question for gay people especially is: will we lose our gayness by being married, or even by being out? Will we lose our "edge"? Will we lose our resistance to "an ordinary life" that is quite boring?

To escape being resigned to nine-to-five dullness, hating life and being depressed, gays like to think [they] have an edge that makes [them] have significance in [their] lives. We decide that most of the world is either simply surviving, or mentally ill, walking around *Stepford Wives*. And it is true that most people are in torture: they are not happy playing the roles society expects. So, no matter what culture you are talking about, people consume or overindulge to get "happy." Gay people sometimes think they are carving out an edge with sexual freedoms, but they resemble those who are consumerists to escape the dull life. Well, we are some of the best shoppers around, gay men! So we have the opportunity to understand consumerism and its possible negative effects.

...

K: *Exactly! This is really a statement of something far deeper that's finally being acknowledged publicly and legally.*

T: Yes, and it's not consumerist. Marriage, at least for us, achieves something beyond the usual economic unit as the basis of family.

A: Yeah. I'm not sure we've spoken directly about it, but we're saying "What do you *lose* by getting into a relationship?" We hinted at the things that you gain by getting into a relationship, and you need to decide which you value more.

T: Yeah—what are your values about yourself and relationship?

A: That's what it really comes down to. If you define yourself through sex or your ability to be completely independent, you're losing a lot by getting married.

T: Or if you define your illnesses as your life, which a lot of us do in our culture—our mental illnesses, our predilections to hurt ourselves and others.

If we define ourselves that way, it's probably not going to include relationship, or it's going to include a relationship that's repetitively the same destructive system. You have to choose health if you're going to choose a marriage that's worth anything.

A: Gay marriage is always going to be responded to differently. I think it would be great if it's completely accepted, but I think the big thing is how we respond to the external world and what we get out of the relationship.

...

T: Exactly.

K: *Let me thank you for taking part in this very enlightening interview.*

Lin and Martha McDevitt-Pugh
photo by Kevin Midbo

Sculpting Something Real
Martha and Lin McDevitt-Pugh

Date: August 23, 2003
Time: 10:00 am
Place: Amsterdam, The Netherlands

A long and steep staircase leads me up to Martha and Lin's place. Their condo looks like it was built around 1650, similar to other properties in Amsterdam. Martha tells me it was built in 1930. I left my camera behind by mistake in Barcelona, where I was before flying here, but I don't need it to capture their radiance. Lin, originally from Australia, has lived in Amsterdam for twenty-five years, a place she respects for its long-standing tolerance of diversity. Martha was born in San Francisco, and despite her denying it, I got the sense that she would want to live there once again with her partner. But San Francisco won't recognize their marriage. [At least not when I wrote this!] Home, after all, is where you feel accepted. Amsterdam is home.

L: By making same-sex marriage legal, it allows us to participate in institutions that have been in existence for a very long time. When we got married, we were able to stand up like my brother and his wife and my sister and her husband in front of all the community and say, "Okay. We're a couple. We intend to be together for the rest of our lives." We're now part of each other's families—we want this whole community to care for us and to make sure that [it] supports us in our commitment to each other. The major thing we said is that we are committed to each other. That hasn't been possible for gay couples to do, ever, until now. When a couple has a registered partnership and they throw the big party, they're asking their parents, their siblings, and their aunts and uncles to play the game with them. The game is one of pretending that this is the same as marriage. [In the Netherlands, they have both a *registered partnership* arrangement, which is legally similar to marriage but without certain privileges and perceptions, as well as full same-sex marriage.]

Now we're able to enter a really important social foundation, if you like, and I think that's it. By recognizing same-sex marriage, we create another functioning object in that society which says, "I'm caring for you. I'm looking after you." These social foundations help build a society.

M: We married in May 2001, which was about a month after marriage was legalized for same-sex couples in the Netherlands. When we were planning our wedding, we crossed our fingers and hoped that it would become legal by then because the proposed legislation had been in process for two years. The government had agreed that [it was] going to move in this regard, but the actual implementation took quite a while. If the government had fallen, it might not have happened. In the meantime, people were buying plane tickets to attend our wedding, we were making necessary arrangements, yet we were not really sure that we would be allowed to marry.

We didn't want to be registered partners because we felt strongly that marriage was our goal. We wanted the same kind of support that any other married couple has. When you become a registered partner, you sign a piece of paper. You don't get up and say, "I do." We're not just living together hoping that it works out. We wanted the people in our lives to understand that we're making a different kind of commitment. That was how we came into it. I was a domestic partner in San Francisco in 1991 with my former partner and although we did it, it didn't mean anything. It didn't give us any rights at all. Lin and I wanted the rights and responsibilities of the institution of marriage.

We weren't sure whether being married would make a difference in our relationship, but it has. Although it is not standard practice in the Netherlands, we wrote vows to each other and read them as part of our ceremony. It's incredible what that has given us. We promised before witnesses to be present for each other every day and to love one another. It seems like an easy thing to promise, but there are times when you are definitely not present to love. But when we're arguing about something and one of us says, "Are you present to your love for me today?", and the answer is "No," we do something about it.

K: *That's fascinating. You actually come back to the vows that you made and state, "Am I being loving to you, as I promised?" Very interesting. One of the things I want to know is the story of your relationship. Where did it begin?*

M: We met in 1982. I was studying and working as an intern in Amsterdam and the person who hired me gave me Lin's name and address. She didn't have Lin's phone number, but I understood from her that Lin's close friend had returned to the U.S. and that Lin was feeling sad and alone. I had the idea that I was being seen as a possible replacement. But I didn't have a phone number. Then one day Lin showed up at my office to use my electric typewriter.

L: This is very important, you see. At my office we also had an electric typewriter, but on that occasion, we had two people that needed to use it. That's why I went to Martha's office.

M: She came and sat behind me. We sat back-to-back and at the time, Lin was a slow typist, typing one letter at a time. I'm a fast typist so it started to drive me crazy and I felt really sorry for her. She returned a month later and I offered to type the newsletter for her.

L: Yeah, so you could get rid of me quicker.

M: No, no, no. But it developed from there.

L: At that point my then-partner was pregnant with our son, Koen, who is now twenty-one. He was born a couple of months later while my friendship with Martha developed. Once Koen was born, Martha became involved with him too and she often visited us. Soon Koen was calling her his third mom. Then after a few years, Martha left Amsterdam for a period.

M: I went back to the U.S. and finished my degree. I was then given another opportunity to return to Amsterdam as an intern, which turned into a job. Those were the years that we were close friends, hanging out together. After a while, I decided to move back to San Francisco with my [then]-partner, and we stayed there for ten years. I travelled back to Amsterdam twice a year, which sustained my friendship with Lin. I always tried to visit in May for Koen's birthday.

In 1998 I split up with my partner after fourteen years and Lin and her partner at the time invited me to go on vacation with them to Greece. Lin and I saw a lot of each other that year. And that was the year we got together—in October 1998. We maintained a long distance relationship for about a year and a half until I returned to live in Amsterdam in 2000.

L: When Martha and I got together, it felt like a modern-day version of Dorothy in *The Wizard of Oz*. Dorothy experienced a long and difficult journey to find her way home, but she did get past the wicked witches of the North or whoever they are. In the long run, all I had to do was click my heels and I was home. When I said to Martha, very timidly, "I would really like to get together, if you wouldn't mind. I think that would be really nice." I was terrified in thinking that she would question why I would want this after so many years of friendship. I mean there she was, this wonderful woman in my life, as she had been all of those years. After sixteen years of knowing her, it was difficult to say that—I didn't want to lose a very valuable friendship.

K: *Given that you were friends for so many years, did you ever think that you would be better off with each other, even though you were in different relationships? Had that thought ever crossed your mind?*

L: Not for a long time. It would have been embarrassing to have that thought because Martha was my best friend.

M: I didn't think about it either. Because of our friendship, it didn't strike me as a possibility. But I always had this idea that when we were old, we would have a platonic friendship and live together somewhere, perhaps on a farm. I knew there was an important connection between us.

K: *What do you value about each other? What is the cement between you?*

M: I think we're quite different, which is nice. I think Lin is an amazing person. She's a pioneer, doing things that other people aren't doing, like having a child in a lesbian relationship twenty-one years ago. There were no books or road maps or anything about how to do that. She's really brave and she's somebody who goes for what's important and what she wants in life. She's a real people person with great networking skills. I love to see her in action, listening to people and finding out who they are and putting them in touch with other people and just enriching people's lives. Amongst everything else, she's an amazing mother. With her former partner, the relationship wasn't always what they would have wanted it to be, but they were incredible parents together. I've never met two people who were so capable of being in sync and bringing the same values to being parents. The result is an amazing young man who is able to do all kinds of things in life because he has parents who really listen, support and love him. This allowed him to grow where he needed to grow, and that's something I really value.

K: *What are some things you value in Martha, Lin?*

L: I've always talked about my friend and now my wife, my wonderful Martha, and all the things that she can do. She's a real inspiration to me. She has a very sharp mind and an incredible ability and willingness to discover things. When she left a fabulous job in the States and came to the Netherlands just to be with me, I was overwhelmed with emotion. She has created really wonderful work here too, and her ability to do this is one of the things I really admire.

K: *I realize that relationships have ups and downs, and it's not all glorious. What are some of the struggles the two of you face?*

M: I think we face the struggles everybody faces, but they take their own form because of who we are. For example, we come from two different countries, so sometimes communication is a struggle. Where to go for Christmas is a challenge.

L: It's not like we'll go down the street to mom and dad's. We've from two countries, Australia and the United States.

M: We have a complicated life because of the fact that we have three countries. When I first moved here, Lin was still Australian, despite having lived here twenty-five years by that point. I thought that she was quite Dutch and pointed that out to her, and since then she's become a Dutch citizen. In the background, we are always working at how to maintain those relationships with family of origin. I find it very sad not to be around my family and not to see my nieces and nephews growing up.

K: *Same-sex marriage was first legalized in the Netherlands on April 1, 2001. How do you see it having changed Dutch society since it was introduced?*

L: Let me first share with you two anecdotes. Last night we went to a concert performed by Mathilde Santing. She is the diva of Dutch song, a wonderful singer and very popular here. She sang a whole series of songs about the risks and the downsides of marriage. She said, "There's a lot of songs that warn you about marriage and I have them all in my repertoire." She was jokingly warning you never to get married. This is a very funny theme because she's an out lesbian woman. Many of her songs have clearly lesbian content, and with now having same-sex marriage here, this is something that she can say now on stage. That's extraordinary.

Another anecdote has to do with how much we wanted to get married on the date we had set, but we didn't know if it would be possible to actually get married then. I had a very close connection with one of the unmarried senators here. She has been living in a relationship with her male partner for more than thirty years and she refused to get married because it was an institution that excluded gays and lesbians. On the day the law changed, she became willing to get married as well.

I think it hurts society to exclude gay people from its many institutions. Look at that wonderful singer, lawyers, doctors, judges and secretaries— fabulous people who have all made wonderful contributions to society. It hurts society by excluding them. Something wrong has now been repaired, and that's how it feels. When the Pope came out with his oppositional statement, closely followed by George W. Bush, about same-sex marriage, people here, including Catholic theologians and Christian democratic politicians, got up and said, "Oh, no—you're not going to do anything to harm our new law." I think people now view it as sacred.

M: Same-sex marriage has now been in place for two years. The sky has not fallen. It works. People are used to it now. I was at a meeting the other night and I was having a discussion with several heterosexual people over dinner. One of my colleagues is Catholic and she sings in a choir at her church. She doesn't like her church because [it is] very conservative. She was really upset about the Pope's comments about same-sex marriage. She said, "I'm not going to get married and I'm not going to change to a new church. The only reason I belong to that church is because of the choir." You notice people really defending what this country has done, and I think underneath there is a real sense of pride. Showing outrage [at] the Pope's comments is a good example of this.

I believe it gives the Dutch people something to be incredibly proud of, which is difficult for the Dutch because they don't generally openly show pride in their country. Contrast that with the Americans who are proud to be American. It's like a slogan for them. They may not be sure what they are supposed to be proud of, but they're proud to be American. A Dutch person would never say that they're proud in general and certainly would never say that they're proud to be Dutch. Nevertheless, I think underneath they really are proud, and they are proud that this country took a step that no other country has taken before. The message to the world is that preventing same-sex couples from marrying is discrimination, and that doesn't work here because the Dutch population believes in and supports equal rights. Essentially, it says that there is no reason to treat one family different from another family. It just doesn't make sense. The Dutch are proud of their stance and they're willing to defend it.

L: There are many individuals getting married to their same-sex partners, including one of the most popular entertainers here. He was on television recently, describing how he would see all these dads walking with babies strapped to their tummies. He wanted that for himself, but felt so angry for years because it wasn't something he could have because gay people were not allowed to adopt. Then he and his partner adopted a baby from the United States, though only one of them is the legal father. A Dutch adoption agency worked with an American adoption agency to facilitate this.

K: *If the two of you wanted to adopt a child who is not biologically related to either of you, is that possible now that you're a married couple?*

L: Not any more, but that's because of our age. We're too old in this country to adopt. It's under discussion at the moment, but right now the maximum age is forty.

M: If one of us were younger, we could adopt a child from another country as an individual, but not as a couple.

K: *But a heterosexual married couple could adopt from outside?*

M: As a couple, yes.

K: *So there's not equity in this right now. You had mentioned earlier that there are some other regulations about same-sex marriage here—something about residency. Can you talk about that?*

M: Same-sex marriage is the same as any marriage in this country. The way marriage works in this country is that one of the partners must be either a resident or a citizen. For example, if we were a Dutch/American couple not living in this country, we could marry here because Lin is a Dutch citizen. At the time we married, we were able to marry because although Lin was still an Australian citizen, she was a resident of the Netherlands. I was also a resident of the Netherlands. You have to provide a lot of paperwork to prove all of this. As a foreigner on a work visa, I had to get permission from the foreign police [also known as "the aliens police" or Vreemdelingendienst] to marry. They have to make sure you're not a criminal, for example.

L: And you had to prove that you hadn't been married before.

M: Which in this country you can prove because all these things are registered centrally and available, whereas there's no system in the United States. In the United States you marry and if you actually were married to somebody else, then you'd get in trouble later for being a bigamist. In this country before you're allowed to marry, you actually have to prove that you're not already married to somebody else.

K: *But this system is the same for heterosexuals who want to marry, so it's equitable.*

L: Yes. What was different for us in 2001 is that the adoption laws were made accessible to gay people at the same time same-sex marriage was legislated. This meant that for many lesbian families, the children were allowed to be legally linked to their non-biological mothers. That was a very moving part of the whole thing. In our case, even though I'd been fighting for the right to adopt for eleven years, it wasn't possible because Koen was too old— he had already turned eighteen.

K: *Somebody told me that there is also some kind of income regulation if you're marrying a non-Dutch citizen, or a non-Dutch resident. Is this accurate?*

L: I think what that person is referring to is that if you want to sponsor somebody to immigrate to this country, irrespective of marriage, you have to prove that you have sufficient income.

M: There's one more thing I want to say about the fact that marriage is equal for heterosexual and gay couples. When we finally went and did all of the paperwork for our marriage, we got a packet of forms to bring home and complete. There was a form where you could say what you wanted your name to be after your marriage. It amazed me that all you had to do was check a box and send in a paper to change your name. We took each other's names, so we now have hyphenated names. If you wanted to do that in the past, you'd have to go to court and go through a whole process to change your name. If you wanted the other person to have power of attorney, you would have to do something else, and something else for your will. It was very complicated. In getting married, all we had to do was fill out some forms. Even for heterosexuals, a man can now take his wife's name, which wasn't allowed in the past. The law changed in general, it wasn't simply a special law for gay people.

K: You've given me the impression that, perhaps, most Dutch are in support of same-sex marriage, but is there a group here that remains opposed to same-sex marriage?

M: Certainly. We're in Amsterdam, which is a very progressive city, so we don't usually run across people who are against it, but there are small, right-wing Christian political parties who would like to see the law reversed. They don't support it.

L: It's not something that you read about in the papers or see on television. It would be like an undercurrent. In terms of communities that wouldn't support it, doubtless [they exist]. What we see now is the education department has decided that there needs to be more education going on at schools about gay people, partly to deal with the anti-homosexual sentiment that still exists.

K: *Has same-sex marriage in the Netherlands lessened the amount of homophobia here?*

M: It has certainly lessened our own internalized homophobia. For us, being married is about being 100% in this relationship—not 98% or 99%. This is it. We'll give it everything we have.

L: Yeah. Before we could marry, I might have thought, "Martha is an amazing and wonderful person, but she's got these couple of flaws and I don't know if I can handle that." Being married takes away the doubts. Nothing about her needs to change—I mean, this is who I married. Likewise, the things that irritate her about me is partly what she married. It's about knowing that those things are there and accepting them. By marrying, you're saying that we're going to put everything that we have into making this work. It will be hard work sometimes, and there's nothing wrong with that. That's the way marriages are. I can't cop out by believing that most marriages don't work out, or that it's hard to be in a gay relationship, or that I can't fathom being in a gay relationship longer than a certain number of years. Being married means we are completely in this relationship.

We're also part of another section of society, like at work. When you're married, you're really out in your relationship and there are all sorts of moments that you think, "Oh, dear—this is going to be difficult," but you do it anyway. I let people know that I'm married. That has an effect wherever I go. I went to Kenya and I was standing in the queue waiting to get a visa. You have to write down whether you're married and if so, the name of your partner. That was a bit nerve-wracking. What's going to happen? What sort of dungeon am I going to get thrown into and oh, I was thinking, nasty things. But nothing happened at all. Perhaps the name Martha didn't cross their mind as being either male or female. I don't know, but I got out of there alive. Kenya is a country that isn't very keen on homosexual relationships.

But other countries are affected by the introduction of same-sex marriage. As people become aware that these changes are occurring elsewhere, it creates a new wave. When someone challenges these laws, for example, they can argue that the law has changed in Canada, in Belgium, in Germany, in France, in the Netherlands, etcetera, so isn't it time the law changed here? I think that's lessening homophobia and limiting its grasp in Europe.

K: *In a social situation, I'm assuming that you introduce yourself as, "This is my wife, Lin," and "This is my wife, Martha." Do you detect any kind of reaction from the people you tell?*

M: There are reactions, but because we have the same name, people often think we're sisters, but we don't see people having a negative reaction. Even when we were preparing to get married and making all the arrangements, people were really supportive and fine about it. Dutch culture is a very commerce-based culture and, frankly, having two brides walk into your shop to buy shoes or order flowers means double business. It's a very practical culture.

I think that by being married, our relationship is very clear to people. There's no explaining, "We live together," for example. Marriage is universally understood—everyone knows what it means, even a small child. It was surprising to find that being married was another opportunity to come out. We didn't realize that would be one of its effects. When I tell people, "Lin is my wife," it's an opportunity for me to overcome my homophobia and think, "Okay. Is that other person going to think it's weird if I say Lin's my wife? Well, who cares?"

As a gay person, I can always imagine that the other person will have a terrible reaction. By being married, we just say who we are and people can react however they react. You know, my mother tells me she is against same-sex marriage. That sounds homophobic but, on the other hand, she got up at four o'clock in the morning on our wedding day so she could call us before we left to go to the ceremony. When we took our wedding video to the States to let everybody see it, a huge Thanksgiving dinner was being prepared so people sat down and watched a couple of minutes and then went into the kitchen. My mother, however, did not let her eyes leave the screen until the video was over. Now that says to me a lot more than whether she's in favour of, or against, same-sex marriage. I mean, she may have homophobia, like we all do, but [she] loves her daughter and nothing is going to stop her from watching the wedding on video.

L: It also says how powerful the institution of marriage is. It forces people to develop a certain understanding, people who might otherwise not feel positive towards gay people. When we entered the States, the immigration official said, "What's your relationship to each other?" and we said, "We're married." He looked up and said, "Huh, is that possible where you're from?" I replied, "Yes, it is. Would you like to see the wedding certificate?" "Oh, no. Don't worry," he said. That is much more powerful than any thought he could have about whether he thinks homosexuality is okay or not.

My parents have never been excited about having a gay daughter. They had a lot of trouble with it. But thanks to the institution of marriage, it's now like, "Okay. Our daughter is married now and this is our daughter-in-law. God bless her."

K: *So, they've come full circle?*

M: Well, they were grappling with the fact that we were getting married. But when they were able to distinguish civil marriage from marriage in the church, it became a lot easier for them because in the Netherlands, same-sex marriage is civil marriage. Marriages in churches don't count.

K: *Is that true of everybody?*

M: Yes. For example, our future king gets married and he has to first go and have the civil ceremony, and then he can have the ceremony blessed in a church, but it has no legal standing at all. That, I believe, is one of the factors that made it possible in this country for marriage to be opened up to same-sex couples. The churches can still do what they want and many of them still don't bless gay ceremonies. The new law doesn't change what churches do or tell them what to do. There was no question of that because it was a clear division between a legal marriage act and a church blessing, and the law only addressed the legal part.

K: *What advice would you give to gay couples who are thinking about getting married?*

M: Having this discussion right now, I'm realizing what a public statement it is and how many opportunities it's given us to step over our own homophobia and create a different relationship with the people in our lives. To let people support us and to let them see who we really are, and to witness our commitment to each other. I'm realizing how powerful that's been for us, having a public commitment that's universally understood.

I think marriage is great, so my advice to gay couples would be to look and see whether it's something for you. I think gay people bring something special to marriage—we don't have as much baggage about it. We haven't felt pressure from our parents to marry our partners. We don't have models for what it is like to be wife and wife or husband and husband. We are defining marriage for ourselves as we go, and in the process changing the institution. It's exciting to be part of that change.

L: I think the advice to [give] people who are thinking of getting married would be the same advice you would give people who are thinking of getting a job. It's just part of life. How do you want to create your life? How do you want to be a powerful person in your life? What's going to work for you and what opportunities does marriage provide you with in that? Martha's niece and nephew came over to be the flower girl and ring bearer in our wedding. So their concept of marriage will include the idea that girls can get married. They might not be sure if boys can get married, but certainly girls can get married. So that's changed in their consciousness. My son went to his cousin's wedding the other day and he's been to our wedding and to his other mother's wedding. That now becomes his understanding of weddings. When he went to his cousin's wedding, he actually found it a bit tacky!

M: Oh, we had style, didn't we! We know how to throw a party!

L: The whole realm has changed.

M: That's right.

K: *Is there a metaphor, image, movie or piece of music that really speaks to your feelings or thoughts about same-sex marriage?*

M: The image that I think of is the one in our lesbian friends' wedding album, a picture of them with their two sons: the family that now has two parents with full legal rights and responsibilities. I've looked through this wedding album a couple of times because it's just so beautiful to see these four people celebrating and being a family. They also live here in the Netherlands. When they travel to the U.S. it's a little bit different because their marriage may not be recognized, but when they're here, it's fully recognized.

L: For me, I've got a crystal clear, mountain spring type of image. It's clear, it's clean, it's beautiful, it's crisp, and it smells great. You know the way people talk about shaping a diamond—you cut a diamond only on the edges that need to be cut. You don't imagine where it's got to be cut. I think it's already there. For example, Michelangelo sculpted away until *David* appeared. What we're doing is chopping away at all sorts of insanities that have made our world not entirely sensible. By making marriage available to same-sex couples, it returns some humanity to our society.

K: *What would you put in a "hope box" for gay people? What needs to happen within the gay community? What changes still need to happen within mainstream society?*

M: In the Netherlands? Getting back to homophobia, it's letting yourself have the life that you deserve and want to have. It's overcoming your own homophobia and allowing yourself to have what heterosexuals can have. I don't need to be different all the time anymore. I can be like the family upstairs or the couple across the street. We need to accept ourselves. This is a country known for its tolerance. You need to ask for and demand that kind of acceptance, instead of waiting for it to come to you. I think that's what's still left—for people to allow themselves to change as the laws of the country change. Gay people need to be willing to take the risk of making a commitment, a marriage commitment, and be willing to succeed or fail. They need to allow their relationship to be public, to have their relationship in front of everybody so that people come to know them and accept them.

L: It is a huge step because gay people cannot be completely out.

M: No?

L: You're still going to have trouble if you're a gay footballer. Changing the marriage laws hasn't affected that. You're going to have trouble if you're all sorts of things.

M: But it probably is general knowledge about who the politicians are that are out and gay, but it's just not that important in this country. As an American, what I've always noticed that in the Netherlands, when people are known to be gay, it's just not a big deal. Whereas in the States, it's like, "Will you go on the record saying you're gay or lesbian?", and then it gets to be published and it's a big deal. Here it's not allowed to be a big deal. It's just the way it is.

L: The other hope is that currently, we are destined to live in this country even though we have two other countries that we could possibly live in. We would like to be able to live in the United States, and we can't. Nothing has changed as far as that's concerned. So the fact that we're married hasn't affected anything there. I'd like the Dutch government to get really angry with the American government and say, "Look, our citizens are married. So you have to accept that our citizens are married and therefore if our citizen wants to live in your country and get a green card, they have every right to." That would be really nice if they got upset about that, but they can't. Apparently Portuguese people don't accept marriages that don't take place in Portugal, so there are all sorts of barriers in the world.

M: Yeah, and so far there aren't other countries, except for Belgium, that recognize our marriage.

K: *Yeah, and two provinces in Canada, right now.*

M: Well, and also the city of New York. New York City recognizes legal relationships from other jurisdictions.

L: But I couldn't get a job in New York.

M: Exactly. Getting a work visa is a federal thing, and the federal government doesn't accept same-sex marriage. It's important to realize that in this modern economy, countries are attracting people from other countries to contribute to their economy. They start early, attracting students with the hope that when you've got a student coming to your country, they'll pay exorbitant tuition, and that helps the education system. Some of these students will fall in love with the locals and will want to stay. When that happens in the United States, it's wonderfully open for heterosexual couples, but it isn't for gay couples. What happens for gay couples is that the

American citizen has to leave the country if the [couples] want to stay together. Gay marriage would provide immigration rights to gay and lesbian citizens.

K: *It sounds like you would really like to be able to go back home.*

M: I would like to be able to have a choice. When I originally came here, we were planning to move to the States in two years and it turned out to be much more difficult. Now that we're married here, moving to the States is not something I want to do. I really like living in a country where our marriage is fully recognized in every way. The idea of giving it up and moving to a country that doesn't acknowledge our marriage is unacceptable. This here is pure paradise.

L: And what you said about choice is so important. I don't think it's important that everybody get married, but I think it is important that they have the choice. The Dutch diva last night was talking about choosing not to go for the wedding bells. It's great that she has the choice.

K: *Exactly. But if that choice was open to you now in the United States, would that become your destination?*

M: I don't know anymore—my head is not really there. We met a couple recently, an Australian/Dutch lesbian couple, and my lack of rights in my own country hit me yet again. These women have two countries they can live in! They met six months ago. The Australian woman lives here, because here you get instant recognition for your relationship. You don't have to prove that you've been together whereas in Australia you have to show evidence that you've lived together for a year. The Australian woman came here where she simply had to show that she's not married to anyone and was then given permission to work and live in this country. It's great. Partner immigration works well in this country and has been independent of marriage for a long time.

L: Yeah. The reason I chose to be in this country twenty-five years ago is that what was offered to me here was not offered to me in Australia.

K: *Thank you both very much for our time here together.*

René LeBoeuf and Michael Hendricks
photo by Kevin Midbo

Living the Spectrum of Colour

Michael Hendricks and René LeBoeuf

Date: September 13, 2003
Time: 9:50 am
Place: Montreal, Quebec

I arrive by taxi at Michael and René's home, a residence we would call a townhouse in Alberta, but with far more character. I learn that they have lived there since 1976, and I wonder how long they have been together. Both seem ageless to me. Perhaps there is something about having strong passion and meaning in one's life that seems to retard the aging process. Here are two activists that have an amazing story to tell.

K: *Normally I start off with a more general question, but I am curious about the current situation here in Quebec. I think it was in June 2002 that a registered partnership of some sort began in Quebec, so that preceded what occurred in Ontario and British Columbia. Can either of you speak to what happened then, what has been your involvement in this, and where is it going?*

M: It was announced in November 2001 that the Quebec government was going to bring forth a form of same-sex civil union that would be akin to marriage. It did not, however, address questions of parenting. Although the [government] announced that this was unique and the first in the world, civil unions between gays or lesbians already existed in Vermont. The initial proposal was, in fact, less than what Vermont's civil union contained.

The final version of the legislation came into effect on June 24, 2002. That is also Saint Jean Baptiste Day in Quebec, which is an important provincial holiday. The first registered unions occurred in July. You have to read the Banns in this process, so there is a twenty-one-day waiting period before the union is recognized.

K: *Was it the two of you who started the legal challenge in Quebec?*

M: Yes, that is correct. We began initial work on this in 1993, although I didn't actually propose to René until August 1998. We are also AIDS activists as well.

R: I said, "Why not?" That began our history of trying to get married. So one month later, we filed for a marriage licence.

K: *What did you attempt to do then?*

R: We didn't know what to do. We didn't know the justice system and we didn't know what to do with our lawyer at the time. It was like starting from nowhere.

M: We sought advice from an American who was of no help at all. He conceived of Canada as a unitary state and it isn't: family law is a provincial matter. At the time, we barely knew what we were talking about. On November 7, we went to Laval University and met up with Professor Ann Robinson and asked, 'What are we going to do?' She gave us a day in her office and laid it all out for us. We subsequently hired her to do the research for us, and we hired a different lawyer to do the necessary court work.

K: *Are the two of you still involved in trying to bring full same-sex marriage into Quebec?*

M: Into Canada, we hope! Our objective is to make civil marriage accessible to same-sex couples from coast-to-coast. I see it as the responsibility of the strong provinces of British Columbia, Ontario and Quebec to bring this issue to all gays and lesbians.

Quebec is somewhat weaker, but if we win in Quebec, it will have a national impact because of the way we have two legal systems in this country. In Quebec, we live under [the] civil code, so if we win marriage under [the] civil code, it will automatically apply to the rest of the country. If it was won in a province under common law, it would not automatically apply to Quebec. Through the many efforts of our lawyers, on September 5, 2004, all Canadian laws that ban our getting married across the country will become unconstitutional.... As of September 4, the only statutes defining marriage as between a man and a woman will become inoperative because they are unconstitutional, and consequently will be stricken. The entire process has felt endless.

K: *Wow—it's been a long road to get to this point. What an exciting time to see it's already happened in two provinces while the debate rages across the country.*

R: I don't think anyone thought that the case would go this far. Now everyone wakes up and has something to say. The Catholics, the churches—everyone has something to say.

K: *Exactly. Now I'm going to shift gears into the psychological realm. I think many gays and lesbians will be questioning in their hearts whether marriage is for them…*

M: If they're questioning, then it isn't! Our greatest fear is that some people will rush into marriage because it is the thing to do. The people who have been married in British Columbia and Ontario cannot be divorced: they are the only Canadians who actually went into a *binding* contract. For everyone else, it's a dissolvable contract.

K: *It gives new meaning to the title for this book that I suggested to the publisher:* Binding Love: A Look at Same-Sex Marriage. *I didn't realize it was* this *binding!*

M: When Michael married Michael, the first marriage in Canada, it was forever, whether they like it or not! Of course, that is a temporary situation.

K: *How interesting. I hope that Michael and Michael aren't fighting, but I'll find out Monday night when I interview them.*

M: Are you kidding? Those two are very tight.

K: *So I'm wondering, what do you think heterosexuals really want to learn about same-sex marriage and what do they need to know? What do they want to know about us?*

R: Maybe that we are citizens like them and that we have a right to get married too. Right now we don't have a choice. We are second-class citizens: we are also part of Canadian society. Gay people are everywhere.

M: I'm not so sure they really *want* to know anything about us. Dignity and full citizenship come with rights and choices as René said. You can't have human dignity if you can't make free choices. Heterosexuals have the full palette of colours to paint their own picture of life. We lack some of the colours and we lack the toolbox necessary to build relationships and ensure that children are born into secure circumstances. If we ever had a child, we would have been accused of being paedophiles when we met in the 1970s. The fact remains, however, that having children happens all the time in homosexual relationships and they are the only children in Canada with no protection—none at all. They have no right to recovery from the other parent and the other parent has no right to visitation. Those things are up for grabs: they need to be negotiated. Death becomes another negotiation.

What put us on the marriage trip? Our great interest was police brutality and murder. What cued us up for it was our work with AIDS because we saw what happens when death comes to a relationship. We've seen people put out of apartments and we've seen people lose everything because the family has the land title. The long time same-sex partner had no rights at all. Even in the hospital setting, the family of origin was called in to make life and end of life decisions while the lover sat in the waiting room. They'd been together twenty years yet some aunt comes in and decides when to pull the plug and what to do. A love relationship of many years was turned away at the hospital door, not because of the stigma around AIDS but because of the stigma around homosexuality. This made us acutely aware that for any couple, whether they are heterosexual or homosexual, the partner should have the right to speak to medical issues once the person has lost consciousness.

K: *With the civil union that's currently in place, if you had a biological son, could René adopt him?*

M: Yes, but only if the mother wasn't present or if she legally surrendered her parental rights. Artificial insemination is recognized and the second parent's name goes on the birth certificate and everything else. Civil union is marriage, without the title, but without access to federal laws and any of that.

K: *Now let's take a look at your relationship. Where did you meet and how did your relationship develop from there?*

M: We met at a New Year's Eve party on January 1, 1973. I was there looking for somebody who didn't show up. René was at the party too and he was looking for a place to sleep, it was late, and I invited him to my house.

R: Yes, and then after that I had to go back home to Quebec City. I was still living with my parents because I was in school. After that, we would see each other on the weekends and in the summertime. This went on for three years until we bought a house here in Montreal. We moved in on June 21, 1976.

M: He only moved one time in his life from his house to here!

K: *When did you start to feel a real connection to each other?*

M: About a month after we met.

R: Yeah, and for the first ten years, we fought like every other couple. There was a lot of adjusting to living with one another. After that, it went smoothly as our relationship entered a different level. After all the fighting, we got rid of our baggage. Then it was fun.

M: When we met we had no civil rights at all. Civil rights came in 1977 with the change of the Charter in Quebec and when sexual orientation was added as prohibited grounds of discrimination. This only applied, however, to employment and apartment rentals. The [government] also inserted a clause later in section 92 of the Charter that prohibited discrimination regarding pensions and insurance.

K: *Was there a time that you were saying to each other, "I have fallen in love with you?"*

R: Yes, since the very beginning.

M: When we moved in together, we were in love.

R: Oh yes, yes. I travelled from Quebec City every weekend to see Michael. I come from Quebec City and there was no role model of gay living or gay anything. Quebec City is like that, a very closed society, so it was very difficult to deal with being gay. Whenever I went to Montreal, gays were more visible. That was very interesting. That's why I wanted to move to Montreal since I was thirteen or fourteen years old. I knew by this age that I was gay. By age fifteen, I knew there was nothing I could do to change that. I moved from Quebec City because I could not be myself there.

K: *What age were you, Michael, when you came out?*

M: I knew I was gay at around age nineteen. Well, I actually knew since around age seven or so, but I didn't look it up in the dictionary until age seventeen or eighteen. I decided that there was no way I could live life like this. When I was twenty-one years old and attending law school, I attempted suicide. I woke up in a mental hospital and realized I had come out because I had left a letter explaining why I killed myself. That was on December 12, 1963. When I regained consciousness in the hospital, I knew that there was no going back. I was, of course, expelled from law school because I was homosexual.

Gay lives where short in those days. People died young, and I accepted that that would likely be my fate as well. People who led great lives often died young, so I thought that the people who had great lives didn't have long lives. Gay life then was kind of a short-term bohemian existence, but I wanted that. I was already on my second life at that point, so I was going to live it to the fullest. It never dawned on me that I would ever settle down with someone. I don't think we even used the word "gay" then.

R: No, the word "gay" became popular in the 1980s.

K: What did you call yourselves before then?

M: "Fags" or "queers." It was a very different world, like a pseudo-culture or an under-culture.

K: *Today we think of those terms as derogatory. Did you see it as a pejorative term when you used it on yourself back then?*

M: It depends on how you use the word. It was the word that heterosexuals invented to call us. Remember, we were technically criminals back then.

K: *You could have been jailed in Canada back then for being gay.*

M: There were 250 people who went to jail in Quebec for homosexual acts up until the passing of the honokous [Trudeau's omnibus bill, which decriminalized homosexuality in Canada]. It was very common. Professor Robinson notes it in her research and she gave us the statistics.

K: *René, when you were travelling from Quebec City to Montreal to be with Michael and you were in love, do you think the love you were feeling toward Michael was any different from how a heterosexual man feels toward a woman that he has fallen in love with?*

R: No, not at all—love is love. They are the same feelings, regardless of gender. I don't think it is different.

K: Do you see any difference, Michael?

M: Well, I think heterosexual men often see women as unequal and inferior. I don't see René that way.

K: *Where were you born, Michael?*

M: In Trenton, New Jersey. I moved to Montreal because the Vietnam War was occurring. I had successfully avoided the draft by being at school. Then the boom fell and I got a notice that I would be called out. I knew that I wasn't going to go to Vietnam and kill people. I could see what was happening on the television every night and it wasn't for me. At that time you could no longer declare you were homosexual to get out of the army because too many people had done it. I mean, the heterosexuals had taken all the good spots! The downside to that was when you did declare you were homosexual, your draft card would show that you were not eligible for service because you were homosexual. Everyone had to carry a draft card in the United States back then, so it was probably easier to go to jail and spend hard time than spend the rest of your life in the United States as a marked homosexual.

So I came here with my lover to visit Montreal before going to jail. Then I discovered that there were many Americans living here to escape the draft and, under Trudeau, you were allowed to live here and they welcomed us at the border in fact. We arrived June 6 and by September, I was starting my life here as a resident. It was easy to be gay in Montreal compared to New York City, where I had been living at the time. It was still underground here, but it was nothing compared to New York. Gay life was so much freer. Your neighbours didn't call your landlord and report you and although you could lose your apartment, it just didn't happen. People had been going to jail in the 1960s, but that was over with omnibus. In many if not most American states, however, homosexual acts were considered criminal acts until just this year! It was clearly a better life in Montreal, but I came because of the war, not because of homosexuality. Five years later I met René.

K: *Most of us think of New York City as one of the gay meccas, one of the places gay people seek out. You're saying that in 1968, it was worse there than being here in Montreal?*

M: Oh yes, definitely. *The Boys in the Band* is what it was like—kind of a bitchy, closed society where everyone knew each other. It was all quite hermetic. People lived double lives. In Montreal, you didn't have to do that as much—it was a lot more relaxed. There were still police raids in Quebec, however. René witnessed many raids. He had the luck of drawing the police—everytime he was at the bar, there was a raid.

K: *What would happen in one of these raids, René?*

R: The police would come into the bar and asked for ID. They stopped the music and because there were too many people inside, everyone had to get out. People were searched and some people would get arrested for unpaid tickets, etcetera. They would check for drugs. Essentially, they just barged in with the intent of arresting people for whatever they could find.

M: They checked everyone's police records, so it would go on for hours.

K: *How often would these raids occur?*

R: Every week or every second week.

M: This went on until 1994.

K: *Until 1994? I thought it would have ended in 1969 when homosexual acts between consenting adults in private were legalized under Trudeau's government.*

M: Oh no, no, no!

R: The gay life was mostly in the west section of the city. Because of the police harassment, the gay bars moved to the east where the village is now.

M: Budd's bar was raided in 1984, and 150 people were arrested for frequenting a bawdy house.

K: *They were arrested because sexual activity was occurring on the premises?*

M: That's what they said, but they didn't see it if there was. In 1993, we had public hearings about the police raids. We publicly accused the police for what they were doing. They denied it all, but then they proceeded to raid one last bar in March 1994 called Katacombes. They arrested 175 people for being found in a bawdy house and we made a fucking huge stink over this one. We asked the police chief if he had informed anybody first. He let all these people, who were innocent in this bar, get arrested. It was like a trap. The police chief agreed with us, and he declared that there would never again be a raid, and there hasn't [been].

K: *As you know, police recently raided the bathhouse in Calgary, and this created quite a bit of media attention.*

M: Some people commit suicide after such arrests! When I was attending [the] Johns Hopkin's University in the early 1960s, the husband of a woman who taught us History of Art jumped off a bridge after the local paper printed an article that he had been arrested in a restroom for engaging in homosexual acts.

K: *Not surprising. What has kept the two of you together thirty years?*

M: He's never met anybody better, that's all!

R: It's obviously his charm. Really, it's because of the past we have shared together. At the beginning, we had a lot of friends. Then AIDS arrived and so many died. We managed to pass through that. The beginning of AIDS was the dark age of gay life.

M: We have a collaborative relationship. We managed to resolve our issues in the early years and we are financially dependant on one another. It hasn't been easy financially, but we are always there for each other. We've always shared our activities, we do things together, and [together we're] involved in society. We figure our best time together was during our four years with Act Up. During that period, we were constantly together and with other people. There was an activity happening every day. We've always had a common project and a common vision. We take interest in each other's activities. We've always shared.

K: *So thirty years later, what do you really value about your partner, René?*

R: I can rely on him. He's very dependable. If Michael says he's going to do something, he does it. There's never any bullshit—he's always straightforward. We haven't fought in twenty years. We argue a lot but we don't fight. There's a difference.

M: If I don't agree with what he thinks, I wait until tomorrow and try again! (*Laughter.*)

K: *At this stage in your relationship, is there still some aspect of growth you need to go through to enhance your relationship still further?*

R: We are growing older, and you know what that's like. There are challenges that go with age. I'm forty-eight and Michael is sixty-two. I think we are more stable and you have a better sense of where you are, what you're doing, what you like, and what you don't like. It's difficult when you're young because there are so many things you want to do. The question is less heavy than when we were young.

K: *If Michael was to pass away before you, have you thought what that would be like for you?*

R: No, I don't want to think about that now.

M: We're used to death. AIDS taught us that life is about living, not about dying. Everybody dies. Living well is what's important.

R: I had dear friends I knew for twenty years, my gay friends from my teenage years, who died one after another. It was very difficult to get through that and make new friends afterwards. I'm talking about the 1970s and 1980s.

M: Our lives changed radically on New Year's Eve in 1990 when one of our friends told us that all of our friends were infected with HIV. We asked, why didn't we know this since everyone else seemed to know it? We were told it was because we are moral people who are coupled. They thought we would judge them so it was better not to tell us. That was such an eye-opening experience—we didn't think of ourselves as being moral.

R: One day your friends are there and six months later they are dead. Nobody was talking about that because it's so horrible. So many of the ones that died were alone.

M: We drove back to Quebec City in January 1990 because we wanted these people to know that we weren't the slightest bit judgmental or shy about their illnesses. In fact, we became very active and that certainly changed our lives. One of our friends who died went through a horrible experience. After his death, his parents came, grabbed his body, and ran home with it. We weren't allowed to go to the funeral or anything. That's why our friends and we founded the AIDS Memorial Park here so that gay people would have a place to mourn and grieve.

K: *When I hear these stories, I'm always deeply moved. People like me, who haven't been out for that long relatively, and most of our gay youth, have no idea of just how bad it was in the recent past. It's hard to believe that there were bar raids in Montreal, the city of acceptance, until 1994.*

M: It's a myth—it's not *that* liberal! Our biggest fight was getting free medication for people with AIDS, and we won that fight. Everyone is covered by medical insurance in Quebec. We won that in 1995.

K: *When do you celebrate your anniversary—is it when you first met?*

M: Yes we do—on New Year's Eve.

R: Each year on our anniversary, we make a point of looking at what's happened during the past year in our work life and our social life. We make resolutions. It's also a day we remember our friends, our life, and we talk about the past, the present and the future. We also set our goals for the next year.

K: *In what ways do you believe your relationship is different from heterosexual married couples?*

M: We're not divorced and we don't hate each other? Really, it's not that different.

R: It's not different when you love—when two people are in love.

M: Two men living together, two women living together, or and a man and woman living together is very much the same. We don't have the tension of not understanding the other sex, so you can't write off problems by playing that old card that "I'll never understand women" or "I'll never understand men." You're stuck with understanding who you're living with. He may be incomprehensible, but it's not because he's a male.

One of our most difficult moments caught on tape is in that silly series called *Out in the City*. We were being filmed doing that usual old fag couple stuff of working in a garden. I managed to get René's goat while the camera was rolling because he had forgotten to bring his gloves to the planting of the community garden. We were planting things with big thorns.

R: So Michael says, "How could you forget the gloves?," and he said that about twenty-five times. The camera is rolling and I retorted, "Fuck you!"

M: Not only did they get that on camera, but they also played it extensively on television. I think people actually enjoyed that part.

K: *How did your friends react when you told them of your intention to fight for same-sex marriage?*

R: At first everyone was laughing, both gay and straight. It was like two men can't do that and the idea is so far-fetched. They didn't understand why we'd want to do that, and they saw it as silly, ridiculous and impossible. Even in the gay community here, they kept laughing at us for three years, but when we had our trial, everyone tried to get on the bandwagon. "Oh yes, we're always been in favour of this, and we always fight for it." Nothing could be further from the truth.

M: These were the same people who said we were causing trouble for our community.

R: They said there would be a backlash [in] our community.

M: These same people then try to get in front of the camera to say that they were supporting it all along. The two of us started out in a kayak with Anne Robinson…. Later we had to get a war canoe and add the lawyers. By the time we finished up at trial, we had Cleopatra's barge onside. Even people who told us months before that we were insane, that we would bring ruin to the community, that we were not a moral couple, that we were living with AIDS, and that this was just a way to legitimize who we are—these same people now brought out their trump card. We learned that you never get a prize or medal for being an activist: all you ever get is shit.

K: *How did your family respond?*

R: My dad is deceased and my mother is seventy-seven years old. I also have four sisters and two brothers. My parents were a very straight couple living together with kids. We never talked much about sex, marriage or anything that was very personal. They saw us on television and they said that we were very courageous for what we had to do. They were open about that and it didn't matter to them. When we told them and when we tell others how much of a fortune this legal challenge has cost, people are amazed.

K: *How much has this cost the two of you up to this point?*

M: We owe a lot, and we could end up losing our home.

K: *Remarkable. Tell me about your family, Michael.*

M: My father died in an accident after a month after I came to Canada. My mother died in 1993. Her last words to me were, "You can find a nice girl, don't live with him."

K: *Oh my God.*

M: She never learned René's name, despite having known him for twenty years. She used to call him "Lenny." She wasn't senile in the slightest. That was her chorus. Over there is a picture of my one sister at our commitment ceremony. She dressed up as a suffragette. She enjoys us a lot and her daughters do too as well. They think it's all impressive and they're very supportive. That's my brother-in-law smoking with the cigarette hanging out of his mouth, holding up the gay banner.

R: My nephew and nieces, and their generation, they enjoyed the commitment ceremony too. They found it fun and they talked about it very openly. The younger generation is much more understanding.

K: *Do the two of you walk hand in hand in Montreal or do you kiss in public? What is acceptable for the two of you?*

R: We used to walk hand in hand when we went to gay pride marches in the beginning and we would kiss in public, which wasn't a big deal.

M: But actual affection? We certainly did that in the early days but we don't walk hand in hand now. After thirty years, it's not the same kind of physical relationship that it was in the first week! You no longer have to prove anything to each other.

R: We are company to each other.

K: *Do you remember when the first gay pride was here in Montreal?*

R: Was it in 1991, Michael?

M: No, the first gay pride parade occurred in 1992. It is always held the first long weekend in late July, early August. In the early 1990s, we would have somewhere between five thousand and fifteen thousand spectators. Now there are hundreds of thousands.

Pride here is apolitical—it's just about visibility. This year, the press or the media decided that it was about same-sex marriage. We've been doing this silly number for years—we wear tuxedos—and we never got any recognition from the media in the past. This year, we got lots of recognition from the media.

K: *Are you known by most people in the gay village?*

M: Oh yeah, we're recognized by most people in Montreal.

R: I work as a front desk clerk at a hotel and even the guests of the hotel tell me, "We saw you on television, or on the news!" The reaction is very positive.

M: We have never had a negative comment. Some men will make comments like, "Don't make the same mistake I did, like with her."

R: Late one night I was coming home from work and I saw this guy looking very seriously at me. He approached me and said, "Hey mister, I saw you on television and I'm very proud of what you're doing. I've been with a guy for three years and we are in love. We want to get married. You're doing good work."

M: On the opposite end of the rainbow, we have had other gay activists tell us that we've mismanaged this whole affair. We get nothing but criticism from them.

K: *Are there any drawbacks to same-sex marriage as you see it?*

M:No, but I don't want to see it done on impulse. One of the things about gay life is that many gay men, before they have sex, ask, "Do you love me?" Marriage cannot be just about sex. We're concerned that marriage will become part of that game. It needs to be thought through carefully and planned. There are advantages and disadvantages to marriage, like most anything that involves such a serious commitment. Because of the element of loneliness and the long-standing feeling of being isolated and excluded, when [gay men] meet they can feel like instant soulmates. I would hate to think that the first [man a guy] meets might seem like the one for life. That occasionally happens, of course, but most heterosexuals already know that this is unlikely. Gay people have always been denied this experience, so their naïveté around marriage may be problematic. Many gay people have a tendency to jump on the first boat that passes and then they start making these silly declarations, which later turn out to be falsehoods.

R: People need to think a lot about marriage and not do it on impulse. Be sure that it's the right choice—maybe live together first and see how that works out.

M:I think we must remember that marriage itself is a contract. It is of no meaning at all in real life until the relationship ends, either by separation or by death. At that point, marriage is very important. You could do very well by having a commitment ceremony or have some kind of engagement when you move in together. Marriage is when it's needed. That's when there are material interests, such as your estate and property. How many gay people have I seen ejected from their apartment by their partner or lover, by the one who has his name on the lease? Marriage protects both people's interests, and it protects the interests of children.

  For us, there will never be recognition for all the years we spent together. Those years have been our marriage, however. Only the legal part of it has been missing. Before I die, I want everything to be neat and clean. In marriage, legally, two people become one. Property becomes fluid between the two of you. When I pass away, there would be no question that the matrimonial home is his. In marriage, there is no question of anyone else having interest. Right now if I was to get Alzheimer's, I could get rid of him and ruin him financially for the rest of his life. He has no protection for what we have built together. That's what marriage is about. Anyone can have a wedding ceremony and it doesn't mean a thing. The marriage contract itself is a very important thing and it guarantees a kind of justice for both persons.

K: *Upon reflection, is there a metaphor, an image, a piece of music, a poem, anything that really speaks to your relationship or your thoughts and feelings about same-sex marriage?*

R: It may sound a bit silly, but two trees that grow together in a garden. They slowly pass through the seasons, the weather, the bad times, and the good times. Our relationship is like that.

M: It's a little unreal for us. It's like inventing the menu after you've eaten the meal—we already did it. It's the end of my life, not the beginning. I can't imagine what it would be like now to be twenty-five and have the option of marriage before me. We didn't choose to marry, we just lived together and it ended up being marriage. We always thought it would end, because that is what would happen to most homosexual relationships. We never saw any that didn't in fact. They would last two to five years, then something would happen, they would drift apart, there might be a big fight, and it would end. Gay relationships were not stable relationships—we had no models to show us any differently. The fact that ours survived was amazing to us and to everybody who knew us. We worked on our relationship like we care for two trees in a garden. We grew together and we became one but we didn't plan it that way. We didn't opt for marriage because that option wasn't open to us.

Everything was illegal when we first met except the sex act itself. Gradually and with difficulty, fights have been won. When they opened the Charter and made it a legal basis for discrimination, they took away the rights for pensions to make sure we wouldn't get that. The same day the Charter was changed, it became illegal to be in a park after 11:00 pm in Montreal. They could easily discriminate against gay men before that and they didn't bother making it illegal. Heterosexuals could go in the parks at any hours but homosexuals could not. When it became impossible to discriminate against us, it became a step-by-step battle. The big thing for us about gay marriage, once this is won, is that no child in Canada will ever have to look forward to the dismal and forlorn future that we faced in 1973 when we met. The options were limited and there was no freedom.

R: Some kids who are gay and lesbian had to leave their family, the only choice being to live their gay life somewhere else. Most people want to stay in their family and in their community. Many gays and lesbians could not because they were not accepted. They could not live as citizens, as real people. This point is very important.

M: That's why it's so important that the law be universal. It's great that it is in Ontario and British Columbia, but it's not there that it counts. Are we going to continue to drain the smaller provinces into the bigger provinces so that people can live more freely? We want them to have rights everywhere so that they can choose where they want to live and settle. If you want to live in some hick town or community, you should be entitled to live there with equal rights and human dignity.

R: We lived the life for everybody else. I think the next generation will understand that.

M: Better than ours for sure. Ours was a lost generation. It's now the future that counts. We didn't produce children but we know that heterosexuals are producing the next generation of gays and lesbians. We don't want them to face the same barren territory that we faced, a hopeless land of suicide attempts where women were dragged to death at fifty and gays died of syphilis and AIDS. These problems are containable, and some of it comes down to ensuring that people have equal rights so that they can mature with a healthy sense of themselves as gay people.

K: *What would you put in a "hope box" for gay people? What still needs to happen within the gay community?*

R: Everything is happening so fast. It took a long time to get here, but we have had little time to realize the impact of what has occurred in Ontario and British Columbia, for example.

M: Like us, our gay community is overwhelmed and no one knows how to deal with this. I have watched with great interest the lesbians that have kids and the men that have adopted and now can get shared adoption. For them, it's not fast enough. What would I put in a hope chest?

I wish that our community could assimilate what is currently happening. You see, there's a hierarchy in the gay community of what's acceptable: it's always existed. It was the more straight appearing that were more acceptable.

The Mark Tewksburys were acceptable. It was very clear when we were young who were the "good" and who were the "bad" homosexuals. Part of that still hangs on today—being too effeminate and putting on dresses was always seen as a bad mark for our community. Some of our finest moments in our lives have been in the company of people in drag. This has always been a part of our lives and we often finish our New Year's celebration in a drag bar. We hope that our community learns to accept itself. It's called "internalized homophobia" and I think we'll be able to beat it quicker in the straight society than within our own community where it has been bred for more than fifteen centuries.

We are taught that we are second-class citizens and that we deserve the "hind tit," as it's called on a farm. We've been given the short end of the stick and told in no uncertain terms that we are inferior people. It's going to take a long time to internalize the fact that we are equal and that we do have the rights of full citizenship. It's hard to believe that it's finally happening. We almost fell off our chairs when we saw Michael and Michael get married. But it did actually happen.

It will be accepted that we are normal, full citizens and that we have full rights. Now we have to use them. Another thing that we've done a lot is excuse our failures because of homophobia. You know, "because of the hetero-sexuals I can't do this and I can't do that." That's obviously not true. Gays and lesbians do remarkable things and succeed at all sorts of things. The first cop-out has been, "because I'm gay I can't." When I was a kid, there were limitations—I couldn't be a lawyer and I couldn't be a doctor. It was illegal.

The three professions open to us were ribbonqueens, hairburners and pinqueens. Pinqueens are the display artists who arrange store windows. A ribbonqueen is someone that sells dried goods out of a department store, and a hairburner, of course, is a hairdresser. We no longer have those excuses…but mind you, we still make the best hairburners and pinqueens, no question about it, we have natural talents for that! (*Laughter.*)

We have discrimination within our community toward others within our community. The hate, such as the misogyny in the male homosexual community, and the hate of men in the lesbian community, is frightening. We know several women who have been rejected by other lesbians because they are "gayest," meaning they hang out with men. This could be a serious problem. One of the beauties of the underground days was that we were all stuck with the same oppression. When the raids occurred, the girls got it and the boys got it. That had a way of equalizing the playing field.

We picketed gay men's bars to get women and transvestites admitted. We broke the line in the bars in the 1990s. The hiding from women is painful for gay men. We've always felt that if women are around then the windows are open for us. It's when the women aren't present in gay bars that weird shit starts happening. (*Laughter.*) I don't think that's necessarily the case in lesbian bars, but surely the presence of women is an improvement.

K: *Yeah. Do you think we've dealt with this topic thoroughly or is there anything that you want to add?*

R: No, I think that's it.

M: I'd just like to add that in 1999 after we declared our intent to marry, the cover of one of our cultural newspapers read, "Have Gays Become Too Straight?" We have to live with this all the time, the notion of main-streaming homosexuality and making it appear straighter. This is an absolute fucking lie.

We became aware of many homosexuals have been living in the closet for two all these years. All we have attempted to do to is to recognize what already exists—that is the status quo. We're not going to change people. There have been about two hundred civil unions so far in Quebec, one-third female and two-thirds male. One third of these have been religious because it can be done in a church and the remainder are civil unions. What this really is, and you'll see it in the Dutch statistics as well, is recognition of the existing state of affairs in life. Nothing has changed: it will not ruin gay culture. If gay culture is having sex in toilets, bushes and parks, then that's not much of a culture. Whatever culture we have is not going to disappear because of marriage. Culture will exist independent of our legal status.

R: Art is art, and culture is culture.

M: It will, however, make it impractical to cry all the time that we are hideously discriminated against. Marriage is the last barrier, legally, in civil rights. The next battle is in the schools. It doesn't start in high-school sex education classes with fifteen-year-olds: it begins in the first grades with Julie and her two mummies. Homosexual families need to be normalized. If you start in these early grades, then there won't be high-school bullies beating up fags and effeminate boys. You don't have to be gay to be Nelly. In fact, most effeminate boys are not gay, and most gay men are not effeminate.

K: *Let me thank the two of you for some wonderful insights into same-sex marriage.*

Addendum, March 20, 2004

The headline in the *Globe and Mail* reads: "Same-sex couple win right to marry in Quebec." The unanimous decision by the Quebec Court of Appeal ends the battle that René and Michael have fought for six years. Thanks to their perseverance, Quebec now becomes the third province in Canada to legalize same-sex marriage. I sip coffee this morning and wonder, "Which province, state, or country will be next?"

Michael Stark and Michael Leshner
photo by Kevin Midbo

The Centennial Couple
Michael Leshner and Michael Stark

Date: September 15, 2003
Time: 7:55 pm
Place: Toronto, Ontario

This is the condo history will remember. The first same-sex couple to legally marry in Canada live inside. A security guard first welcomes us before calling upstairs to announce our arrival and receive permission to let us enter.

I thought the Michaels were an unlikely couple to charge the cause—that is, until Michael Leshner began talking. Sometimes overpowering in conversation, his inner strength and conviction spilled out for the next three hours I was there. I think it takes these qualities to become a national hero.

I leave feeling tired and drained. I know we sometimes expect our heroes to actually be superheroes, somehow above the rest of this human condition. But Michael and Michael are like the rest of us, and twenty-two years of being together has not created the perfect relationship. They still have issues. After all, we don't change a person simply by cohabiting with him or her. Instead, we learn how to manoeuvre ourselves such that the end product, when it is working, appears to have mutual respect and a type of tolerance for the things we don't like in our partner. As the Michael's said, a relationship is hard work. But their work paid off for all of us.

ML: We've been together for twenty-two years. It was love at first sight, or at least it was sex at first sight! In 1981, you first had sex and if anything else developed, that was like having the cherry on top. We met just before the AIDS crisis was recognized. Most gay men and lesbian women in Toronto were horribly in the closet still in 1981, the pain of which was palpable. Gay people were afraid that they would lose their jobs and afraid that their parents and family would find out. The amount of internalized homophobia was equally obvious. The pain of acknowledging [internal] homophobia…was worse than living with the fear that [you'd] get fired, disciplined and rejected for being overtly gay.

MS: Also, there weren't many positive gay role models back in 1981 when we met: actually there was zero. The public perception of gay people was entirely negative. There weren't a lot of things to pin your hopes on. When Michael and I met, I don't think we ever thought that we were destined to live a lifetime together. We didn't think we would go down this political path either of making history and working towards achieving political equality. [These things] didn't develop initially, but [they] began to develop after the first third of our relationship. It wasn't planned: it just kind of happened.

   We met on the long weekend in May, and my Baptist aunt was visiting from Nova Scotia. I remember I spent the weekend with Michael and the big question was would I call Michael after she left. She was visiting me for a week and for me to call him was a big thing because I hadn't been out for a year.

ML: Well, the truth is, my dearest, you hibernated for six months of that year...

MS: Michael, can I speak now?

ML: Okay, okay.

MS: We do this all the time because he's such a control freak. So anyway, back to my story. It was a big thing for me to call him because I was very shy and he was a lawyer—with all kinds of issues. (*Laughter by all.*)

   I heard afterwards that Michael was so nervous wondering if I'd call back after the week. Well, I did call back after Auntie left and we got back together. Then we started seeing each other on the weekend and one night a week, then two nights of the week, and it grew from there. We didn't start living together for two and a half years. Part of that was time, and the other part was the ten-year age difference between us. I wasn't sure if I wanted to commit to one person at that point. Michael was more willing because he had already been out for a while and he was more ready to settle down.

ML: The understanding we had from day one was that we wouldn't see other people.

MS: Neither one of us had ever lived with anyone, except when I was attending school at Ryerson. I was thrilled to have my own apartment after that and I wasn't willing to give [it] up at first. Michael had lived on his own for quite a few years and to give up that independence was not easy for either of us. I think we are cautious people as well. We [eventually] saw each other through so much that the writing was on the wall....

ML: We met May 23 and in the summer, he already wanted to break up with me. He said he didn't want to be in a relationship, but could he stay for dinner? The breakup lasted for three hours.

MS: I think for me the inner turmoil was that I hadn't been out that long. I hadn't experienced life as a gay male, I was insecure, and I didn't know how I fit into the big picture. I wasn't sure I wanted to make a commitment to someone else so early in the coming out process.

ML: I was roughly twenty-two when I came out. It was around 1975 when I started to come out. I was just called to the bar and I was about to start my first year of practice. By the late 1970s, I was involved in deep therapy to deal with the aftermath of coming out of the closet. I met Michael when I was still going through a dark period in my life at age thirty-three.

I was already out to my family by then. There was a great deal of anger in me then as I dealt with internalized homophobia and the pain of having lived in the closet. I suffered from a significant obsessive-compulsive disorder which [took] ten to twelve years of therapy to overcome. I attribute the obsessive-compulsiveness to the trauma of the closet and trying to emerge from it in order to reach a level of comfort with myself. I learned that I needed to do it my way. I couldn't look for other role models because there were none. Every time I attained a level that I thought I would be comfortable with, I was still obsessive-compulsive, agitated and anxious. In hindsight I was never "out enough."

The longer I was in a relationship with Michael, the more the obsessive-compulsiveness came under control. I was very angry with gay men, particularly those who wouldn't come out of the closet and tell their employer or their family. Michael didn't come out to his family until around 1983 or 1984 either. I felt very alone in a jungle of hostility. I bled intensively back then, but I was very good at hiding how traumatized I was. The good thing for both Michael and I was that we were in a healthy relationship.

Michael and I agreed that he couldn't go home to his parents in rural Nova Scotia unless he took me. I could not be my boyfriend's dirty little secret to his family. I'm afraid that Michael had lucked onto a guy who placed many demands on him. You also have to remember the context was 1984. We were already living together by then and things were going along well.

What would be the effect on Michael's family? Would he come out to his family without acknowledging me? Well, my inability to compromise was pushing Michael into a corner while his parents pleaded, "Why aren't you coming home?" Michael can tell you the rest of that story.

K: *Let's switch back to you, Michael, for a minute. I hope both of you are okay with swinging back and forth.*

MS: Yeah, you have to cut him off because he speaks forever.

ML: Okay, okay, you don't have to be diplomatic. Trust me, we've been through this many times.

MS: We moved into our condo in 1984, so I don't think it was until 1985 that I told my parents. I wrote them a letter. I didn't want to deal with them head-on. I knew I couldn't get everything out verbally that I wanted to say. My father was in the Armed Forces and my mother was raised by nuns. I knew that when you tell your parents, friends or siblings, they have to go through their own coming out process. I got letters back from both my parents that were very negative and hurtful to me.

ML: It was the first time I had seen Michael cry. They were profoundly angry, horrible letters. He had a much closer relationship with his mother than his father. The father's letter was worse than his mother's.

MS: In hindsight, I think it rocked their world. I'm the oldest of five children and I was the kid who was perfect and who never upset the apple cart. I turned out to be the first in the family to upset the apple cart and give them an issue to deal with. It did get better eventually, but ironically, of all my siblings, I have the longest and the most secure relationship. My family couldn't imagine what our relationship would become over time. They had never dealt with anything like this in their life and so a lot of the anger was directed at me. I put them in a situation they never wanted to deal with.

Although Michael and I share a lot of core values, we are very different people as you can tell. The biggest source of conflict between us is that we approach life and problems differently. I avoid confrontation whereas Michael revels in it. He loves the thrill of the hunt and I think part of being a prosecutor is that he does this all day. I've gotten much better with it, but especially back then, I knew I wasn't ready to take on my parents. I knew before I told them that I would need to be strong enough to withstand the rejection.

ML: I dubbed him John Boy from *The Waltons* when I met him. He was that sweet young man straight off the mountain. I told him I wouldn't go home with him unless he came out to them first. I said, "You have to choose. Are you going to stay as John Boy to your mother and father or are you going to get beyond that? Even if you're rejected, you know I'll always be there for you and protect you. You're not going to be alone." Michael always perceived me as stronger than his parents, despite the fact I was in intensive therapy. I think Michael always saw himself then and his parents as the little people of the world.

MS: They still are and that's what you still don't get. My disclosure rocked their foundation and it had a huge impact on them. They remained angry for some time.

ML: His mother had no one to turn to. She couldn't turn to the church and she wouldn't raise issues like that with her friends. It resided within her and her husband. They floundered because there was no self-help available then.

MS: After I came out, there was no opportunity to help re-educate them about what it means to be gay. I'm sure everything they knew about gay was very negative and immoral. My mother said to me, "We wish you had told us earlier. We would have sent you to see a priest." Seeing a priest would be the last thing I'd ever want to do. For a year, we didn't talk. I think they thought it was a phase I was going through and that if they played hard-ball, I'd change. After a year, I called and said, "I want to come home." They said, "Fine." The next issue we had to deal with was that Michael wanted us to stay in the same bedroom. He forced me into confronting my parents with this issue. My mother said, "No, I'd rather you didn't," and that caused a big conflict.

ML: I wasn't allowed to discuss it with them. No discussion—period. The worst thing I had to accept in therapy was no discussion. I saw it as a form of punishment. Michael said, "You're stronger than they are and we've gone this far. Look at how much they've changed in the course of a year." It felt like it cost me another year in therapy. I was so angry that I wasn't allowed to talk.

MS: I could see everybody's perspective and I felt truly stuck in the middle—I was trying to keep both sides happy.

ML: Michael knew I was immovable, but they won that one.

MS: My parents had met Michael once before, but he scared them.

ML: I didn't scare them because I'm gay, but…because of my personality. Michael tells me that I don't appreciate how intense I come across.

MS: Well, Michael took on my parents because he got upset with them for not pushing me into becoming a professional. We hadn't known each other very long at that point and I was not out to my parents. Michael, to them, was no more than a friend. My parents were proud of me because I was the first child in the family to go on to post-secondary education, and from their perspective, here is this guy telling them that they didn't push me hard enough, that I should've been a doctor, a dentist or an architect. They didn't know where he was coming from.

ML: I was their first Jewish contact. I only mention this because there wasn't anyone like me in Greenwood, I can assure you, which is where they grew up. I want to underscore how intense it was for Michael to have to choose. One night we were in a restaurant with a friend and this issue came up. I said, "Are you going home? You can't go home without me." Michael exploded, and he rarely does that. He broke into tears and ran out of the restaurant. After witnessing this, our friend simply stated, "I'm never getting into a relationship if this is one of the joys of being in a relationship."

Michael had never disappointed his parents, and I was putting tremendous pressure on him to assert himself. In retrospect, I understand that I was dealing with those painful issues myself. I believed that my love for another man was supposed to be therapeutic: not upsetting and primal. You know, if we were a man and a woman, we would not have had any of those issues. We would've had different issues, but not those ones. These issues were society-made.

MS: We bought a house in September 1986, and my parents came to visit us for a week the next summer. We had a dog, we had jobs, we had to buy groceries, we did laundry, we had a nice home, and we were very responsible. We also slept together. I think it was very therapeutic for them to see us living as a regular couple.

Then we went to their home about a year later. The rule was, if they don't let us sleep together, we're not staying with them. We'd stay at a hotel instead. I called home and asked, "Can Michael and I can stay in the same room at your home?" My mother kind of laughed and said, "Of course."

ML: We were never allowed to ask why or how, but I have always been fascinated by the transformation. I knew I could learn something from how they were able to get as far as they did so quickly.

MS: I believe that their love for their eldest son was stronger than any religious or prejudicial attitudes that they had. They looked at what they believed it meant to be gay, which was a terrible picture, but they saw their son and the two beliefs didn't jive. I think they came to realize that they would need to disregard certain teachings and beliefs.

ML: The wonderful success story was that we would not be in a gay marriage today if people like us hadn't come out to their parents and continued to come out to others. Through the media attention we received, we became everyone's son, daughter, cousin and nephew by putting a human face on discrimination. As long as gay people remained in the closet, others could pretend that they [didn't] know any gay people. Once you personalize the issue, it becomes everyone's issue and that is the wonderful silver lining in all this original pain.

In 1984 and before that, [there] were painful years. That was before there was any family, societal support, books, movies, *Will & Grace, Queer Eye for the Straight Guy,* etcetera. There was none of that back then.

K: *The way I see it, you were grooming Michael S. for something bigger. Really, I suppose, you were both being groomed to be grooms.*

ML: We didn't think that then. It was really one step at a time. We came out to family, we came out at work, and we formed a monogamous relationship. There was no road map. For a monogamous relationship back then, the joke was you take a bit of penicillin because it cured everything. It was pre-AIDS. The road map was to screw your brains out, stay in the closet, have a lot of fun, and let someone else deal with gay rights. The gay community then was incredibly selfish and homophobic. It was downright ugly, and the ugliest part was the sense of victimization. People revelled in having as much sex as they wanted, thinking there was little cost. The cost would have only occurred if you came out, or were outed.

MS: I think that's a natural part of development for a movement. …[A] movement begins with the first steps of freedom. You cannot go immediately for the brass ring—you have to go through various steps first. For whatever reason, Michael and I chose a more unorthodox way of doing it. In the long-term, however, the rewards from it have been amazing. In our twenty-two years together, we've achieved more than we ever dreamed possible.

K:　*Michael L., when did you come out to your family?*

ML: It would have been 1974 or 1975, and I came out to my parents first. I had no problems with them or my five brothers around my disclosure. My mother simply said, "That's fine, but don't have sex." I had had a terrible relationship with my father, [but] from that point on it became better. He seemed more comfortable with me as an out gay son than as a presumed heterosexual son who was disappointing him in so many ways. My mom is now ninety years old, and my father passed away when he was eighty-three.

　　I never had gay sex until I came out, or any sex for that matter. I'd always feign a headache if a woman wanted to kiss me. That's a true story! If I was on a date and it came to the crunch time of a kiss, I'd say, "Oh, I'm sorry, I've got to leave immediately!"

　　I had been influenced in my formative teenage years by the black civil rights movement and the women's movement, the suffragettes' movement. I always read a lot when I was younger. My overwhelming heroine in my formative years was Eleanor Roosevelt, for heaven's sakes. I blame Eleanor for what I became!

K:　*Was your mother at your wedding?*

ML: Yes, she was.

K:　*How did she react when you told her, "We're getting married?"*

ML: We didn't—we got engaged first. We won our first court case in 2002 at the Divisional Court level, which was the first court win on the marriage case. They said, "Yes, you can get married, but there will be a two-year delay. We're going to give Parliament time to bring in new legislation." That's when I proposed to Michael on national television.

K:　*When you say Parliament, do you mean the legislature?*

ML: Yes, the Court meant the Federal Parliament because "who can marry" is federal jurisdiction exclusively. We brought the marriage case to the Divisional Court of Ontario and after about eighteen months, in July 2002, [the Court] decided that gays and lesbians would be able to marry because it was contrary to the Charter [to not allow it]. The court said they would suspend the operation of judgment and give Parliament two years to bring in legislation. That was ruled by two of the three judges. The third judge said we could marry right away. Then we appealed that decision to the Court of Appeal, and their decision was made on June 10, 2003, which said, "Yes, you can marry right away." We got married the same day, and the rest is history.

In July 2002, after we won at the Divisional Court level, I said on television, "Now I can turn to my sweetie and ask him: will you marry me?" Most of the media picked up on this because I didn't want anything to do with commitment ceremonies or anything less than marriage. It was all or nothing because anything less would mean that I was participating in prejudicial treatment toward gays and lesbians. Michael and I were fighting for equality—plain and simple. I would not accept a homophobic premise of "less than."

K: *When did the two of you decide that you were going to start the fight for marriage?*

MS: We didn't decide to start the fight: I think we were contacted.

ML: That's right. In 1999, we were contacted by one of the lawyers, Martha McCarthy, for the *M. & H.* case. We also won common-law equality for gays and lesbians in 1999. I had known Martha for years and she was looking for litigants. In 2000, she said, "Go down to the new city hall, apply for a licence, accept their rejection, and bring the licence back. I'll then get you to sign an affidavit."

I [go] down expecting to fulfill her instruction. I [say], "I'm applying for a licence to marry my gay partner." They [say], "We can't issue you a licence," and I [ask], "Why can't you?" They [say], "Because you're gay." I asked them to put that in writing because I needed it for our court case, and they said "No." I said, "Okay, I'll be back in an hour with the media, because if you're ashamed to put it in writing, you tell it to the media." All hell broke loose.

I have many connections [in] the media from over the years and they usually know it's a good story if I'm ready to blow. I told them what I was doing, and asked them to come down and meet me in an hour. They all [showed] up and I said, "Look, here's the media. You tell me I can't get a licence because I'm gay, but you won't put it in writing. I need it in writing for the court case." Of course, they were embarrassed to death with the media all there. I said, "I'm not leaving here until you give me a letter." They said, "Okay, we'll give you a letter in a week." A week to ten days later, they decided they weren't going to take the position of refusing to give a licence. They announced that they had to go to Superior Court and get directions of what do with Michael Leshner's request for a marriage licence.

That propelled the case way ahead because it was no longer being fought by individuals like Michael and I and the six other litigant couples. Now the City of Toronto in the year 2000 was asking, "What do we do? We need the law to tell us." The *M. & H.* case in the Supreme Court of Canada had already given us common-law equality. This is an example of how an individual can move an issue, against [a] lawyer's best instructions. She was thrilled, though, with what transpired.

The publicity generated by the media meant the issue of fundamental equality and principle was now out there for all to see. When they told me I couldn't marry Michael, the person I love, without even putting it in writing, what am I supposed to do? Walk away with my head between my knees? That's what gays and lesbians did in the early 1980s and the early 1990s.

I was living my life according to my principles. I was neither acting as a victim nor internalizing homophobia. Instead, I was demanding of them what I perceived as my right. How much more empowered could I be? I couldn't lose! Even if they refused to do it, I had won because I had found the road map out. It's such a simple road map if you can do it. It entails demanding what you are entitled to. With the media there, it was empowering and exhilarating. I could tell my lawyer, "See, I told you so." The story has a happy ending.

Many people are afraid that if you do that, something bad or something negative is going to happen. My message is that you do need to fight for your beliefs and your principles without backing down.

MS: Michael is who he is, and he just keeps pushing the envelope. He is colourful and the media love him. He is also very articulate. When we finally did marry, even though there were six other couples, we became the poster boys for same-sex marriage because of our history. There have been literally hours and hours of media tape over the years.

ML: In 1992 when I won same-sex benefits and pensions for all gay and lesbian employees of the Ontario government who were in same-sex relationships, we were all over the media because that was the first time anywhere in Canada that we existed constitutionally as an entity, as a couple. That was my media debut and our couple debut. After that, I was often called on by the media to comment on gay and lesbian issues, partly because of what Michael calls my "sound bites"—I tend to be a very open and direct—and partly because I'm like an intelligent Ralph Klein, if there is such a thing.

MS: Michael is not politically correct. Gay advocacy groups [don't] know how to treat Michael. They always try [to] rein him in and try to script him. But you can't script Michael—you don't need to. He's got a history of success that most groups would envy. He has had huge success.

ML: You have to understand that institutionally, any group wants everyone to sing from the same hymn book. The song is usually the one that the committee believes is politically correct. As Michael said, my language was not politically correct. I spoke to the committee in a language that they could understand—at times I was funny, at times I was angry and sarcastic.

MS: It would make some people uncomfortable.

ML: But as time went on, society was evolving and what may have made people uncomfortable in 1992 was becoming less and less uncomfortable. People change as society changes.

MS: That's true—more and more people were coming out of the closet. The gay movement really took off and it needed people like Michael who would lead and who would keep pushing the envelope.

ML: Because we were in a stable long-term relationship, we were a good source of information for media in Toronto. Toronto is the media capital of the country and they would come to us to visually show a long-standing couple. I also believe that the public still pays more attention to what a lawyer says. Also, because I am a crown attorney, they knew I had both feet on the ground.

MS: The amazing thing too is that we only received three hate phone calls on our answering machine in all our years together. We have never been harassed on the street either.

K: *This is Toronto, after all.*

MS: There are a lot of bigots in Toronto, like everywhere else.

ML: By the time gay marriage passed, it was a real love-in in Toronto. Complete strangers on the street, gay and straight, would stop us and offer congratulations. They still do. If they're driving, they'll honk their horn or say, "Are you the gay guys who got married? Congratulations!"

Perhaps something you don't see in Alberta or in many other parts of Canada is that I was never uncomfortable about holding people in authority accountable. I would say to people on TV or the print media, "The premier is a hypocrite," or worse. Whatever the movement is, it is important to speak in a language that people understand, using everyday vocabulary. I don't make a distinction because I believe I'm always telling the truth.

MS: Everything Michael says to the media is the truth. It might be a little bit exaggerated or more colourful, but it remains couched in truth, and people connect with that.

ML: With same-sex marriage, we've immortalized the gay version of *Romeo and Juliet*.

K: *Where did you guys meet?*

MS: We met at a bar on Church Street, called Buddy's. It is now defunct.

K: *At what point did you start to think and/or feel that your connection was more than sexual?*

MS: I think it was quite early. Michael was the first person I had been with that had his head on his shoulder. I had been with a lot of duds initially. I suffered from low self-esteem at that point and it was refreshing to be with someone who was stable. Michael helped me to find out who I am. I think we helped each other. I remember when Michael first told me about his obsessive-compulsiveness. I had no clue. I'm very down-to-earth and practical. I've helped him to smooth his edges and he's brought mine out. He's helped me grow in self-confidence as well.

We are opposites in many ways, but that helps us bring each other closer to the centre. I knew there was always a bigger world out there. I was raised in rural Nova Scotia and I had never lived in a big city before.

ML: But when did you fall in love with me? You're stalling. When was the first indication that you were in love?

MS: I think we were very old-fashioned in our dating and courtship. We didn't fall madly in love initially—instead, we got to know each other. We were late bloomers in the sense that neither of us knew sex as adolescents. The odd thing is this is the first long-term relationship for either one of us so we were exploring this without a point of reference.

Michael has mentioned the road map a few times, but we were more like explorers. We had no points of reference so we reacted as situations evolved. Once we started seeing each other every weekend, our relationship evolved very quickly. I don't think either of us would have seen [the] other as [his] ideal prior to meeting. I never thought that he would be the person I would end up with, and vice versa, but there was always a bond there.

There were a lot of issues that I was dealing with, centred on my identity. Who was I? What did I want to do with my life? What did I want to do as a gay man? I think I was dealing with this for the first seven to ten years of our relationship. Michael has taught me to communicate rather than bottle things up until they fester and become major issues.

On the flip side, we were also notorious for our arguments. Our first trip together was in 1983: we fought our way through the capitals of Europe. We had a terrible argument in Venice where we went to some recital and I huffed out. Michael was the most complicated person I had ever met.

ML: Whatever the case, I deal with it and move on. Michael analyzes things to death. My attitude was like, "Just leave me alone and just get over it. Let's have a good time." Why does everything have to be so deep and heavy? I just wanted to go out and do things.

Within the context of being gay, you need to know that I alienated a lot of people. We'd make friends and we'd lose friends because they weren't sufficiently out of the closet for me.

MS: You would lash out at anyone who didn't live up to your standards. In retrospect, it's amazing we did survive because I didn't think I could ever live up to those standards. When I achieved something, the bar would get raised higher. Michael was never content.

ML: Yeah, one could vacillate between calling me Moses and Preston Manning. This refers to the certainty of my views combined with the intensity with which they were expressed.

MS: There are so many facets to every relationship, and I've only picked up on certain ones. I think the important thing for people to realize is that relationships are hard work, but when they work, they force each of you to grow, and to grow closer together. I hope the reader can see some of this [in] our story. We fought, and continue to fight, on many levels—but ultimately, we also win.

K: *When did you begin to feel committed to this relationship, Michael L.?*

ML: I recognized early on that there was something very precious about Michael. Part of how I knew I loved him was that I wanted to show him off to my friends. You don't stop and do a chart regarding what I love about this guy and what I don't like, and then add up the points and decide if you are going to stay. Despite our differences, there were so many good times. The bad times that tested our relationship were mostly created by our work in gay rights.

I was disciplined for bringing in same-sex benefits at work and for speaking out about gay rights at the Ministry of the Attorney General. They said that I brought the administration of criminal justice into disrepute. That made me crazy because I thought there was nothing better as an employee than to fight at the Ministry level for equality before the law. When I returned to work, there was a letter of discipline on my file. I couldn't stand the letter. It is never easy to truly fight for what you believe in. I sued the Deputy Attorney General, borrowed money for the lawsuit and won 3:0 in the Divisional Court. The letter ceased to exist by court order.

MS: He was very proud of his cute boyfriend. My friends would say, "Oh, Michael's got a boyfriend," and that was cute as well because most gay people hadn't achieved a relationship yet—they were still doing the one-night stands.

We've had both a conventional and an unconventional relationship. We've experienced so many amazing highs that most people never experience. We didn't work toward those moments: they just happened when we were doing things for a bigger purpose—doing things that created fulfillment.

ML: If you look at the marriage case, for example, the simple issue really boils down to, "Why shouldn't the Michaels marry if they want to?" The only reason that would preclude this is blatant discrimination, with the prejudicial attitude that gay people are not equal to heterosexuals in marriage. If that's how you feel, fine, but it's blatant discrimination that cannot be sustained by the Courts. Michael and I lit a match and it illuminated the world. The illumination wasn't there the day before. ...

The final anecdote I offer refers to Benjamin Franklin at the Constitutional Conference in 1773. A woman reportedly asked Ben, "What kind of government did you give us, Ben?" and he said, "A democracy, if you can keep it." That was the challenge to me—what [kind] of democracy did I want to live in? What kind of democracy would I fight for? What kind of democracy wouldn't I live in or be a party to?

This story is first and foremost a love story. Without love, you wouldn't have had people striving toward a better society, or toward a just society. I often have said, "Will anything stand in the way of my love for Michael? Nothing can that is known to man. You'd have to put me in a cell, tie me up, and muzzle me." Besides my love for Michael, I love Canada and human rights. I also love myself, and when people say, "I just don't know how you do it," compared to the pain of the closet, this is a snap!

MS: There is great satisfaction in knowing that you've contributed to society. We're very big on giving back.

K: *You said earlier that there were no role models for gay people in the early 1980s. Today, the two of you are role models. What advice would you give to gay couples that are thinking about getting married?*

ML: It was the land of the dark where dinosaurs roamed.

MS: We would hate it if people got married on a whim, because it is still marriage. There are implications to it. We always said that we would take the responsibilities that come with the rights. Getting married is not like going out and buying a shirt. Is it something you want to do? Obviously you have to love each other and know that, in theory at least, it is supposed to be forever. Marriage is a serious commitment.

ML: In the end, I don't thing that gay men and women will necessarily have a better key to longevity and the meaning of happiness compared to heterosexual couples. Relationships are hard work: it's communicating, it's trusting, it's listening, and it's enjoying one another. I'd advise you to get a dog because each dog we've had doesn't like it when we argue. When we say to each other, "Look, our dog is getting upset," that usually means it's time to stop the argument.

I'm sure there are people hoping that we'll fall out of love and divorce, but it won't prove anything other than the Michaels tried hard at something that didn't work out in the end. What you make of your life is your own.

Don't whine and don't cry to anyone. I'm not talking about a sixteen year old trapped in a dysfunctional, homophobic family. I'm talking about adults in Canada. You are the only one keeping yourself back. Gay marriage is fundamentally about the democracy that you live in. What you make of it is something you own.

K: *Is there a metaphor, an image, or a piece of music perhaps that speaks to your feelings or thoughts about same-sex marriage?*

ML: Our theme music from our wedding was the song "Somewhere" from *West Side Story*. It's about "somewhere there's a place for us," and "hold my hand, and I'll take you there." When you think of most gay men and women who grew up closeted and you listen to those lyrics, it reminds you of where you were, what the struggle is, and offered "hope" when in the dark days the best that could be offered was nothing more than "hope." It was that bleak.

MS: It's actually quite powerful. We've always liked the song and when we were planning our wedding party that was the song we wanted for our first dance. They kind of screwed up but whatever.

ML: They were supposed to play "Somewhere," but they somehow screwed up and played "Some Day My Prince Will Come" instead.

K: *What would you put in a "hope box" for gay people? Where do we still need to go as a gay community?*

MS: I would say people need to maximize their potential and become themselves. We have helped to give gays and lesbians equality, and from that can come self-confidence and integrity. You cannot dismiss your potential because you assume you will be discriminated against, or because the laws are against you. It can be a justification for not moving forward, and you can hide behind that. The more that people come out, the more that society learns we are everywhere. The more you maximize your potential, the more you contribute to the gay movement and to society at large.

ML: In the hope chest, the lawyer in me would want to put the Charter of Rights because it is truly a tremendous gift. Our Charter of Rights is better than the American Bill of Rights because ours is much more effective. In the hope chest, I would also put Donna Summers' "I Will Survive," the song "Somewhere," Martin Luther King's "I Have a Dream" speech and the film of black people at the lunch counter from Mississippi. I'd show the suffragettes to remind people that there is a continuum through history of images of people struggling for self-respect, dignity and equality. Many people before us have suffered much more horrible difficulties than we have. As horrible as it was, most of us were not thrown in jail, most of us didn't lose our jobs, and most of us weren't beaten up. The hope chest should reflect the historical continuum. Without that historical context and perspective, the content becomes too superficial.

K: *That is all of my questions, but are there other important pieces that you think are missing?*

ML: I think you've got the essentials. We've shared our strengths and opposing weaknesses that are complemented by one another. It takes very special people to do this, and we've given you an honest, accurate picture of ourselves in relationship to one another.

MS: I agree. A title for our story could be the *Centennial Couple*—we married this year, and right now, our ages equal one hundred. Thank you for the interview.

K: *Thank you both for agreeing to participate.*

Angie and Lynn Keen
photo by Kevin Midbo

I Can't Stop Loving You
Angie and Lynn Keen

Date: September 16, 2003
Time: 1:00 pm
Place: Toronto, Ontario

Angie and Lynn came from Kitchener for this interview. They define themselves as a "dyke" and a "fem," respectively, titles not shared by all members
of the lesbian community.

L: We didn't formally meet each other until one night in a bar. Angie was
leaving, I was coming in from outside, and…it just clicked between us. I was
with somebody else at the time, but meeting her was like, "Oh my God!" I
immediately struck up a friendship with her, and I knew I couldn't let her
go. I liked her look and I wanted to be with her. I could tell from looking in
her eyes that we could have a great time together. My relationship at that
time did fall apart because she was in the closet and wasn't ready to come
out. I, on the other hand, was really out and proud. I was so happy to be
finally free of the mask I had on around my family and friends. At one time,
I was straight to them and gay to everybody else; until I finally had to be
myself. From that point, our friendship developed into a great love affair,
and I don't regret anything since we got together.

K: *When did you two first meet?*

L: We met in August 2000 and we started going out on September 18.
Our official anniversary of our first date comes up in two days! Our relationship developed like a whirlwind—we tried to slow it down, but we
clicked so well and we couldn't stop the love from growing rapidly and
steadily.

A: By the time we said, "Wait a minute," we had already gone too fast, and it was too late—we were already in love. We were already intertwined because Eric, her son, lives with her and we were already doing everything together as a family before we knew it.

K: *It sounds like Lynn's connection to you was immediate. She just saw your eyes and lost herself inside. What was it like for you when you first met her?*

A: The first thing that grabbed me was her smile. When she smiles, her eyes light up the whole room and it is very infectious. My connection with her was also immediate.

...

L: I had several male friends that attended the club where Angie and I met, but I wanted to have more gay women as friends. It wasn't until I started going out by myself that I started meeting more women and I was basically just looking for more friendships. I was also learning more about gay people and the community. I had tried dating another fem girl and we constantly fought over stuff like who was wearing whose shoes. I am very feminine and when I met Angie, she was someone I was looking for, but it took me a while to find her.

K: *Does the lesbian community still embrace a difference between dykes and fems?*

L: The distinction may not be as prevalent as it once was, but in our own circle of friends, we can tell who is which. The feminine woman will wear makeup, shave her legs, have her hair in line, will wear skirts, and stuff like that. The butch, or dyke, tends to go toward the masculine side of [herself] instead of the feminine side. [She] will wear [her] hair short and may not want to wear a skirt. Angie will dress up in jeans and a dress shirt. Angie works as a forklift driver, while I work in an office.

A: You will never see me in a dress or a skirt.

K: *If someone who's straight called you a fem, Lynn, and you a dyke, Angie, would you see that as derogatory?*

L: I think so, but it's what we have always been called.

A: No, I don't think so, because I don't really pay attention to what people say.

L: My seventy-eight-year-old grandmother is Roman Catholic and she lives in Newfoundland. When she met Angie, she didn't know how to ask me so I told her that Angie and I were a couple. Then grandma said, "Well she's rather mannish, isn't she?" We both found that rather funny. I've always been honest with my grandmother, so I told her everything about our special relationship. She then told me, "All I worry about is that you are happy."

...

K: *Now I am curious because both of you have a child. Were you each married at an earlier time? How does this tie into your coming out?*

A: I have been out for eleven years and I knew that I was different since grade three. Even then, I was looking at the girls in the class instead of the boys. In high school, I stuck to myself because of how I felt. I did my best to hide in the locker room because I wanted to check out the other girls. When people ask me, "When did you know you were gay?", I always tell them that when you walk into a room full of males and females where you have no need to talk to anyone in particular, if the first person you can't take your eyes off is a female, maybe that is telling you something about which side of the fence you should be playing on. It is a good indication. A heterosexual male or a heterosexual female would naturally first see the opposite sex. For me, I always noticed the girls far more than the boys: in fact the guys didn't exist. It was like that for years until I finally got tired of living my life for everybody else.

K: *How old were you when you first starting dating guys?*

A: I was about sixteen when I dated my first guy. But even then I knew that I was supposed to be gay. I found out I was pregnant at twenty-one. ...[M]y son, Brandon is sixteen years old and I am glad that I have him in my life.

K: *Did you intend to have a child?*

A: Yes I did, but there were other reasons behind it. Unfortunately for me, [Brandon] lives with his father, although his father and I get along really well. There is no animosity between us. Once I decided to come out, his father was almost the first person I told. He was okay with it.

...

K: *Okay, let's switch over to you for a bit, Lynn. Tell me about your experience. Were you married? When did you know you were a lesbian?*

L: I was never married before I married Angie. I have known that I was a lesbian most of my life, but the community that I lived in Newfoundland was very tiny and anybody that was different didn't have an opportunity to come out. I knew a couple of gay couples that lived in the community and I tried hard to talk to them, but in my town, I was well-known because of my parents and I couldn't come out. It was not until I moved to Kitchener in 1998 that I was able to explore my sexuality. I first classified myself as bisexual because I wasn't quite sure if this was what I wanted or if it was the right choice.

I always wondered why I was so grossed out by men. I was disgusted by the entire male persona. When I started dating women, it felt right to me. I was a jock in school, like a real rumble, tumble person. I would be with the guys ogling all the girls in the school hallway! The guys would be like, "What are you doing?" I'd say, "I'm one of the guys, right?", and they'd respond, "Yeah, that's right."

I was afraid of my feelings for girls growing up. I didn't let my parents know how I felt at all, or anyone else for that matter. I didn't want anybody to find out, which was very difficult because it meant I had to keep myself hidden for years. Like I had to basically stay in myself instead of being who I wanted to be. I knew I was different for a very long time. I'd love having sleepovers as a kid because the more girls I had around me, the better I felt about myself. We didn't all sleep in the same bed, but we slept in one big room in sleeping bags. After I came out, one of my best friends asked me, "Did you ever find me attractive?", and I said, "No, because you're my friend. I wouldn't take that to the next level with you." She then asked, "Why, what's wrong with me?" After I explained it, she said, "Oh, now I understand."

My parents took my gayness extremely hard, especially my dad. Dad was worried about my son. Eric is his first grandchild and he was completely happy when I had him, despite the fact I was only nineteen. I have two sisters and a brother and Eric was his first and only grandson at that time. My brother's all grown up with two boys of his own. Eric is still my dad's special boy.

K: *What age were you when you started thinking that you might be bisexual?*

L: I was either ten or eleven, but by age twenty-five, I knew I was a lesbian. As I look back, I was unfortunately very promiscuous with guys because I couldn't handle having them in a relationship. My philosophy as a teen was, "Love 'em and leave 'em." It didn't give me the best reputation in the world, but it helped me decide who I was. When I got pregnant with my son, it was with a guy I had been off and on with for two years. After giving birth to Eric, I didn't date anyone for four years. I totally dropped out of society and did a lot of soul searching and thinking.

I knew I didn't want to get married to a man and I needed to get away somewhere where I could be myself. My sister moved to Cambridge for a job, and six months later, she asked me to move there with her. That was the opportunity I needed. As soon as I moved here, my life changed for the better because I could finally be myself.

...

K: *In two days, you celebrate your fourth anniversary. What is it like being together?*

A: It's about everything that is good in life. We argue about things and we agree on other things, although that seems rare!

...

Lynn represents everything that I need and everything that I have searched for. We are two parents, we have two kids, two cats, and two goldfish: we are a family.

K: *What is it about your perspective, Lynn?*

...

L: Having someone to help you through the good times and the bad times is very important. Eric feels like he is part of a family now. He was so proud when we got married. Our pictures were in the paper so he went to school the next day and said, "Oh yeah, these are my parents." He was completely ecstatic about it. When I met Angie, I knew she would stick by me regardless of whatever happens in life. She exemplifies total unconditional love. I mean just sitting alongside her on the couch gives me…I can't say anymore or I'm going to cry.

K: *I can see that.*

...

Take a minute, Lynn, that's fine. That is ultimately what your connection is about. You both are in sync with each other. Angie, when did you know that there was a solid commitment between the two of you?

A: I think I knew after the first time I did something really stupid. It was probably one of the dumbest things I have ever done, but when it was all said and done, she was still there. … It happened before Christmas of our first year together. I said something that was really stupid and she didn't bolt.

...

L: … I just looked at her and said, "You can try whatever you want to get out of this. If you can't work on this with me, pack up your stuff and go." We sat down and talked things through. We have great communication skills. That took getting used to because I used to bottle things up inside.

...

Angie ended up losing the place where she was living, and she had nowhere to stay. She was planning to stay at either the YWCA or at Mary's place, and I said, "No you're not—it's almost Christmas. I want you to live with me." I had a three-bedroom apartment and my brother, his wife, and child were living with me at the time. I wanted to give her a choice to respect her individual needs—either the couch or my room. I had never lived with anybody before that I was involved with, so this was all new to me. Before she moved in, we never stayed at each other's house. We dated, went to movies, parks, talked on the phone, and so forth, but being with her face-to-face, 24-7, was different.

K: *How do you see your relationship as similar to and different from a hetero-sexual marriage?*

L: There are similar traits in terms of the way we raise our family, except we have a different outlook on life in general. Our children are not prejudiced because we tell them the truth about everything. We want them to learn that everybody out there is practically alike, despite having different views or different opinions on different subjects.

...

There is more love in our household than I have seen in many heterosexual households. We treat our children quite differently from the way Angie and I were raised. We don't hit our children, for example.

...

Brandon has been unfortunately struck with teenage acne, which gets worse in high stress situations. He lived with us for three months when he was having problems at school and at home. Within a short while, his face cleared up, he was happier, and he couldn't wait to come home after school was over. He worked on his homework in front of us and we were checking it over to make sure that it was done. Once he returned to his father's, his face started breaking out again. We have also received a couple of phone calls saying that he is skipping classes again. We think maybe he should have stayed with us.

Rob has completely good intentions, and he is an honourable man, but we wonder why Brandon has such a bad reaction to staying with his dad. We are strict about having the kids do their chores and their homework before listening to the cds, watching television, playing on play-station or playing on the computer.

I know that Brandon loves coming over to be with us. He calls me mom, and when he introduces us to others, he says, "This is mom #1, my biological mom, my dad's wife is mom #2, and Lynn is mom #3—I always save the best for last." That is what he says to people. Both he and Eric are charming. Eric is completely infatuated with women and Brandon has had a girlfriend for the past several months.

Eric's dad has not been in the picture since he was three months old unfortunately. Since the legalization of same-sex marriage came in, we don't have to go through as much red tape for Angie to adopt Eric. Eric wants to have his name hyphenated to keep [the] identity of his birth.

I changed my last name to Angie's so that we could be the Keen family. Brandon's name is already hyphenated with his father's name and Angie's name. When Brandon is with us, we are Keens, and when he is over [at] his dad's, he is a Le Drew.

K: *Did one of you propose to the other?*

A: I proposed to Lynn. Just after I moved in.

...

L: It was on December 12, 2000. There was a raging snowstorm outside and we went inside to make hot chocolate. While I was busy in the kitchen, Angie called Eric into the bedroom for a second to talk to him and all of a sudden I see them walking back and forth. I asked, "What are you guys doing?" They were bringing candles and everything into the bedroom. Little did I know that Angie had earlier bought rings for the three of us: one for herself, one for me, and one for Eric. The three of us would have the same ring! Brandon was in and out and we were just getting back into a relationship with him. He opted to have a necklace and a cross when we got married. He was not there unfortunately when Angie proposed. I will let you take over the rest because it was really nice what you said.

A: I had already asked Eric for permission to marry his mom. He was really happy about that, and of course he said yes. I took Lynn into the room because the way I had intended to ask her wouldn't work because of the snowstorm. I lit all the candles, I sat Lynn in the chair with Eric standing beside her, I got down on one knee, and I proposed to her. I asked her to be my wife, and she and Eric both cried. Eric had no idea that I had a ring for him too. After I asked Lynn to marry me, I looked at Eric and said, "I love you very much and I want you to be my son."

L: Later Eric said, "I'm engaged to my parents."

...

K: *Same-sex marriage was legalized in Ontario on June 10, and you two married on June 14. How did you pull off a wedding with pictures and everything in four days?*

L: We had already been planning [a] commitment ceremony for two years, and we had actually planned it for June 15, 2002.

...

K: *Do you believe there are any drawbacks to same-sex marriage?*

A: I don't think so—that is like asking a heterosexual couple if there are drawbacks to being married. I do not see any difference other than we are two women. We still think about not having enough money and we have our little quirks in the family unit. Everybody has a job to fulfill in the household, no matter who they are. We both go to work everyday and the children go to school everyday.

L: The only drawback to same-sex marriage is the public's view of it. We are still the same two individuals that we always were. We love being together and I miss her when she goes to work on her night shifts. It takes me a long time to fall asleep because she is not there. I couldn't have dreamt of a better life than to have married Angie. Eric's teachers are so happy that he has two parents that care for him a great deal. I haven't seen a negative side to same-sex marriage: everything has been positive since we got married.

K: *What advice would you give to same-sex couples that are thinking about getting married?*

L: Don't enter into it lightly. Marriage is marriage: it is two people committing their lives to each other. You can't go into it after only knowing someone for six months. You have to make sure that both of you are ready for this commitment. Another piece of advice is just keep talking to one another—communicate, communicate, communicate. That is most important.

A: Always let the girl win. Communication is the key because there is so much between people that if you don't talk, you aren't going to make it. You have to know how [the] other [person] feels. Also realize that it has nothing to with the bedroom—nothing.

...

L: We know several lesbian/gay couples that are thinking of getting married, but they are working through some major problems right now because they can't communicate with one another. We were encouraging them to work together on some stuff before they think about making the big step into marriage. Before Angie and I married, I said to her, "If we get married, you are stuck with me for the rest of your life because I don't believe in divorce." I take my vows very seriously.

K: *Is there a metaphor, a poem, an image, a piece of music, or something else that really speaks to your feelings or thoughts about same-sex marriage?*

L: One day I sent Angie an electronic card that had Phil Collins singing a line from his song, "I Can't Stop Loving You." My inscription was, "I Miss You Every Moment Of The Day." The card was really sappy. When I came home from work, Angie was on the computer. She turned around and tears were just falling down her face. I got her [that time], because I am usually the one doing the crying. Another song that had meaning for me was k. d. lang's "Summer Fling" because we originally started out as a summer fling, but it turned into something wonderful.

K: *What would you put in a "hope box" for gay people? What still needs to happen within the gay community?*

A: We need to gain an overall acceptance of each other. I've noticed in the gay community that gay men don't like lesbians, lesbians don't like gay men, bisexuals are supposed to "get off the pot," and nobody likes the transgendered people. We need to stop judging each other and find ways to start connecting with each other. If we can't accept our own, how can we expect heterosexuals from the outside looking in to accept us for the way we are?

L: We belong to the gay bowling league, and Eric goes with us some of the time because he loves it. He knows most of our friends. He handles it very well, but it is hard having a straight kid grow up in a gay family. He does get teased and tormented, although he is beginning to develop some good comeback lines. When a kid says something like, "Why doesn't your mom go like bleep on my dick," he'll turn around and say, "Well, no, because your mom is busy with my mom right now." Eric has learned to turn the whole thing around. He used to shut right down and walk away. Now he has the attitude, "No way, my mom deserves to be happy too, and Angie is what she needs."

...

We have two great kids. They are open and honest with everybody. They are not ashamed of their parents. Even Brandon boasts to kids at school that are in gangs, for example, "You know I've got three moms, which means I can't get away with anything." Eric is doing fine without a dad. He has a big brother from the Big Brother/Big Sisters organization, which provides him [with] a positive male influence in his life.

K: *If same-sex marriage sweeps the country, what do you think will need to happen within mainstream society?*

A: We need to educate straight people. Unfortunately, straight people still think it is a bedroom issue, which is very closed-minded. We could look at them the same way. We have to stop crucifying people for who they are.

L: I do believe that education is the key. There is not enough information out there for straight people. They need to learn that we are just like they are, except she's with a woman and he's with a guy. We are just people.

...

Some even put us in the same category as child abusers and paedophiles. I overheard some colleagues at work say, "They shouldn't be allowed to get married—they are child abusers." I went out and confronted them, "Listen here, I have two teenage kids. Do I look like a child abuser to you? How dare you say that!" I had to get a little angry with them.

A: I would like to see where the literature is to back up that statement.

K: *The literature indicates that between 90 and 95% of child abusers are hetero-sexual males. Do you think that there is anything that we missed that still needs to be said?*

L: No, I think all the bases have been covered.

A: I agree.

K: *Thank you very much for taking part in this interview.*

Kevin Alderson and Kevin Bourassa
photo by Kevin Midbo

Penhaligons of London

Kevin Bourassa and Joe Varnell

Date: September 16, 2003
Time: 4:15 pm
Place: Toronto, Ontario

I feel especially honoured to meet Kevin. Unfortunately his partner, Joe Varnell, was not available at the time of our interview. The two of them published a book called *Just Married* following their marriage through the Proclamation of Banns process in 2001. We head off to a coffee shop where we conduct the interview on the outside patio. It seems like only minutes later, Kevin has to leave for another commitment. He reminds me that a great deal of information can be found on his and Joe's Web site, www.equal-marriage.ca.

K: *How did you guys get to this point?*

KB: We met in 1997, but the story of our marriage really began in 1998. One night Joe and I were wrestling around in our living room and suddenly he proposed to me. We both knew that marriage as a legal entity wasn't ours to embrace, at least not then, so I knew he was really asking if I would have a type of holy union or commitment ceremony with him. We were both members of the Metropolitan Community Church (MCC) of Toronto, so in the absence of legal recognition, we thought at least something resembling the best of what we wanted could be achieved through MCC. We approached the [church] and sent out invitations to family and friends with a picture of the justice minister on the back of it. We asked those who were coming to our holy union to write and protest that we couldn't actually have a true marriage, which is what we had wanted. The church remembered that invitation when lawyers advised [it] that couples could receive a record of marriage without requiring a licence by going through the Proclamation of Banns process.

The Banns process is a means of getting married whereby you announce on three consecutive Sundays to the community the intention of a couple to marry. The community is not just the congregation, but it includes the community at large. They can object to the marriage according to the legal provisions in the Ontario statutes. These objections included things like being related by blood, being underage, not having the mental capacity to make the decision, or [being] currently married.... It is a Christian practice that existed before civil marriage—it is the original form of marriage. In Ontario prior to 1847, you could not get married outside of the Church of England. What that meant is that some people did not have the right to marry.

The church called and explained the Proclamation of Banns to me. [It] also explained that not allowing people to marry who had been married before was in [the] fine print and that [it] had not noticed this before [it] selected other couples to be the test cases. It turned out that one of the men in the male couple had been married before and one of the women in the female couple had been married before. Consequently, both of them were disqualified from the process so the church went back to the boards and selected Joe and I as potential candidates. We were happy to learn that the female couple who [was] simultaneously chosen in the effort to bring in equal marriage to Canada was Anne and Elaine Vautour. We already knew Elaine because she was the deacon in our church and she had ministered to Joe's mother while she was dying in hospital. Elaine counselled us during that period. We only had a few hours to make up our mind so I called Joe and left a message for him on his voice mail. If we agreed, CBC news was going to be at our home that night. Our lives changed very dramatically within a matter of hours. We really didn't understand the impact of the journey that we were about to embark upon.

K: *How interesting. Tell me about the book that you and Joe wrote?*

KB: *Just Married* is the result of the period immediately following our marriage. We had been on the front pages of several daily newspapers in Toronto and nationwide. Our lives had been inundated with media coverage. We then had the opportunity to either walk away and only show up on the courthouse steps for photo opportunities when our case appeared every once and a while, or we could maximize opportunities to work in-between those major dates to further advance our case. Our lawyer, Douglas Elliott, explained his role and our role when we first met him. Our job was to be the "human" in human rights. We both looked at that with the intention to tell a very personal story. Our book presents the broader perspective, including a mix of the personal, the political, the spiritual, the legal, and the many aspects that same-sex marriage touches on that we are now debating in society at large.

K: *Does the reader gain a comprehensive picture of the relationship that you and Joe have?*

KB: I wouldn't describe it as comprehensive as it is not strictly an autobiography but some people, including reviewers, were surprised at how personal we were in the book. Its intent was certainly to give an intimate glimpse of our existence so that the reader would perceive us not just as friends but as spouses. We didn't want to write a book that was unidimensional, bidimensional or even tridimensional. We looked for ways to interweave our stories so that it had some literary potential. One of the important aspects of writing the book was that we wanted to show what it means to be an activist and an advocate. Joe and I in the past volunteered for certain things, but we had mostly written cheques as our form of helping causes. We had never really taken [a cause] to heart and used all of our competencies and skills. We write about that journey and about what activism means. My parents were transformed from people who used to say to us, "Why do you have to hold hands in public?" to parents who went to five bakeries in small town Ontario to find a baker who would bake a cake with two men on it. That is a journey my seventy-year-old parents went through. I think that is similar to what other Canadians are going to experience if we achieve national recognition of same-sex marriage.

K: *I don't want to include the same material in my book that you and Joe have already included in your own book. However, I also know that as a writer, sometimes once the book is published, you think, "Jeez I wish I would have remembered to include this or that in it." Is there a piece that you now wish you had included in* Just Married *that we can get into this book?*

KB: No, we didn't have that experience. We used a highly structured approach to the work as a whole. It was mapped out page by page, chapter by chapter, and then written. Nothing was left out by chance or by circumstance. It does, however, cover a very limited time frame of six weeks between when we were asked to get married and when our lawyer announced the intention to sue for registration of our January 14, 2001 marriage. I am interested in the legal aspects of the journey, and this story will lead off in our second book.

K: *Your second book will cover more of the legal side of what happened?*

KB: Yes, we will take a look at the legal debates that have occurred and the political debates, which are hand in hand with the legal. I am outraged at the way our Charter of Rights and Freedoms has been taunted and debased by those who oppose same-sex marriage. I'm equally outraged by the way our courts and judicial system have been slandered and with the politicians who have allowed this situation to be so mishandled because they weren't willing to face the difficult questions early on. Given that this is happening with same-sex marriage, you can be sure that it is happening in the federal budget, the management of the Canada Pension Plan, and so forth. I would like to [cause] the Canadian public to be more conscious in how [it] monitors the activity of [its] governments. Just as the first book was intended to inspire people to step up to personal advocacy, I would like the second book to inspire people to vote. I also want to inspire them to get engaged in the political process because if they don't, some jerk—who is bound and deter-mined to ruin your life—[will]. The second book will be a little more about political awareness and engagement.

...

K: *I understand that some individuals from other countries are coming to Canada to marry and then returning to their own country where they begin the legal challenge to have their same-sex marriage recognized. Is that correct?*

KB: Right. There are treaties that have been signed and countries are expected to oblige. The treaties are only as good as the rights and protections that exist in the resident country. If you've got a weak charter, constitution or bill, then you'll have a weak case in court. Typically Commonwealth countries have a stronger base from which to launch a marriage challenge. New Zealand and South Africa are examples of countries where the drive for same-sex marriage has gone a long way. People are coming here, getting married, and then returning to their country to challenge, launch from a constitutional basis, or exercise one of their singular rights as a married couple. It may be as simple as requesting a name change, or getting a drivers' licence [with a] new marital name if one has been adopted. They will be taking the challenge from various perspectives. In the United States, it is a slightly different approach in that they are coordinating a mass challenge state by state because of the constitutional legal differences between states. For example, we are looking at Massachusetts, New Hampshire, New Jersey and California. All of those states are making strong progress towards delivering equal marriage.

K: *Tell me, how did you get to this place of having so much passion to do what you are doing now?*

KB: It's like anything: when your car muffler breaks down or your carburetor, you suddenly become an expert on how to work on that piece of your car. If you have an illness, you look it up on the Internet and become an expert on how to manage that illness. We had a problem fall in our lap and we've tried to approach that problem as comprehensively as we could, and that problem was to achieve marriage equality. We have had counsellors and advisers and our own inherent capabilities to pursue it. Remember that we married on January 14, 2001, so it's been two and a half years of living this every single day.

K: *When the two of you married in the MCC church, did you also have to get a marriage licence?*

KB: No, the Banns process doesn't require a marriage licence from city hall because it's not a civil marriage: it is a religious marriage. You sign marriage documents exactly like what you saw in church today. You are given a government record of marriage with a number on it. That was given to us on the day of our marriage. A second half of that document is torn off and sent to the appropriate ministry for registration. At that point we became the first couple to actually have a record of marriage. There were eighty news organizations at our marriage because the media around the world understood that this was a legal marriage because we had the legal record signed, sealed and delivered in our hands. The only thing we didn't have was that number registered in a book. Eventually the Ontario Court of Appeal and the divisional level both ratified that our marriage was legal at that point. On June 10, 2003, the Ontario government was ordered to register our marriage, so it was done shortly thereafter.

K: *Does that mean that the two of you are really the first same-sex couple to marry in Canada?*

KB: What's important to stress here is that the significance of the day of our marriage is not whether it was the first or not. The significance was that it put equal marriage on the map in Canada, and this sent a message around the world. [Legally] speaking, we became the first legally married same-sex couple in the world in the modern era. If you read [John] Boswell's work, there were legally married men in the eyes of the church when the church controlled marriage in medieval times, but that stopped in the 1500s. There have been registered domestic partnerships in places like Norway and Sweden for some time, but these are marriages minus something, such as adoption rights, inheritance rights or other rights. So yes—Joe, Anne, Elaine and myself were the first to legally marry in Canada.

But it's like those figure skaters that got their gold medal: it's by judge's decision. The two Michaels are certainly the first to have a legal civil marriage because our marriage was not a civil marriage. They were also the first to be married after the law took effect. Our church continued to marry people after us, and so did the United Church and many others. In that regard, there are many people who became legally married who predate the two Michaels.

The important story is how I think those first marriages were celebrated in the smaller local papers across Ontario. When the story of couples being showcased as a first marriage began to appear in the local papers, I knew that same-sex marriage basically had been won. Dr. Kees Waaldijk, the father of same-sex marriage in the Netherlands, told us at a conference that when the local small radio stations and small newspapers started covering stories about marriage in Holland, the equal marriage fight was over. That is what has happened in Ontario as well. God bless the *Globe and Mail* and the Canadian Broadcasting Corporation for their support. The national carriers are not the only ones anymore, however. Now the small community newspapers with local voices and faces resonating with local meaning are being shown on their front pages. That's the miracle that has happened since June 10. There are many people still continuing the fight, like those who have got married in Ontario and who are struggling for that recognition in New Brunswick. There is more work that needs to be done.

K: *What do you think is going to happen at the federal level?*

KB: They'll kick and they'll scream, but they basically have three choices. They can either give us equal marriage, leave marriage completely to the religious groups and get out of the marriage business altogether, or declare that people like Joe and I are less than full citizens of Canada who are not protected by the Charter by invoking the notwithstanding clause. I don't believe the notwithstanding clause will be used. Getting out of marriage is equality with vengeance. That would be like saying, "I don't want you to swim in my pool so I am shutting down the pool rather than let you swim in it," or "If I have to let you in the park I would rather close it than let you in." So that's not going to happen either. There is a lot of squawking because they don't like the medicine but they are going to have to swallow it.

K: *Are there any drawbacks to same-sex marriage?*

KB: I think a better question is whether there are drawbacks to marriage. There are benefits to marriage and there are drawbacks to it as well, depending on the make-up of the couples. It is a personal choice and marriage in its structure and execution is individually defined. We define our own roles and what works as a couple, so marriage is both good and bad. Joe and I haven't seen anything bad except that we have had to fight like the dickens to get it. We would eventually like to reclaim a large part of our lives that we have given up and focus our energies elsewhere. Don't get me wrong—our advocacy work has developed us and made us grow and we are grateful for this tremendous opportunity.

K: *I think a lot of gay men and lesbians are going to look to this book for role models and advice. What advice would you give to same-sex couples who are thinking about getting married?*

KB: It needs to be thought through very carefully. It is neither a marriage petition nor a political statement. It is a legal entity that you are creating with protections and obligations. Any couple needs to seriously consider [this] before [marrying]. We counsel many people, especially people from outside of Canada who are coming here to marry, to be serious and really think about it. In terms of role models, Joe and I categorically reject that kind of label because all people are basically the same with varying strengths and weaknesses. The person you marry should be your role model and you should be that person's role model. Then you know you are on the right path.

K: *Very thoughtful. Is there a metaphor, a piece of music, a song or an image that really speaks to your feelings or thoughts about same-sex marriages?*

KB: I can only think of our experiences on the road. Joe and I have travelled over one hundred thousand kilometres this year and almost as many last year. That has been a fascinating experience for us. What comes to mind for me are visions of the people that we've met through our travels and what it has meant to them. People project their feeling onto us and they often assume that Joe and I are motivated by the same things that motivate them. They pour their hearts out and share their motivation with us, and sometimes it is very touching and surprising. What has defined marriage for us have been people like parents, both straight and gay, who have told us that the work happening here in Canada and elsewhere will allow their children to grow up in a different world. Making the world a different place and the evolution of culture in society I see as a major component of same-sex marriage.

We have an advertising agency, Zig Inc., that is starting the production of same-sex marriage public service announcements on our behalf. They, and their partner companies, are donating around a million dollars worth of production time and real dollars to build three television commercials and three radio spots for us for free. They don't want their kids growing up in the world that we now have where they hear that one family is better or worse than another. For me that's what happens. We have had sixteen-year olds and eighteen-year olds giving us little pride flags, showing us that they have had the courage to come out. Our family has relayed stories from their small towns of children whose marks were bad, doing poorly in their social and school realms until they finally told their parents that they were gay. Their lives then turned around. People have told us they wanted to commit suicide before hearing our message. Those are the things that come to mind because equal marriage is not strictly a personal thing. You have to realize Joe and I work almost every day meeting the public, talking to people, and writing about it. It's not just a favourite song for us.

On a personal level, London resonates very deeply because that was where we had our first honeymoon. For Joe and I, there are certain smells and brands of champagne that remind us of our romantic honeymoon in London. There is a cologne that reminds us of this [time] called Penhaligons. It's a men's perfumery that was launched in the 1800s. We were having champagne on a side street in London one morning when we saw this Charles Dickins type store. We entered and there were all these scents, and that is how we found it.

K: *Those are all the questions I have, Kevin. Thank you.*

Nelson Ng and Roddy Shaw
photo by Kevin Midbo

Train Ride

Roddy Shaw and Nelson Ng

Date: September 17, 2003
Time: 10:45 am
Place: Toronto, Ontario

Roddy and Nelson came to Toronto from Hong Kong to get married. Upon their return home, they plan to begin a legal challenge to have their marriage recognized in Hong Kong. I wait at the Second Cup on Church Street and Wellesley for Roddy and Nelson to arrive. I talk to a woman editing a paper for someone attending York University. She says that she attended a gay male wedding recently, a couple together for forty-seven years. I gave her contact information and asked her to pass it onto these two, never expecting to hear from them.

Roddy and Nelson arrive at 11:10 am. I get them coffee and a snack, and we begin the interview.

K: *It was such a privilege to be at your wedding yesterday, although I arrived late because my taxi driver ended up with a speeding ticket en route to your wedding. At least you two were not late for your wedding. I'm curious, how did this come about, that the two of you would come all the way from Hong Kong to get married in Canada?*

R: We are gay activists in Hong Kong, and we have been following the legal reform developments that are occurring throughout the world. We have followed the changes in the Netherlands, in Belgium and in Canada. What has happened in Canada is really amazing, and there is a difference between the developments here and the changes in Europe. In Europe, there are a lot of legislative changes. Parliaments have taken the initiative, with some pressure from gay organizations and individuals, to legislate same-sex marriage. In Canada, by contrast, you have gone through a path of constitutional challenge. That also occurred in Vermont in the United States in 1993. The outcome of that challenge, however, was not same-sex marriage, but a civil union.

These are constitutional challenges, so North America is taking a judicial path of reforms rather than the legislative path of the Europeans. I think the Canadian model is really interesting and I can see Hong Kong taking that path because right now, we don't have a fully elected Parliament. We call it legislative counsel in Hong Kong, so I think it would be beneficial if we had a judicial or constitutional challenge. By getting married in Canada and having it recognized in Hong Kong, this will set the precedent so anybody coming after us should be protected. That is why we came all the way from Hong Kong to get married here.

N: We travelled to Vermont in December 2001 and went through the civil union arrangement. When we returned to Hong Kong to ask for recognition of it, however, the Hong Kong government said that the union was not equivalent to marriage. They recognize marriage, but not civil unions. That is why we needed to become legally married here.

K: *Does this mean that the two of you are the very first gay couple to marry in Hong Kong?*

R: We think so; although there is a remote possibility that somebody did it secretly without publicizing it. We are at least the first couple from Hong Kong that has been acknowledged by the media.

K: *I wouldn't think that most people in Canada or the United States know much about Hong Kong. Do you know the population?*

R: It is six or seven million people [and] more than 95% of them [are] Chinese. The British ruled us until 1997, so we follow a common law system. We have a mini Constitution and a Bill of Rights that guarantees human rights to citizens of Hong Kong. We will have to evoke that for our marriage to be recognized because it provides marriage rights, family rights and other similar matters.

K: *What has happened in Hong Kong since the British ended their rule in 1997?*

R: Hong Kong was handed over to China, or from China's point of view, we were reunited. Although we are again part of China, Hong Kong preserves its own legal, economic and social system. Consequently, it is a capitalist state rather a communist state. It has the premise of one country with two systems. In this way, it preserves what Hong Kong has been.

N: So that is the reason why we call Hong Kong...a special administrative region.

K: *If same-sex marriage becomes legalized in Hong Kong, could the Communist government of mainland China enact legislation to prevent it?*

N: They can, but they probably wouldn't. They want to be known as liberal, or at least not as ultra- conservative. They also want to maintain their reputation of non-interference with Hong Kong's policies.

R: There are three areas in which the central government can interfere with Hong Kong. One is related to diplomatic relations, second is military defense, and third is anything that is related to or has a direct impact on the central government. The third criterion is a bit unclear.

K: *What is it like to live in Hong Kong right now?*

R: Because we were a British colony, we had anti-sodomy laws until 1991, which were called Buckley laws in our country. Basically, the criminal code before 1991 said that men having sex with each other is illegal. The British abolished that law in their own country in 1967, so we had a huge gap in bringing this legal reform to Hong Kong. Since 1991, it has been okay to be gay publicly. Since 1991, more than twenty lesbian and gay organizations have been established in Hong Kong. Consequently, a lot has happened in Hong Kong concerning liberation for gays and lesbians over the past ten years. It is becoming increasingly more acceptable to be gay. For example, we express public affection all the time in our neighbourhood and it has been okay. We feel safe to hold hands and even kiss on the street.

K: *How and when did your relationship start?*

N: We met each other nine years ago through our activism. We worked for two different gay activist organizations. I was working for the 10 Percent Club and the Black Minority Christian Fellowship, which is a gay church in Hong Kong. Roddy was working for Horizons. This meant that we had a lot of chances to meet each other, although we weren't interested in each other at first. We came together to organize some conferences five and a half years ago, and it was then that we finally got into each other.

R: At first, we thought it was only going to be a one-night stand, but by the end of organizing the conferences, we worked out quite well together. Nelson moved in quite quickly following this and that is how we started our relationship.

K: *Do you have a date that you celebrated prior to your marriage, recognizing when you started dating?*

R: Yes we do—June 15, 1998.

N: I am not the kind of person that would commit to someone for the rest of my life easily. From the beginning, however, it seemed right that I would stay with Roddy. There is always a chance that our lives will change, our personalities, our habits, or whatever. At this moment, we are very connected to each other's lives, but there could come a time when we need to separate.

R: I think our lives blended gradually together. I wouldn't say there was a point where I would have said, "Oh, this is the guy." Nelson is quite a gentle guy and he has provided our relationship a lot of space. We gradually realized that there was room for us to grow in this relationship. We are lovers and soulmates. We share many interests, such as activism and travelling. In our first year, we went on more than six trips together.

K: *How did you propose marriage to each other?*

R: I am Chinese and there may be some cultural differences that you need to understand. I have spent most of my life in Hong Kong, which is quite a Chinese society, and I do not adhere to the Western model of dating, getting married, and having kids. We didn't actually propose to one another. We decided that we had been together a significant amount of time, and we felt strongly for each other. We thought that we could continue to live together for a long time, so we talked about getting married.

N: When we travelled to the United States and ended up in Vermont, we weren't initially planning to have a civil union. We started out by travelling to Boston to visit a friend. We learned about civil unions in Vermont from a Web site. We went to Boston and New York and then decided to drive a bit further to Vermont to get the civil union done.

R: At the time, I was studying and he was working full-time. We thought if the civil union were recognized in Hong Kong, it would give us the legal protection and tax breaks that we wanted. That is why we went for the civil union.

K: *What was it like to come out to your family?*

N: There has been a lot of tolerance and acceptance of homosexuality in Chinese culture and throughout the long history of China. The main aim of the family is to produce offspring for the next generation. If that is done, anything else will be all right. After a man has his offspring, he can have either a homosexual or heterosexual relationship—that is acceptable within the family system. Chinese people are conscious of creating the next generation, and this takes precedence over erotic desire.

R: Basically, Chinese people don't care what happens in the four walls of your bedroom. The long history of same-sex love in China is well documented in literature. It is not so well-known in the West.

K: *I'm aware of this, but I understood that in contemporary Chinese society, they had adopted more of a modern-day negativity toward gay people. When you look at Communist China and Hong Kong, are the cultures pretty much the same?*

R: No, they are not the same, but mainland China never had any sodomy laws: they never criminalized sexual behaviour between members of the same gender. I think that is one area where you can see a greater tolerance for same-sex relationships. When you say modern China, they still don't have the baggage of homosexuality being a sin or a crime.

This is not to say that same-sex marriage will be welcomed in Hong Kong. There is still a gap because marriage for the Chinese is very much about procreation. There is a need to have your own children by blood—adopting children is not sufficient within the Chinese value system. It is a duty that you bring offspring to your family line, and that is the idea behind so-called Chinese tradition.

K: *Do you have living parents back in Hong Kong?*

R: Yes.

K: *I assume your mother knows you were coming to Canada to get married. How has she reacted to that?*

R: She is cool about it. My mom is quite unique—she is not the average over-sensitive sixty-year-old woman in Hong Kong. She is quite unconventional, despite being born in a small rural village in China. Although she is not highly educated, she always did unconventional things. For instance, in rural China, women are not allowed to work in the field. My mother, however, was somebody who would volunteer to do that because our family needed another person to work in the field. Some relatives despised her for doing this. I think I have inherited part of her unconventionality.

K: *When did you tell your mom that you are gay?*

R: At roughly age twenty-five—I am thirty-six now. There are eight children in my family, including myself. All of them are very supportive of who I am.

K: *Excellent. Let me now switch to you, Nelson. What was it like when you told your mom and dad?*

N: My dad is quite a traditional Chinese family man. We never talked a word about homosexuality, but he is showing support to Roddy and me. My dad always asks me to bring Roddy to festivals and family gatherings. I could sense that before we came here, he received a lot of pressure from friends and relatives to my family. It is okay in my family to get along with a same-sex partner, but not publicly. It is the public displays in the media that pressure my dad.

I have a younger sister who is very supportive. I told her I am gay fifteen years ago, and she comforted my mom and dad with they found out. I never talked to my dad about my homosexuality so there is no official time that I came out to him. I think he is okay now with accepting my sexuality.

K: *What about your mother?*

N: My mother is divorced with my father, and she is very supportive of Roddy and me. She never had an issue in supporting our relationship. I think it is common that Chinese men are more homophobic than Chinese women, perhaps especially in the case of my family. My dad was not accepting for the first two to three years, and then it gradually improved.

K: *When did you tell her?*

N: About eight or nine years ago.

K: *At what age did you know that you were gay?*

N: I'm not sure because I used to have girlfriends. My first gay relationship started ten years ago. I had relationships with other boys when I was in high school. I remember having a crush on another boy when I was fourteen years old. I was attending an all boys' school at the time, so perhaps that's why I only had crushes on boys. That school is called Queen's College. (*Laughter ensues.*) I never had sex back then, but I did hug and kiss other boys.

K: *You mentioned earlier that 95% of Hong Kong is Chinese. Is the religion then mostly Buddhist?*

R: No, I think it is mostly atheist—same as mainland China. Communism suppresses religion.

K: *Do you come from a religious belief system, Roddy?*

R: Yes, I am a Christian. Our families are mostly atheist, however.

K: *I imagine that atheism in general is fairly positive toward homosexuality because judgments are not coming from a Bible or some other religious document. Buddhism is also supportive of gay people. If I was living in Hong Kong and got a job there, would I be able to tell my employer and my co-workers that I am gay, or would I want to keep that to myself in 2003?*

R: I think it is okay to tell your employer.

N: But that depends on the job you're in. If you are a professor, a hairdresser or a fashion designer, it is probably all right. However, if you are a physician, social worker, dentist or secondary-school teacher, you should keep it to yourself.

R: You can tell your employer, but people don't feel the need to know. People don't feel the need to come out in Hong Kong.

N: That may not be part of their identity. Their identity may be built on their title, their job, or on other things unrelated to their sexual orientation. The Chinese gay people that we know are somewhat indifferent about their sexual status.

R: Their sexual orientation as an identity is not as strong as in other places because it is just one of their many identities. For example, I am a man, I am Chinese, I am middle class, and I am a lawyer. These are the identities that have more significance to people in Hong Kong and China.

K: *When you attend a social function where you are meeting other people, you would have no hesitation in saying to other people, "This is my husband, or this is my partner, whatever the expression would be?"*

R: No, not for the two of us.

K: *The two of you are gay activists. Do you think most gay couples would be as forthright?*

R: It may be an issue for some. Some people may not be as forthright in admitting that. Some people may not be in a relationship, so introducing their partner becomes a non-issue.

K: *You said earlier that procreation is an important part of being in a relationship in Chinese culture. Would it be better for the two of you if you were to have children by either donating your semen or by directly impregnating a woman?*

N: What family name would we give to our child?

R: We can give the child both of our last names, but in my case, I don't have to fulfill that expectation because I come from a big family. I need to be more precise: so long as there is somebody in the family who has children, they will be fine—especially if it is the eldest son or daughter.

N: Mainly the son because the son will have offspring to carry the family name.

K: *Roddy, you have older brothers, but you do not, Nelson. Is there an expectation on you to have a child?*

N: I think the expectation has vanished already. My dad no longer expects that I will have a child, but I think he would be pleased if we did have one.

K: *If you are a married man with four children in Hong Kong, and you later realize that your stronger attraction is toward men, how would Hong Kong society look at you?*

R: Let's talk about China. I understand there are a lot of gay men in China that are married to a woman, perhaps mostly because the entire social system surrounds an ocean of marriage and family. If you are not married, you don't receive public housing—you don't get a place to live. Men have to get married to have a place to live. There is also a high expectation from society to get married.

Hong Kong is different. If you get married as a gay man, that will camouflage you and people will stop asking the embarrassing question, "When are you going to get married?" However, if they know you have a lover and you are married to a woman, they will [pass] more judgment on you. They will think it is not right to be married and have a lover, concubine, or mistress at the same time.

N: I see loyalty as the issue that people would focus on. Many bisexual individuals would not be seen as loyal to either gender. If a man has a wife and a boyfriend, I think the main focus from others would be on [his] lack of loyalty and fidelity. In that example, society would judge that man more harshly than a monogamous gay man with one boyfriend. Furthermore, I don't think the wife would accept it if she found out her husband had another lover—whether the lover was male or female, although it would probably create a worse perception if his lover was another man. The end result will likely be divorce.

K: *I see. Is there a metaphor, a piece of music, a poem, a piece of art or a story that speaks to your feelings or thoughts about same-sex marriage?*

N: I think of a train as a metaphor. I feel quite safe within the train, and there is a destiny I am going to with the train. The same is true of marriage, although I am not sure where it is going, but I feel quite safe in it. It will transport me to some place.

K: *Thank you, Nelson. Do you have one that speaks to you, Roddy?*

R: There is a movie starring Julianne Moore and Dennis Quaid, circa 1960. It was called *Far and Away*, or something like that. [NOTE: The movie is actually *Far From Heaven*, set in the 1950s.]

K: *What would you put in a "hope box" for gay people? What do you think still needs to happen within the gay community in Hong Kong?*

R: Personally, I believe that every gay or lesbian person should come out within his or her capacity. For some, that would mean coming out to their friends or families only. I think this is very important because when real people come out, it makes an impact on the people who know you and respect you. Media portrayals of gay and lesbian people are great, but they are distant stories to most viewers. If more people come out in Hong Kong, it will create a big change in our society. It will produce less discrimination and greater acceptance of legal reform, including same-sex marriage.

K: *What is your sense, Nelson?*

N: I think gay and lesbian people need to celebrate. We are not doing something according to tradition—instead, we are breaking a lot of boundaries and I think that is worth celebrating. A lot of people used to stay in the closet, and now when we come out, we need to recapture the fun that we lost when we were closeted or in denial.

K: *Do you have gay pride marches in Hong Kong?*

R: Not yet, but we did have a parade on July 1, 2003. It was an anti-government parade, although we did include a gay and lesbian procession. It wasn't a gay parade per se, however. There is still a problem with visibility—many gay and lesbian people do not want to be visible.

K: *How many gay and lesbian bars are there in Hong Kong?*

N: We have around twenty gay bars and others that include a gay and lesbian clientele.

K: *How many bathhouses would there be in Hong Kong?*

N: Somewhere between fifteen and twenty.

K: *It sounds like, in terms of religion and family, Hong Kong is more accepting than Canadians are presently. But in terms of visibility, it is less so right now. I could keep asking questions, but I know your time is limited today. Did you have anything else that you think should be said that I haven't asked you?*

R: There are several high-school aged activists that are gay, lesbian or bisexual. They go to other high schools and colleges telling people what it is like to be gay and lesbian. A lot of that is occurring in our society. We have got to know many of them, and they often come to our house to have dinner and hang out. Sometimes they ask advice from us because we are the older generation. They call us dads and we treat them as our kids. They are younger and we share this relationship with them. They enjoy our company and they refrain from treating us like babbling parents. In this sense, we have created our own family, a self-chosen family of people we value and care about. We have created a space for them to hang around, because space is a scarce resource in Hong Kong. They feel comfortable being themselves when they are with us.

K: *Let me ask you one other thing—what are the stereotypes of gay people in Hong Kong? If you were to ask most North Americans, "What are gay men and lesbians like?", they would probably describe a feminine man and a masculine woman.*

N: I think they would describe gay men and lesbians similarly to the North American stereotypes.

R: I have to disagree. I think that in Hong Kong, the stereotypes or expectations of men and women are not as polarized as in Western culture. Many Westerners would view Chinese men as tender, gentle and soft. This means the difference between the genders is not as great as compared to here. Consequently, I don't think Chinese men and woman are as polarized regarding the gender roles of masculinity and femininity.

K: *Okay, another question—in Chinese culture, it is traditional for the husband to be head of the household and for younger people to show respect to the elders. With the two of you getting married, who will be the head of the household?*

N: That depends on the task at hand. We have strengths in different areas, so if it is about gardening or our pets, I become the head of the household and I give the orders. If it is about computers or technology, Roddy will give the orders.

K: *Okay, let's say you're purchasing a new house—who will have the final say?*

R: Whoever pays for it. I see our relationship as very dynamic, and [it] changes depending on our life circumstances. The beauty of marriage is that we can really share our resources. You can support each other when you have different financial and emotional needs. We somehow shift roles about who is the breadwinner, who is the head of the household, and who makes decisions for the family. We try to treat each other as equals, with both of us contributing in a responsible, fair manner to each other.

K: *Thank you very much. I really appreciate the two of you being here today.*

Robert Berry and Leslie Sheare
photo by Stéphan Grégoire

Oscar and Felix

Robert Berry and Leslie Sheare

Date: September 28, 2003
Time: 10:20 am
Place: Telephone Interview (couple lives in Mississauga, Ontario)

Coming across Robert and Les was most serendipitous. While waiting at the Second Cup in Toronto at Church and Wellesley to talk to the couple from Hong Kong, I noticed a woman sitting at the next table editing or marking what looked like an academic paper. A kindred spirit I thought, perhaps even a professor. I started talking to her and mentioned why I was there that day. She said she knew of a gay male couple that had been together for forty-seven years. I said I would be delighted if she passed on my e-mail address to them, and by the time I returned to Calgary, their message was waiting for me....

Robert and Les met before I was born, and by the time of my birth they were already in love. That's remarkable because, back then, in the eyes of the law and in the eyes of the mental health field, Robert and Les were criminals with a mental illness.

Robert and Les are neither criminal nor disturbed. But they are two opposites. Love is what brought them together, and love is what keeps them together. Funny how society forced them to have a courtship of forty-seven years, while most other adults across the country were allowed to marry immediately if they so desired.

R: It has been just wonderful for the two of us over the years. There is more to love in each other every day. It was kind of rough and tumble in the beginning, however. Our relationship is a give and take situation. Somebody has to say he's sorry if something goes wrong so that everything can start running smoothly again.

K: *Where did the two of you meet and how did your relationship initially develop?*

R: I met Les when I was leaving Parkdale [one day] when [it] wasn't the best part of town…. I met him on St. Patrick's Day, March 17, 1956. He was staying with a friend of his that he grew up with in Thunder Bay. His friend had called me and mentioned that he had a very nice fellow there that I should meet. I invited Les over to my little bachelor apartment to have a drink and chat, and he kept coming back each day, and each day he would get another parking ticket….

After a month or so, someone broke into his car and took completely everything out of the dash. At that point, I said to him, "Why don't you just move in with me because then you will have a decent parking spot, and we could be together on a regular basis." In the beginning, it was more of a physical attraction, but then it grew much more into love.

K: *What was it like to be gay in 1956?*

L: Well, you had to keep things secret about your personal life. We were called names many times by different people. They would call you a "faggot" or a "queer" as we walked down the street together. We had an awful time trying to get an apartment together. With two women it was fine, but two gentlemen trying to rent an apartment was taboo. Other than that, we just went along with our daily lives.

K: *Was it common for men to be in long-term relationships back then?*

L: No, they were very short-term relationships. Most people met at bars downtown, which usually resulted in one-night stands. There weren't any stable relationships that we knew of at the time.

K: *Were there gay bars then?*

R: They weren't really known as gay bars, however, many gay people frequented them.

L: Well, there were some, Robert, like the Letrose, the St. Charles, and the Westbury Hotel in Toronto.

K: *It was a different time because homosexuality was illegal in Canada until 1969.*

R: That's right, yes, until Trudeau stepped in there.

K: *What could have happened to you back then? Were you concerned that the police might arrest you?*

R: Well, several things could have happened to us, Kevin. For one, we could have gone to jail. Thankfully, we never came across that.

L: We could have lost our jobs and everything else, you know.

R: Yes, we would have definitely lost our jobs.

K: *Was it common practice back then that people would lose their jobs for being out?*

L: Yes, and even so today.

K: *That is fascinating. How did the two of you persist knowing the view of most people in society?*

L: Well, I guess we condescended to the way that heterosexuals lived. (*Laughter.*) We lived in the same apartment buildings as all of them, and we kept to ourselves. Whenever there was a heterosexual function requiring a date, we knew young women that would accompany us. We didn't want to go by ourselves because it didn't look right or proper.

K: *Who did know that you were a couple?*

R: Very few people—mostly those in the gay world. Friday nights or Saturday nights were the nights to go out, so we would go to the bar and talk with different people. We always made sure our physicians knew that we were gay.

K: *What about your family members?*

R: I had a more difficult time with my mother than Les had with his family. Les' family was more understanding of the situation. My mother constantly hounded me to get married and have children. She never fully accepted Les, although Les was always there for her no matter what.

L: Yeah, she felt that I was leading her son astray. (*Laughter.*)

K: *Well, you probably were—didn't you know Robert was really straight? He has just been going through a phase! (Laughter.) When did you come out to your family, Robert?*

R: When I started dating Les, my mother was in total shock. She sat in the living room and said, "What have I done wrong? Where did I go wrong?" You hear this from so many mothers. I told her that she had raised three children with no support and with no father. That was tough on her, and I tried to explain that to her. She had suggested that I see a psychiatrist. I said, "It won't do me any good to speak to a psychiatrist. This is the way I am and you're just going to have to accept it." Les' parents were much more understanding and they have accepted me as one of their sons.

K: *You told your mom in 1956. What age would you have been then?*

R: I was nineteen. I had only come out to myself a year earlier. There was an incident around that. I was out with my mother, her friends, and a married gentleman who was a little older than me. He followed me into a washroom and we touched and felt each other. I realized then that I was gay. It was clear to me that I preferred men to women, despite having dated some girls before.

K: *Les, when did you come out to yourself?*

L: I was out at age eleven.

K: *Oh, you little tramp. (Laughter.)*

R: Seriously, he was!

L: I knew I was different and I knew that I liked men more than girls. All the girls I knew used to come to me for advice on their boyfriends.

K: *Did these girls know you were gay?*

L: I think so.

K: *When did you come out to your family?*

L: I think my parents always knew that I was a bit different. I told my mother when I was about sixteen. I thought she was going to pass on, but she didn't thank goodness. From then on, she always clipped things out of magazines and put them under her favourite chair cushion. When I was around, she would say, "Do you see what you can get with this, or what's this, or do you know about this?" (*Laughter.*)

R: I remember taking her to Minneapolis, Minnesota, for a weekend with us. We stayed at a hotel and Les went down to the restaurant while she and I sat on the bed watching a movie. She started lecturing me on how different we were, "You know you have to look after each other, you know you're different from most people, you only have each other, etcetera." She was just wonderful.

L: She was being protective of me.

K: *Les, was your father in the picture as well?*

L: Yes. I had a stepdad since I was twelve months old, an absolutely marvellous man. He told me that he didn't care what my lifestyle was—I was his son and he loved me.

R: I was accepted as part of his family. Whenever we went out together, I was always introduced as the other son.

L: He was introduced as their "adopted" son.

K: *You were sixteen when you told them. What year would that have been?*

L: That was in about 1954.

K: *Did either of them threaten to send you to a psychiatrist or get you locked up?*

L: My mother confided in my aunt, her sister, and they decided I should go and see a shrink. So I went to a woman and she just turned around and told my mother and my aunt, "Your son is perfectly well-adjusted. Leave him alone, he's fine."

K: *Yeah—he just happens to be a queen. (Laughter.) Nothing we can do to cure that.*

L: Exactly—all I need to find is a prince.

R: And you did.

K: *I think it's hard for most people to appreciate what things were like back then. Our young generation really hasn't got a clue.*

R: You had to be so cautious.

K: *Do either one of you have siblings?*

L & R: No.

R: Back in the 1970s, Les and I legally raised my niece from the time she was fifteen. I had legal guardianship of her. Her stepfather had abused her and my sister didn't want to press charges. My niece ran away and we took her in. We got her through high school and she turned out to be a very well-adjusted young lady. She stayed with us for five years, and now lives in Vancouver.

L: While she stayed with us, we made her do chores for her allowance. We taught her responsibility.

R: She also gave us some of her money each week toward the house. She was a little sweetheart.

K: *You are still in touch with her, right? Does she view you as her parents?*

L: I think she views us as her aunt and uncle. (*Laughter.*)

K: *And I won't ask which one of you is the aunt...*

R: It's Leslie.

L: No, it's Robert.

K: *I said I wasn't going to ask. What has kept you two together this long?*

R: Our love and caring for each other. Les is a very giving, kind soul and he has a good sense of humour too. We do have our little bickering sessions like every other couple. We used to have serious arguments at one time, but now we're just down to bickering.

K: *When did you guys get married?*

R: August 9, 2003. We were saving for our motorhome, but we thought what the hell. We've been together forty-seven years and I think that we should make the wedding a big splash. We spent the money, and we don't regret one bit of it.

K: *I think you've had the longest courtship I've ever heard of! (Laughter.)*

R: That's true. I sometimes wonder how we ever managed to stay together this long without killing each other.

K: *Do you celebrate anniversaries of some kind?*

R: Yes, we celebrate March 17 because that's the actual day we met. We did have a commitment ceremony in 1972 at Holy Trinity Church, but March 17 is the day we celebrate as our anniversary. Our friends, including our straight friends, throw us a party at the local pub each year.

K: *Now that you're married, are you going to have a second anniversary each year?*

R: I think we're just going to leave it at March 17 because most people are aware that that's the day we normally celebrate it.

L: That means I have to buy two anniversary cards a year?

K: *That's what I was thinking, and then you can also celebrate the commitment ceremony, and have three anniversaries. You'll never get that motorhome, you know.*

L: We do haunt a family-oriented pub here in [Port Credit] and everyone there accepts us, including all of the married couples and children. It's just wonderful. Even the owners, their daughter, and her fiancé were at the wedding. We deal with law firms in our business and the lawyers were at the wedding as well. One of the senior partners gave a speech. These are all heterosexual people, and it feels marvellous to be accepted by them.

K: *Well, I think most people would have a hard time discounting your relationship given its duration.*

L: The straight people we know say they haven't reached forty-seven years. I think some of them are a bit amazed.

R: Kevin, did you say that you just turned forty-seven a week ago?

K: *Yeah, on September 20.*

R: We were dating when you were born.

K: *I know—I find that astounding. Most people my age don't even think about being gay before the 1970s.*

R: Oh, you're still a neophyte then.

K: *Exactly. Do you see your relationship as the same or different from heterosexual married couples?*

L: Oh dear. Well, one difference is we can't have children, which is kind of a nice thing.

R: Gay couples are now allowed to adopt, but at our age, we are just too old to start raising children.

L: Oh goodness, I don't want children at my age—the stretch marks would never go away! (*Laughter.*) I think gay male relationships might be more challenging than heterosexual or lesbian relationships. Males tend to be more aggressive than females, and it can be challenging to have two male personalities living together. You have to have a give and take situation and understand that there are going to be problems and talk about them when they arise.

R: Les and I are definitely opposites, though. Les is a typical Taurus and I am a Pisces.

K: *My partner is a Taurus and that means certain things to me. What are these traits that make the two of you quite different?*

R: Les's temper and his aggressiveness. He tries to be dominant, but it doesn't work.

K: *Now I know who's on top.*

R: Yeah. (*Laughter.*) He does look after all of the finances, and if I'm nice, he gives me an allowance. (*Laughter.*)

K: *Les, what are some of the qualities that make Robert a real Pisces?*

L: Well he's OCD [obsessive-compulsive disorder]. He picks everything off the rug—I never have to worry about the place being dirty. He's easygoing, and a bit of a dreamer, which I like. He is also dependable and steady.

R: And I make sure he looks nice and neat all the time.

L: Yeah, he dresses me.

R: I'm the Felix and he's the Oscar. That's what they call us all the time.

L: You got that right.

K: *None other than The Odd Couple—great. (Laughter.)*

R: Les is the also the cook, but these days, we eat out a lot because of business. We are too tired when we get home to do anything.

L: I also fix the cars if something goes wrong.

R: Yeah, she's a tough babe.

L: In my younger years they called me the "diesel dyke" because I was always working on cars.

K: *I wonder…you two have been together so long, why did you even bother getting married at this late stage?*

R: We thought we would like to make it legal. We had talked [about how] if it ever did become legal, we would probably do it. We feel more strongly bound to one another than we did before. Marriage also includes pension benefits, which means something to us as we age.

L: We always protected each other with a crossover will. If something happened to one of us, everything went to the other one.

K: *You said earlier that there weren't many couples in relationships when you first started dating. We often think that we learn how to relate to each other through role models. Who taught the two of you how to relate to each other?*

R: I think it was just ourselves.

L: Yeah, just common sense. When you have been around the track a few times, you develop an idea about what you are looking for in a soulmate, and what features you want in a life partner. Everybody is looking for a Prince Charming, but he never appears. You have to settle for a little less.

R: I beg your pardon! (*Laughter.*)

L: My mother passed away in 1988, but she bought us a little squirrel holding a nut that we still have. She said, "Every time you get into a little tiff or a battle, look at the squirrel and remember it's me telling you that you're both nuts."

R: All of my family, including my mother, my brother and my sister, passed away within five years of each other.

L: We're orphans.

R: We had a few tough years there when our parents and my brother and sister were ill.

K: *I can imagine. When was the last time you were called a derogatory name for being gay?*

R: Three weeks ago actually. We were with our friends at the pub. There [was] a man and woman sitting behind us, and they were very rude. They especially centred out Les and called him all kinds of terrible names. It was very embarrassing. One of the girls we were with was ready to slap the woman if she didn't stop mouthing off to her. Then the man came over and put his arm around Les and that did it.

L: I said to the man, "Excuse me, did I invite you over here?" He said, "No," and I said "Well then, take your arm off of me before I smack you one in the kisser!" (*Laughter.*)

K: *Perhaps this is the aggression you're talking about, Robert?*

L: Well, they obviously had one or two too many.

R: Then the owner came over, gave them their cheque, and asked them to leave. They said they would never come back there again, and we all shouted, "Goodbye!" (*Laughter.*)

K: *Great. Do the two of you ever walk hand in hand?*

L: No, no.

K: *Do you kiss in public?*

L: No.

K: *Should I go on?*

R: No.

L: You were leaning all over me in the bar the other day.

R: Well, a little peck maybe, but not something big or obvious.

K: *Do you think you are still holding back more than straight couples do?*

R: Yeah, to a point, because I don't think we ever walked hand in hand down the street.

K: *What if you're on Church Street on Toronto, or Davie Street in Vancouver?*

R: No, we've never done that.

L: All you do is put your hand on my ass all the time. (*Laughter.*)

K: *Yeah, but you don't hold hands, because that would be too out there.*

R: That's just to get him to move a little faster.

K: *We all need a push from time to time. What advice would you give to gay couples that are thinking about getting married?*

R: I'd certainly say, don't jump into it right away—that would be crazy. Get to know that person very well before you even begin thinking about marriage. If you just meet someone and you've only gone out for a couple of months, you can run into all sorts of problems, especially if you are younger.

K: *At what point do you think the two of you would have been ready to make this commitment?*

R: I think maybe after five years.

L: Yeah, five years from now. (*Laughter.*)

K: *Yeah, after about fifty years together, one is almost ready to seal the knot.*

L: Seriously, I would say at around age thirty, but you also need to know that person really well too.

R: We attend frequently at various courts throughout Ontario to file and process court proceedings regarding civil actions. We've seen several cases where heterosexual couples have been married for a week and then they apply for a divorce a week or a month later. It's amazing.

K: *What do you think will be the impact of same-sex marriage on the gay community?*

R: I think we will see more gay couples getting married. I'm sure there are other couples that have been together for many years that are now thinking seriously about it.

L: We have neighbours upstairs who have been together for thirty-three years. Perhaps they will consider marriage.

…

K: *Do you think that straight society will come to see us differently?*

R: I don't think we will see that in our lifetime. A lot of progress has been made since we first came out, but I don't think it ever really will be accepted.

K: *I often think about women and minority groups, and despite legislation protecting their rights, they still suffer prejudice and various forms of discrimination. Is there a metaphor, an image, a movie, a piece of music or perhaps a poem that speaks to your feelings or thoughts about same-sex marriage?*

R: The song "I Am What I Am" says it well for me.

K: What about you, Les?

L: I don't know of one. My thoughts are I'll live my life and you live yours. I have nothing against heterosexuals, bisexuals, homosexuals or other sexual minorities. We need to live together and enjoy each other's company. Actually, a movie that does come to mind is *Torch Song Trilogy*. That was a wonderful movie.

K: *What would you put in a "hope box" for gay people? What still needs to happen within the gay community itself?*

L: Gay guys have to realize that sex isn't everything.

R: I agree there.

L: It may be the physical attraction that gets you going in the beginning, but it will not sustain a relationship. There's a lot more to life than sex, like experiencing everything around you.

R: I find that more so in gay men then in lesbian women. The physical thing seems to be more with the males.

L: I see you look out of the car window every once in a while! (*Laughter.*)

R: Well, there's no harm in looking, right?

L: Well, there is if you're driving.

K: *We've talked about some of the changes that need to happen in the gay community, particularly with regard to gay men. What changes still need to happen in mainstream society?*

R: I think they need to give more consideration to people like us.

L: I think it's a two-way street. Gays also have to realize that heterosexuals have their space also, and the gays have to have theirs. We need to live in harmony with one another and forget the sexual differences. We need to accept each other as human beings.

R: That's right. We should be able to intermingle with one another without hassles.

L: I think any male that is down [on] homosexuals probably has the greatest curiosity in [his] own mind as to what it is like, and [he's] scared of [his] own feelings.

R: Perhaps [he is] afraid of [his] own sexuality.

L: Yeah, because when you find a heterosexual that is perfectly happy with his heterosexual life, he doesn't feel challenged by a gay person sitting next to him.

K: *Exactly. Those are all the questions I wanted to ask the two of you. Is there something that I missed that really needs to be said about same-sex marriage or long-term gay relationships?*

L: Live your life to the fullest and be open-minded: life is changing everyday.

R: This is 2003, yet we have a long way to go in terms of becoming accepting of everyone who is unlike ourselves. Although a percentage of gay people live around Church Street and are accepted there because that area is known as the centre of gay life in Toronto, others may not feel that way where there are mostly heterosexual people living.

We have people in the building where we are that give us that "look." You can sense that they don't like us or at least frown on us because we are gay. I'm sure there are many people in the building who have heard about us getting married.

L: That's just because you ordered the limo up to the front. (*Laughter.*)

K: *I think many of us from Alberta assume that now it must be quite good to live in Ontario and B.C. because of legalized same-sex marriage. The fact that you still get snarky looks and derogatory comments suggests that all is not necessarily well in Ontario.*

L: Well, the people we get the looks from and the comments are usually over age thirty-five. Younger people are more into what's happening. They are also more accepting of the changes occurring in the world. It's the older group that refuses to change. Those that are calling us "faggots" in private have likely had their own same-sex experiences. In our condo complex, we only know of one other gay couple. The model sometimes comes to our door.

K: *You have a model living there?*

L: Yes.

K: *I obviously should have interviewed you guys at your own condo, and of course your neighbour would have to be invited—I'm trying to do comprehensive interviews, after all. (Laughter.) Is there anything else that either one of you would like to add?*

L: No, I think you have the gist of our story.

R: I agree.

K: *Thank you very much for the interview.*

Brent and Steve Scheuerman-Stallone

On Common Ground

Brent and Steve Scheuerman-Stallone

Date: October 5, 2003
Time: 1:00 pm
Place: Telephone Interview (Kansas City, Kansas)

This is my second telephone interview. While talking to Brent and Steve, I couldn't help but feel disappointed that I wasn't actually meeting these fine men in person. The relationship that develops between us in less than two hours is real, however. What's missing is a hug at the end. Brent and Steve are on common ground more than most couples, as you will soon discover.

S: Our marriage brought us much closer together. I'm sure we live our lives differently compared to heterosexuals, but the feelings are the same inside. We are also different people with differences of opinion. I don't care that we happen to be two men: we want to have the same rights as everyone else.

B: Although we are now legally married, we have been married for a long time. We have been together for twelve years, but [have] known each other far longer.

K: *Where did you guys first meet?*

B: We met about twenty-five years ago in Topeka, Kansas (about sixty miles from where we live now and the capital of the state). There was kind of a tight gay community in Topeka where everybody knows everybody. I was with my current lover, and when that relationship broke up, he started going out with Steve. I hated Steve immensely because I thought that he took him away from me. Unbeknownst to one another, we both ended up living in Kansas City. One night we met at a bar, but we didn't recognize each other at first. Steve is the one that first remembered who I was. We dated for about one month before we moved in together.

K: *It sounds like the connection was fairly quick between the two of you.*

B: Yeah, we realized that's the way it should have been a long time ago. We just made the wrong move.

K: *I am not familiar with what's happening in Kansas currently. Is same-sex marriage now legal in Kansas?*

B: NO, same-sex marriage is not legal anywhere in the United States.

K: *I didn't think so. Where did you guys get married?*

B: We married on June 28, 2003, in Toronto, Ontario.

S: The unusual thing about this is that one of the lawyers who made marriage possible in Canada said that if we file any documents and do not put down that we're married, we are committing fraud, whether it is recognized or not. There are a lot of legalities that we've never crossed yet, such as how to now file income tax returns.

K: *Do you have a sense that there are a lot of Americans coming up to Canada to get married?*

B: There are quite a few, but not as many as you might expect because it is still a symbolic act for us in the United States.

S: While we were in Toronto, we were requested to be part of the Gay Pride Parade. There is a picture of us riding with half of our bodies out of a limo. At one point in our shop back home, one of our customers congratulated us on getting married. We wondered how he found out. It turns out AOL, which is the largest ISP in the United States, had us on [its] welcome screen for two days with this picture.

B: Everybody saw it.

S: So there we were, two guys that went to Canada to marry privately and it ended up being very public. We were interviewed by *Newsweek*, the

Philadelphia Enquirer, the *New York Times,* Canadian TV, Korean TV, Japanese TV and several others.

K: *You'll be making more news with the release of this book. What do you most value about your partner?*

B: Unconditional love. I know without a doubt that we will be together for the rest of our lives.

S: Yeah, I agree—it's too hard to train a new one.

K: *What are some of the issues that the two of you have had to work through?*

S: We have had to deal with our differences of opinion and family issues. They weren't gay-related: they were just general family issues. We had to work through them, but we have done it. I am the sole survivor in my family, so Brent is it basically.

K: *Steve, how old were you when you first came out to yourself?*

S: I knew from the time I was probably about five or six years old. I was raised in Western Kansas, which is an agricultural society. You were either white Protestant or white Catholic. There was neither a gay community nor a black community. Other than that, it was fairly typical of America. I had to keep most of my gay experiences to myself. I never got to come out like many other people. When I moved to Topeka…and began college, I began to live my life as a gay man.

K: *How old were you then?*

S: I graduated in 1965, so I was probably about twenty-three or twenty-four.

K: *Brent, what age were you when you came out to yourself?*

B: I was twenty-seven when I came out. I had a boyfriend back in junior high school and dated throughout most of junior high and high school. At the time, my adoptive parents were extremely religious right. I went to church every night and twice on Sundays. Whenever the church was open, I went to church. They were Pentecostal.

K: *Before you came out at age twenty-seven, did you ever date women?*

B: I dated two women and then I got married. The marriage lasted about eighteen months.

K: *I did something similar before I came out. I was married for ten years.*

S: Oh my.

B: I have two adult children from the marriage, ages twenty-four and twenty-six.

K: *After you came out, were you still involved in their lives as they were growing up?*

B: Yes, pretty much. Their mother was totally against me and the kids reflected that. Legally, however, I got to see them and stuff like that, but I don't have much contact with them anymore.

K: *Have they accepted your same-sex marriage?*

B: I don't know if they know—I haven't talked to them in three years because of their choice.

K: *What day did you celebrate as your anniversary before you got married?*

B: We used to celebrate March 1. Now that we're married, I think we will have two celebrations each year.

S: There is a sweet girl who works for us, and we treat her as our adopted daughter. When we decided that we were going to get married, she looked at us and said, "I want to throw a reception for you." We had a huge reception in our backyard with nearly eighty-five people in attendance most of whom were straight couples with some children also in attendance. It was just wonderful. We wondered how our customers would respond to it.

We own a jewellery store called Southwest Jewels. The other day I was walking by our shop and one of our customers was driving by and waved to me. He suddenly braked, backed up and yelled, "Congratulations—my wife told me. I'm so proud of you!"

K: *Excellent. It sounds like you have had a lot of positive reaction, but have you experienced any negative reaction?*

B: Yes, we have, but almost all the negatives have been from gay people.

K: *From gay people?*

S: I think we became larger than life with all of the publicity, which incidentally was not our intention. We were simply going to have a small reception. I think the gay people who don't support us are a bit edgy. By putting us down, perhaps it makes them feel better. And some think that we should have waited until it was legal in the United States.

K: *Do you also have gay friends that have been supportive?*

S: Oh yeah—we have a large circle of acquaintances, but we are mostly private people.

B: On a balance sheet, however, we have still received more positive feedback than negative. My brother is also gay, and he had asked, "Why did you bother since it's not legal?" Now he's thinking about it. He has been in a relationship with a guy for three years.

K: *I imagine that if it does become legal in your state, your marriage date would be retroactive.*

B: I would imagine so too, but I don't expect to have same-sex marriage in the United States for quite a while.

S: You know, it's been great to get married. I will fight for it as part of my rights as an American citizen. If need be, with the circumstances and time being right, and/or if appropriate gay activists need us, we will be there to fight.

K: *Are you presently involved in any legal challenges regarding your marriage?*

B: No, but if we thought that getting involved in a joint action suit would help, we wouldn't hesitate.

S: We probably would have hesitated in the past because we aren't the kind to go up to our new customers and say, "I'm gay, and I'm glad you're here." By the same token, if a customer asked me if I am gay, I wouldn't lie. I think our perspective changed after we were in our own newspaper and in international news as well.

K: *Right. In your shop, do you both work largely the same hours?*

S: Yes, we were just talking about that in fact.

B: Yeah. It takes a special relationship to be able to work together, and live together, where you're never apart.

K: *Absolutely. You said earlier that your marriage is like any other marriage, but that there are some differences between your relationship and heterosexual couples that marry.*

S: There are differences, such as showing affection in public. We live in Kansas, which is in the middle of the Bible Belt of the United States. Some people are very redneck but most are pretty much Ma, Pa and the kids. We choose carefully whom we tell. If I held his hand as we walked into a restaurant, we would certainly get a lot of weird looks.

B: Until a year ago, we were one of thirteen states where the police could come to your door and arrest you for sodomy, even though they didn't actually do that in Kansas. However, this was done in another state. In four of these thirteen states, the anti-sodomy laws only applied to same-sex acts while in the other nine states [they] applied across the board to any act [of] sodomy. It was these sodomy laws that the U.S. Supreme Court overturned.

K: *When this is done at the national level, then it is automatically carried into every state?*

B: Yeah, but this creates a backlash. I think the government's response to same-sex marriage is partly a reaction to [the court's decision]. I don't know how you folks are raised in Canada, but here in the United States, we are raised with a belief that religion is always right, regardless of what your religion is. This creates conflict for a lot of us. If you challenge that religion, you are considered to not be religious. The President of the United States does not separate church and state. Nobody will challenge the President in

Kansas because then you would be seen as anti-religious, and nobody wants that label.

S: It's becoming a major problem in our country. It was different under Clinton's administration. Religion was not the driving force then.

B: George W. Bush wants to amend the American Constitution to define marriage as only between one man and one woman.

K: *How easy would that be to do?*

B: An amendment to the constitution is not easy—in fact it's very hard. But with enough religious groups saying, "If you go along with same-sex marriage, you are going against God," it is possible that George W. could pull this off, especially if he [is] re-elected.

S: The gay community and others who support human rights must be vocal. Otherwise, [Bush's proposed] legislation could simply slip through. Few gays as well as many heterosexuals do not realize the vastness of this amendment and how much they will lose. It is the first time that the constitution is [going] to be amended [in order to] discriminate.

K: *Were either of you ever the subject of discrimination, harassment, abuse or gay bashing?*

B: I have never been physically bashed, but verbally for sure. I have been fired twice for being gay, which they can legally do in Kansas. We run into discrimination here and there, and there are people that treat you differently. Steve has had some recent verbal ones. I've had rednecks come in, but many men prefer that Steve or I wait on them.

S: Recently I had a run-in with a salesperson. We have a no soliciting sign on our door, and I had just returned, walking inside with a customer. The salesperson entered, introduced himself to me, and said, "Can I show you what I have?" I said, "I'm really not interested." I was being polite. He said, "You won't even look?" and I replied, "I'm really not interested, and there's no reason to waste your time." He then attempted to forcibly push literature into my face so that I had to look, and I said, "I told you, I am not interested, now there's the door." The man looked angrily at me and said, "Are you a faggot?" I retorted, "Yes, I'm gay." He then took his middle finger from a clinched fist and jammed it into my chest at heart level. While pounding with his finger, he said, "You need to get God in your heart."

He jabbed me so hard it almost knocked me backwards. Then my temper got the better of me and I physically made the man leave with threats of calling the police. There were two women in the store during this incident. This was a dear friend of ours and our "adopted" daughter. Both were ready to intervene if need be to protect me and to witness his stupidity.

A lot of people tell us that they don't judge gay people or same-sex marriages. We have touched so many lives through our shop. A lot of these people probably wouldn't have responded so affirmatively at first, but we have changed their minds as they have come to know who we are as people.

K: *What do you think would be the societal impact of same-sex marriage if it were someday allowed in the United States?*

S: The social impact would not be as great as the legal impact from my point of view. However, there would be a definite social impact. One of the main ones that readily comes to mind is that many currently unheard or silent voices would be heard when it come to politics, rights and many social issues. These voices are presently, in many cases, afraid to come out and speak openly. They fear they might lose so much more than they could potentially gain due to non-protection on the job and negative social and police factors.

K: *Absolutely. What do you think would be the impact on the gay community if same-sex marriage became legal in the United States?*

B: We would finally have legal protections that right now we have to arrange through lawyers. An inexpensive marriage licence would take care of these matters. Although Steve and I are legally married in Canada, the United States considers us strangers to one another. Right now we have no rights.

K: *Do you think there are any drawbacks to same-sex marriage?*

S: You can't sleep around? (*Laughter.*)

B: No, I cannot think of any drawbacks at all. It would be no different from opposite-sex marriage.

K: *What advice would the two of you offer to gay couples that are thinking about getting married?*

B: Be sure you are ready to get married—contemplate on it very seriously. It's not something to be taken lightly. You are vowing to be with that person forever, whether it's a religious or a civil marriage. Make sure it's what you want.

K: *Good advice. Is there a metaphor, image, movie or a piece of music that speaks to your feelings or thoughts about same-sex marriage?*

B: I like the movie *Common Ground*. It's one of those movies shown on cable TV. The town fathers give their blessings to a gay couple, which effectively marries them. At the ceremony, he says, "Is this equality? Too many times we contemplate on our differences and we don't realize the common ground."

K: *That makes sense to me. What about for you, Steve?*

S: I think that it is the word "same." Even though it is labelled same-sex marriage, I feel that we are the same in all respects. Two adult humans, loving and committing to each other—the same as any other marriage.

K: *What would you put in a "hope box" for gay people? In other words, what do you think still needs to happen in the gay community?*

S: It's important to be yourself in whatever life you live. Living a lie is not what the creator ever intended for us as humans to do. I would put in the hope box two items. The first would be a message of encouragement to pursue your own personal life with its expected highs and lows. Secondly, I would like to put in a road map to follow daily so that we do not become uninterested in the needs of all gays in our community as well as ourselves. We need to be persistent with our eyes wide open for any deceitful curves in the road.

K: *How about you, Brent?*

B: Gays need to come out and show everybody that [they] aren't that different—[they're] just regular people.

K: *I agree. People don't need to go around screaming that they're gay, but they need to live their lives with integrity. If they're in a relationship, they shouldn't change the pronoun when they are referring to their partner. Be yourself and don't try to hide. Do you think we have dealt with this topic thoroughly, or is there anything else that either one of you would like to add?*

B: You know, it is Canada that's doing this—not the United States. I think this is something your nation ought to be very proud of. Many gay Americans are waiting to get married, but they are waiting for it to become legal here as well. Thank you, Canada, for what you have started!

K: *Those are very kind words. Thank you so much.*

Rich North and Chris Vogel
photo by Richard F. J. Wood

My Sunshine
Rich North and Chris Vogel

Date: October 5, 2003
Time: 3:00 pm
Place: Telephone Interview (Rich and Chris live in Winnipeg, Manitoba)

Rich and Chris have been together for more than thirty years. It struck me while talking to them that they have worked out most of their issues and are each other's best friend. They married on February 11, 1974, in a Unitarian Church, before their friends, family and the law. They began a fight with the Manitoba government for legal recognition, and they lost. But they are still together. Perhaps the law has just been slow in realizing their commitment is actually real.

R: Our marriage was an incidental sort of thing—we were already in a long-term relationship. We were out to our families and friends from the start. Our interest was in public education and law reform, and getting married was the one thing we could do in those days other than holding demonstrations. Our marriage received a lot of media attention, so it was very successful in that regard.

C: It also had other effects: everyone knew early on that we were gay and that we were a couple. Basically our families and friends didn't have a choice: it was either you accept us, or too bad—so they accepted us. I think the honesty we brought to our relationship was unequivocally the best way to approach the whole issue of being gay and being in a relationship. Also it had the effects generally common to marriage, by involving family and friends. Some of our friends and some people from the congregation attended it, and also Rich's parents and sister.

R: We were inspired by Jack Baker, an activist in Minneapolis, Minnesota. He was an early and very prominent gay activist in the United States. He had been elected president of the Students' Association at the University of Minnesota. He and his partner attempted to get legally married, and that received a lot of publicity in Canada. Even before I came out, I remember hearing him on the radio talking about it. He had also come up to the University of Manitoba, invited by the Campus Gay Club, to speak about it, and this created an awareness and provided us with the idea of doing it ourselves.

C: He wasn't the only one, actually. We subscribed to *The Advocate*, and read of other examples there.

K: *How many people did you have at your ceremony?*

R: We had our ceremony on February 11, 1974, in the Unitarian church in Winnipeg with fifty or sixty in attendance. It was an attempt to obtain a legal marriage. We had gone down to the Registrar of Vital Statistics to apply for a marriage licence, but were refused. When we applied, the officer saw that we were of the same sex, [and] his immediate response was, "This is a joke, right?" and we replied, "No." He then sent us a letter saying that they would not issue us a licence.

C: The Unitarian minister suggested a "Proclamation of the Banns," which we did. For three Sundays in a row, he proclaimed the banns and the congregation [was] invited to attend the ceremony.

K: *What does the "Banns" refer to? Many readers may be unaware of this practice.*

R: Manitoba allows two ways to initiate a marriage; obtaining a licence, and a Proclamation of the Banns. The latter is an older and more community-based procedure whereby the minister proclaims the intention to marry before the congregation for three consecutive Sundays and invites expressions of objection. This obviates the requirement for the issuance of a licence.

The marriage ceremony included the vows and pronouncement which are required by law, and the Marriage Certificate was completed and witnessed. We sent in all of the forms, but the Office of Vital Statistics refused to register the marriage. We took the Registrar to court but lost the case. The judgment was based on the premise that marriage, largely defined in common law, provided only for a man and a woman. Both the Manitoba and Canada marriage statutes did not say this. In fact the minister who married us had just previously participated in a rewrite of The (Manitoba) Marriage Act that removed sexist references, so there was nothing in Manitoba statute law which prevented same-sex marriage. Consequently, the judge had to rely on common law. He resorted to dictionary definitions which defined marriage as the union of one man and one woman. On this basis, the judgment was that no marriage had taken place.

C: The federal act defines who may and may not marry (e.g., you cannot marry a first cousin or a sibling), and the provincial law sets out the procedures for solemnization of marriage and registration.

K: *When did you take the province of Manitoba to court?*

C: October 1974.

K: *How long did it take before it concluded?*

R: It was some time after the case was heard; our lawyer found enough instances where irregular marriages were accepted that the judge felt obliged to reserve his decision, but in the end it didn't do us any good.

K: *In the Proclamation of the Banns practice, after the minister asks on the third Sunday if there are any objections from the congregation, does the marriage occur right away?*

C: No, and that was interesting too. The minister had to send in the forms a certain number of days before the ceremony would occur. He was concerned that if he did this immediately, they would be forewarned that it was going to happen, and might interfere. For him to conduct a legal marriage, he has to be a licenced clergy. He was afraid they might cancel or suspend his licence. He scheduled the marriage for a Monday evening and went out to the country to mail the forms on the Thursday or Friday beforehand. This meant the officials would not receive the forms until after the marriage had taken place.

C: If they were to do some kind of statistical reconciliation for 1974, there would be at least one marriage counted by the Unitarian church that wasn't counted by the Registrar of Vital Statistics.

R: As far as we know it was the first [gay] marriage in the Unitarian church in Canada. That church had been performing same-sex marriages in the United States since the 1960s.

C: The Unitarian church married all kinds of people who would not be allowed to marry in their own congregations. For example, back then most churches wouldn't marry a couple if one of the individuals was divorced or from another denomination. Catholic priests wouldn't perform a marriage if one partner was a Protestant, for example. The Unitarian church became the final resort for all these couples who couldn't marry elsewhere. While we attended our marriage preparation course, we met another couple. The woman in that couple was a reporter for CBC radio, so she came in with her technicians and taped our marriage. The radio station broadcast portions of it the next morning, which created a great deal of publicity without us having to make any effort. We got national publicity through this, with little effort on our part. It was certainly a lot easier than the trouble we had to go to, to get attention for demonstrations about human rights legislation, for example.

R: It was on the front page of the *Winnipeg Free Press*, and that was highly unusual because they didn't cover gay stories back then. The headline was "Homosexuals marry in city." I think it seemed incredible that homosexuals would be marrying right here in Winnipeg, as opposed to some place exotic, like California.

C: The other issue that we dealt with for ten years or more was The (Manitoba) Human Rights Code. In 1974, you had to explain what a human rights act was, and many people you explained it to didn't know whether it was a good idea. Marriage, on the other hand, was a very straightforward issue, so saying that you were getting married or that you were attempting to get married explained itself, and, of course, it applied directly to the situation of being homosexual.

A few years earlier, there had been a couple of fellows who'd been married in a nightclub in Montreal. An article appeared in one of the rotogravure magazines that were included in most dailies on Saturdays, either *The Canadian* or *Weekend*. However, for that issue, the publisher of the *Free Press* had that article ripped, by hand, out of every single issue. I wanted to read it, of course, so I went down to the Provincial Library where they kept all kinds of papers and hunted. It was difficult finding one that hadn't been torn out, but I did find it, in a New Brunswick paper, I think.

K: *Hum, just thinking—you guys married in 1974. Does that mean that the two of you are the first to marry in Canada, at least in the religious spiritual sense?*

R: It's the first case in Canadian law involving same-sex marriage, but I suspect there were earlier instances of same-sex commitment ceremonies.

C: We certainly know of many people who have had commitment ceremonies since we married. One of the organizations that we helped establish and worked with, the Council on Homosexuality and Religion, regularly directed people to clergy who would do that, either in their own denomination or as close as possible.

K: *Now let's look at when the two of you met. Where did it start for the two of you?*

C: It was on June 16, 1972, and we met in a restaurant that was here at the time. Gay people routinely occupied the cocktail lounge upstairs. It was called the Mardi Gras, but it has been gone for years.

R: We both had been out for about half a year. I came out at the end of January 1972, and Chris had been attending the University of Saskatchewan and came out in December 1971.

K: *I assume then that neither of you had dated many other guys prior to meeting.*

R: I had had sex with six other guys.

C: I had had a short relationship with another fellow named Richard. What brought me out was attending a meeting of the gay group at the University of Saskatchewan. My motives were a little ulterior. I tidied up my dorm room and picked the best-looking guy from the group. We met on a Friday afternoon and he asked me over for the weekend. Our relationship lasted until April, although long before that I realized I was in lust with him, not in love. I think I hurt him pretty badly, although we have remained friends ever since and I see him once a week or so because he now lives here.

K: *Rich, when did you fall in love with Chris?*

R: During our first summer together, and when we went to Europe that fall. The following spring Chris returned to live with his parents in London, Ontario, for a couple of months. We had both run out of money, so I moved back in with my parents as well. When Chris and I eventually moved in together in Winnipeg, it became clear that we wanted to become life partners.

K: *What about you, Chris—when did you fall in love with Rich?*

C: After about three hours of first meeting him. We met at the one more-or-less gay bar in Winnipeg, the Mardi Gras, then Rich invited me back to his place. He made me a fried egg sandwich and then we went down to the basement and had sex. By the time I left, I was in love with him.

K: *Wow, so he hit a real impact right away. Now you guys have been together for thirty years. What is it that you most value about your partner now?*

C: There are so many things. Rich is a wonderful person: he's honest, kind, thoughtful, decent, intelligent, and he makes me happy every time I see him. I haven't found or met anyone else that compares to him. We are each other's best friend.

R: Well that is quite a testimonial. I hope you caught every word of that.

C: I have always felt that way.

K: *It's nice to hear these words because we don't always say them to each other.*

R: No, Chris has always been good about that. I have always felt valued, and that is one of the things I value about Chris as a partner. I have never had the sense that I wasn't loved. My relationship with Chris is by far the dominant relationship in my life. I was a bit of a loner when I was a kid and I don't have a lot of other friends. When I look at the people in my life, Chris is front and centre. I certainly care about my parents, my siblings, and Chris's parents. But by far the dominant relationship in my life is Chris: this relationship is what my life is about and has been since we got together.

I think we have been closer than many other couples. We have shared almost everything in our lives. I trusted Chris from the start, and I always felt loved. Someone that loving doesn't come along every day, and naturally I was drawn to that capacity to love. He is also an extremely honest person, he has worked incredibly hard every since I met him. He has devoted himself to the gay movement, spending countless hours trying to effect change. He had a weekly television program for more than a decade. He's also been the leading light in the gay resource centre since we became involved in

1973. He has devoted himself to the welfare of others in a way that very few people do.

K: *Wow—tell me about the television program you had for ten years, Chris.*

C: It probably sounds more impressive than it was. It was broadcast on one of the cable channels here. It was a half-hour program that started in September 1980 and broadcast weekly, and sometimes twice weekly, until November 1994. There were more than 750 broadcasts in total. The program was called *Coming Out*, and it dealt exclusively with gay and lesbian issues.

K: *Outstanding! I am so pleased to hear that someone did this.*

R: It had an enormous impact on the city too. Every week for more than a decade, there was a gay program that people could watch in the privacy of their home. Remember this was in the 80s and early 90s, and things were different then. By comparison, this past summer you could not turn on the television without seeing stuff about same-sex marriage. Today there is an enormous amount in the media about gay issues, but that wasn't the case ten or fifteen years ago.

K: *After thirty years, are there still issues you are struggling with as a couple?*

C: In the summer of 1973, we talked about and then began having a sexually open relationship.

R: It was trendy in the early 1970s to have open relationships. We subscribed to that from the very beginning, at least in theory.

C: So we did that and it worked out fine, and we have ever since. I think there are several things that might happen if you don't do that. I believe that many people begin to feel stifled or bottled up if they are only allowed to have sex with their partner. I have read that sexual interest in each other tends to wear off in some couples, which must be very frustrating. Other people seek out covert sex with others, and this violates the trust that is absolutely essential for maintaining a successful relationship. I think that if you can't trust your partner on the issue of sex, it has a corrosive effect.

R: I also think that if people are determined to be sexually exclusive, it becomes easy to confuse sex with love. Part of the gay male experience traditionally has included recreational sex. The love that develops in a substantial long-term relationship is something quite different. It seems to me that if people get all worked up about casual sex, you are headed for trouble.

K: *Interesting. When you told your parents back in the 1970s that you were planning to marry, how did they receive the news?*

R: We both came from liberal secular backgrounds, so we didn't have the same obstacles that many gay people face. In both cases, our parents were a little upset in the beginning, but you must remember that this was the early 1970s when attitudes were very different. Soon both sets of parents embraced the relationship and have been supportive ever since.

K: *When you guys are out in public are you comfortable holding hands or showing other forms of affection?*

R: It's not something that I would do, although I have no objections to other people doing it.

C: We are physically affectionate in private, but it seems odd to do this publicly. It is nice to see other people doing that, however.

K: *If I heard you correctly, even if you had turned out to be heterosexual, you probably wouldn't be holding the hand of your wife either.*

C: I've never thought about it in those terms, but probably not, especially if my wife had Rich's attitude.

R: To me, it's associated with youth—we were fifteen when we listened to the old Beatles' song, "I Wanna Hold Your Hand."

K: *What do you think is going to be the societal impact of same-sex marriage in Canada?*

C: I think people will get used to it, and it will help them accept gays and lesbians. Both here and abroad, it will motivate gay and lesbian individuals to come out, and over time, more people will begin to think positively about same-sex marriage.

R: I think it will have an enormous long-term impact, both in Canada and throughout the world. Marriage is the ultimate institutional expression of the sexual/romantic dimension of human experience. Less than forty years ago, homosexual activity was against the law in Canada, and now we are on the brink of same-sex marriage. That's an enormous change, and I think it will have a profound impact on people's expectations of homosexual relationships. Belief systems tend to be self-fulfilling, and this positive attitude of equality will encourage long-term, stable same-sex relationships and create greater tolerance and acceptance of homosexuality. On the international stage, Canada is well-respected. With same-sex marriage, we will become leaders in the international movement for equality for homosexuals. Soon the rest of the world will be able to point to Canada as the enlightened nation in which one can chose to marry someone of either sex. Nothing we could do in Canada would speak more powerfully to the rest of the world.

K: *Do you think there are going to be any drawbacks to same-sex marriage?*

C: I've heard some objection to same-sex marriage on the grounds that both partners' incomes will be taken into account in determining income-related government payments made to one of them. To object to marriage on that ground is to advocate welfare fraud. As adults we should expect to have the same responsibilities, as well as the same rights, as heterosexuals.

K: *What do you think is going to be the impact on the gay community of same-sex marriage?*

R: I think over the long term it will create the sense that homosexual relationships are equivalent to heterosexual relationships.

C: I think it will motivate gay people to think seriously about establishing a long-term relationship with somebody, and about treating the other person well enough that the relationship can persist. This will create a change of philosophy for many gay people. Many gay individuals have learned to be pessimistic about the possibility that gay relationships will last. For years, I led something called *rap* sessions, which were structured discussion groups where everyone talked. I heard a lot of people tell me that they wanted to settle down and live happily ever after, but what they expected would likely happen was quite different. I think we still have a long way to go.

R: Traditionally, within a heterosexual context, the honourable form for a sexual relationship to take was marriage. Even when I was growing up, living common law was considered dirty and second-rate. I think same-sex marriage sanctions homosexual relationships in much the same way, and removes the sense that there is something shameful about homosexuality.

C: Gays and lesbians who come out to their families and friends will surely be motivated to take a positive attitude toward the idea of same-sex marriage. I suspect we will see a 180 degree change with parents who were once heatedly opposed to same-sex marriage now insisting upon it. All of a sudden they will accept it, and even insist on it.

K: *You are probably correct because marriage is an institution that straight society values.*

C: Well, it's an institution of control and the people I'm talking about believe others need to be controlled.

K: *I think many people that read the book will be gay or lesbian and contemplating marriage for themselves. What advice would you give to gay couples who are thinking about getting married?*

R: I think our parents were our role models. The way we have organized our sex lives is very different from our parents because I am sure they have had lifelong monogamous relationships. In other respects, though, I suspect that our relationship is very similar to our parents'. Our parents were not traditionalists in that they had egalitarian marriages.

C: I think some people will marry because they think they ought to because of some form of social compulsion. That is what I meant when I said marriage was an institution of control—not for us, and perhaps not for most people these days. In religious environments, marriage was traditionally a mechanism that controlled how people behaved sexually. You were disgraced if you didn't marry or if you had sex outside of marriage. I think you should do what you think is best and not what somebody else wants, including your family. There are a variety of options available and people should select the one they think will suit them. I can see people living together for a number of years and then getting married, or not getting married at all. People should be introspective and determine what they and their partner want for themselves.

K: *Upon reflection, is there a metaphor or a piece of music that speaks to your feelings or thoughts about same-sex marriage and/or long-term relationships?*

C: Well, like many couples, we do have a song. Ours is "You Are My Sunshine."

R: For me, what comes to mind is the opening line the minister read in the ceremony we put together for our marriage. It began with the Shakespearean sonnet: "Let me not to the marriage of true minds / Admit impediments...."

C: It is rumoured that Shakespeare wrote this sonnet to another man.

K: *What would you put in a "hope box" for gay people? What still needs to happen within the gay community?*

R: Ultimately that being homosexual will be seen as a personal characteristic that has no negative connotation. If same-sex marriage becomes legal throughout Canada, we have pretty well achieved legal equality, but we are still a long way from achieving genuine equality.

C: With all of the human rights campaigns, the bottom line is not to judge people based on categories to which they belong, but rather on their individual merits. If a relationship is to be successful, it has to be conducted with a liberal generous spirit.

R: I guess the hope is that one day, there will no longer be statements like, "God hates fags," and the religious right will lose interest in trying to stigmatize homosexuality. Instead, homosexuality will be looked upon as a neutral fact of life.

C: The gay and lesbian movement won't matter anymore.

K: *Do you think we have dealt with this topic thoroughly, or do you think there is more that needs to be said on this subject?*

R: I'd say we've just about covered it.

C: One of the things that strikes me is the simplicity of this issue—everybody knows what's going on here and almost no explanation is required: we want to be treated equally because we think we are entitled to that. Our constitution recognizes that and mandates it. What strikes me about the opposition is that they assert things for which they can provide no evidence. For example, there is no evidence that gay people are harmful to children or that same-sex marriage will be harmful to heterosexual relationships. It would appear that they simply don't want us to be equal because they want to be superior to us. They are angered whenever their own superiority is brought into question by the demand for equality. It is not a religious conviction or a Christian conviction that supports hostility toward same-sex marriage: that is pure fraud, self-indulgent malice.

K: *Thank you for this insightful and thought-provoking interview.*

Marla Kavalak, Keigan and Michelle Livingston

The Power of Two

Marla Kavalak and Michelle Livingston

Date: October 6, 2003
Time: 5:00 pm
Place: Telephone Interview (Moncton, New Brunswick).

Meeting over the Internet is not uncommon today, and this was the beginning for this couple who found connection, and five years later married in Ottawa. They have a twenty-two-month old daughter, a child who will grow up knowing that love is what makes this world a better place. And this child is loved by two good-hearted women who know how to care. Their story is called *The Power of Two*, after a song by the Indigo Girls. Coincidentally, they wrote down the song title independently of each other while trying to think of an answer to my metaphorical question. Amazing how in sync one often becomes in long-term relationships.

MK: Michelle and I have been together for five years and we have lived together for most of it. In our hearts, we always felt like we were married. We talked a lot about getting married and even attended marriage preparation classes with two of our friends. We had talked to a minister in the United Church about having a commitment ceremony, and although our friends might refer to it as a marriage, it would not be legally recognized.

I have attended a commitment ceremony and it was nicer than most heterosexual marriages I've been at. We had talked near the beginning of our relationship about the possibility of having a commitment ceremony in five years if it wasn't legal to marry at that point. Low and behold, it became legal in Ontario in June, which was about six months short of the five-year mark for us. Since we married, people have asked us, "Now that you're legally married, does it feel any different?" I don't feel any different at this point because we have not had to write it down anywhere. They don't currently recognize same-sex marriage in New Brunswick. We are trying to tread the political waters so that hopefully Michelle will be able to change her name. Are you aware of the fiasco that has happened in New Brunswick regarding name changes for same-sex couples who have married in Ontario?

K: *No, I am not familiar with that.*

ML: There were three couples from Moncton who married in Ontario within a three to four day period. Upon their return, one of the couples started pushing the buttons: he wanted to hyphenate his last name. For heterosexual couples, all they need to do is show Service New Brunswick, which is a representative of the Vital Statistics Office, the marriage documentation, and they make the requested name change. Service New Brunswick refused to do it for the gay couple. He finally met with the justice minister and some other people and their response was, "We are not letting one person push us around. We will wait until we see what the feds do." The culmination of this was when he decided to stage a peaceful protest by chaining himself to a chair. He overheard a woman say within hearing distance, "I wish these gays would just go home," and he went bananas and demanded an apology. He became very upset. The woman would not give him an apology and it escalated from there. She called the police and they came and arrested him. He pled not guilty in court and a trial date will be set on December 24. That incident has made lots of news.

MK: The interesting thing is that federally, they changed his name on his social insurance card, but all provincial documentation still includes his non-hyphenated name. Because his identification does not match, that is causing him unforeseen problems. Michelle and I have often talked about changing our name. We eventually decided that Michelle was going to take my last name because our names are simply too long: too long to start putting on tax forms and other documents.

We haven't received our marriage certificate from Ontario yet, but on it I will be listed as the "groom." We are hoping that because my first name is uncommon and the authorities might assume I am a male, they may change Michelle's last name without havoc. Consequently, we are quietly waiting for our marriage certificate to arrive.

The other key issue is that in New Brunswick, second-parent adoptions are not legal unless you are married. The province has already denied my access to adopt Keigan, our daughter, unless Michelle relinquishes her parental rights. We lodged a human rights complaint and the tribunal date is currently set for January. Once we receive our marriage certificate, however,

I intend on reapplying for the adoption again and then we'll see what happens. We fully anticipate that they will not recognize our marriage because we have already heard that through other couples who are going through similar processes.

Personally, I don't feel our marriage has changed anything for us yet, but politically, we hoped to help create change. Our families know that we married, but it doesn't feel official because we packed everything into a car on a Sunday and drove off to get married on a Tuesday. Most of our family were not there, so the whole thing seems a bit surreal to them. Our plan was to have a big reception, but we have not had that yet because Michelle was in a car accident and we haven't had the extra cash.

ML: A month before we got married, my mother said, "We have been thinking of buying you a wedding gift." That felt fabulous that she was thinking about what we wanted. That is really cool because my mother hasn't wanted to talk about this whole "lesbian thing." I've been out for seven or eight years at this point. When we were in Ottawa for our wedding, we stayed in a hotel and a package arrived from my mother. It was the most meaningful and sentimental thing my mother has ever done for me. In the note attached, my mother wrote, "Although we can't physically be there, your family is with you both." She sent pictures of my brother and me from when we were little, a locket, the garter from her wedding, and a napkin from her wedding back in 1965. I was touched so deeply that I immediately burst into tears. In many ways, it was a simple gesture, but it meant so much to me because for the first time, she really showed some validation to our relationship. When we arrived home, she wanted to see pictures.

When we decided that we wanted to have a big reception, we hadn't considered how much money it would cost. I think people are holding back because we have told them there is going to be this reception, and we haven't arranged it yet. We certainly have experienced a range of responses to our wedding, however. Some [people]have shown no response, while…others… have told us how fabulous it is. Some also wondered why we had to go to Ontario to get married.

MK: It is really amazing that some people don't know that gay people can't get married.

ML: Probably many people we know have assumed we were already married because we have worn matching rings for four years.

MK: I remember having a conversation with one of Keigan's teachers at her daycare. Both of the women in that class thought that same-sex marriage was already legal, and they were totally amazed to find out that it isn't. I work for the federal government, and even my colleagues are amazed that we don't have the same rights. Unfortunately, people might be amazed, [but they are not] yet moved to the point where they will write letters to politicians. Often those who write the letters are the people with opinions that are polar opposites in their views on an issue. The people who have the most moderate views don't write the letters because it doesn't personally impact them.

K: *Exactly—most people are not browbeating these politicians. Michelle, could you tell me more about your experience of coming out?*

ML: I have a unique coming out experience from the perspective that I was in University at the time as a mature student. I met my first real live gay person when I was twenty-five, and from that moment on, I was amazed by the fact that he was not this bizarre, weird creature. He was a normal, intelligent, attractive man and that stunned me because growing up in rural New Brunswick, I had the impression that gay people were freaks. At the time I was in nursing school and I ended up doing a seminar course in January. We were doing our seminar on hot button issues, like lesbian parenting and abortion.

I thought I could never be gay because I believed that gay people were all weird, and I also assumed that they could not be parents. For the seminar, however, I was reading about several lesbians who have had kids, and I was identifying with every single one of them. That created a crisis of sorts for me, and for the next two weeks, it consumed all of my time. I called up the only counsellor that I knew at UNB and said, "I need to see you and I need to see you now." I went to see her and she gave me some direction.

I'm like, "No, I couldn't do this, and I couldn't do that." Within two weeks, I was ready to identify as a lesbian. That's all there was to it. It began as an intellectual awareness for me initially, and by the time I met somebody, it felt totally normal and right: it made so much sense.

It took me a long time to get through school because I had a hard time staying focused. In retrospect, I think it was because I did not know [myself] and I was out of touch with my feelings, so it was hard to know what I wanted to do. I am also thankful that I didn't come out as a teenager because that would have led to harassment from peers and so forth. By the time I came out, I was secure in my feelings of worth as a human being.

K: *Did you end up losing any friends when you came out?*

ML: No, but some of my friends acted a little weird initially. When I was attending school, I became really out there. I worked within the residence system, and I was the "gay" proctor. Whenever anything happened on campus, I would get the phone call, like, "Somebody wants to come out in the guys' residence. Oh my god, what am I going to do?" It was bizarre when I left school because I had to step back in the closet as I entered the working world.

K: *How did your mom react initially?*

ML: I told my mother on the phone and I asked her not to tell dad or anyone else. My parents were funding some of my education and I knew I could not afford to pay it on my own. I was afraid because I come from a narrow-minded family. My father, especially at the time, was sexist, racist and homophobic. He has improved a lot since then.

   The next day, mom arrived at my residence with a psychologist. The psychologist was a family friend and my mom brought her along mostly to act as a mediator. She didn't bring her alone to try and "fix" me. Mom and I are very much alike, and this has led to some communication problems between us.

   My mom is one of those people that researches to death anything she does not understand. By the time I told my father, his response was, "Whatever, no big deal." I was expecting this big reaction from him, and it was the opposite of what I expected. Maybe he just had an inkling that this was the case. Apparently when I was three, my mother took me to a psychologist because I wanted to do boy things, like play with trucks, be bare-chested, and play aggressive games. That was in the early 1970s, and the psychologist's response was "don't let her play with trucks." Good try, but it didn't make a bit of difference!

K: *Let's move over to Marla for a bit. When did you come out and how did people react?*

MK: I always knew that there was something different about me. Since elementary school, I remember having crushes on my female teachers and never on my male teachers. I always enjoyed male activities, like climbing trees. I realized in grade six that I had a huge crush on my best friend, and that horrified me because I grew up in a small town in Nova Scotia. I thought, "I can't be this way because this isn't normal." There were some gay people in town, but they were rarely talked about, and when they were, it was like, "He's gay so stay away from him." It was a coalmining town and there is a penitentiary there. People there aren't necessarily going ahead with formal education, and the "isms" were common (e.g., racism, sexism).

I thought that if I dated guys and met the right guy, these feelings would go away. I dated men all the way through university, but it didn't work out. I had a crush on my best male friend so I thought maybe I am in love with him. When we explored this, I realized I was not in love with him either. That led to a lot of soul searching because after I graduated from university, I returned to that small town. I started working for the Correctional Service of Canada, and frankly it is not the most open environment. I heard many homophobic comments from my colleagues. Eventually I realized I had to accept who I am. Luckily I had a cousin who was a lesbian and I spent a lot of time with her. We used to go to the local gay bar together in Moncton, but there was never any talk regarding my own sexual orientation. I finally told a friend from the U.S. that I was gay and that felt like a big weight off my chest. I was twenty-six or twenty-seven at the time.

Meeting Michelle was good for me because she is a bit of a pusher. I am a low-risk person and Michelle is like, "Let's jump off a cliff and see what happens." After a couple of months of dating, she said, "I am moving to Moncton, with or without you, and you decide what you want to do."

Little did I know that my mother had already suspected I was gay, and she had discussed this with her doctor, who happened to be a lesbian. She asked her doctor if she should ask me if I was gay, and her doctor dissuaded her from doing so. In the meantime, I was living at my parent's house and Michelle told me that she would not come to visit if I didn't tell them. Over the course of five hours, I eventually told my mother by giving her a copy of the book, *Now That You Know*. She read the front page and started laughing. She said, "I've known this forever." I was a little disappointed because I had expected her to react the same way she did when her best friend's son came out, and she didn't. Mom has been very cool about it, but I wasn't at the time. I told her not to tell anybody else, which in retrospect was a selfish thing to do because I came out, dumped it on my mother, and then told her to stay in the closet with it. I think that has caused some difficulties with my parents and my relationship with my mother because I created some shame around it.

Eventually my father found out. He is an electrician and I asked him to check out something in the house we were buying. When he returned home, he asked my mother if I was gay. My father said, "Well, Marla is a smart girl and if this is what is right for her, then it must be okay." But he never acknowledged it to me until my parents attended a party in this small town. Somebody said something malicious about me coming out of the closet. My mother handled it supremely, but I think it hurt her. It really drove home to my parents that others are not all cool with this. When we became pregnant, my mother congratulated us, but she was also very concerned. She knows that Michelle and I have a solid foundation in our relationship, but she was concerned about the impact of our baby being born into a family being raised by two women.

My brother-in-law told her, "That baby is going to be loved and Marla and Michelle are going to be great parents. Who cares what other people think?" I think that helped my mother, and then Michelle and I gave her a lot of material to read. Then I realized that I had put my mother in the closet, and now we are pregnant and how is she going to explain this? We decided that we needed to take that closet away from her.

We wrote a letter that confirmed our relationship and we informed people that we were pregnant. We tried to counter some of their anticipated concerns, including the fear that our child will get teased and this will happen and that will happen. We also wrote that we don't expect others to do anything different from what they would do if we were a straight couple having a child. We wanted to encourage them to support our child and help our child build strong self-esteem and self-confidence so that he or she can deal with whatever teasing may result. We basically said if they don't feel they can do this, then they won't be part of our circle. We wrote that we can't stop the hateful words that people say on the streets, but we don't have to have it at home. The letter was sent mostly to people in my family because I was not out to everyone yet.

ML: I forgot to mention that after I came out to my father, I also sent out a letter to my extended family because I was sick of answering questions like, "When are you getting married? Who's your boyfriend?" I sent out a mass letter and told them what they needed to hear. It doesn't leave them anything to talk about.

K: *When did you decide that you wanted to have a child?*

ML: We talked about having a baby before we got too serious in our relationship.

MK: But just to clarify: we weren't going to run out and get pregnant. We just wanted to make sure that we were on the same page in terms of what we wanted out of life.

ML: In my previous relationship, it was part of the reason we split up. I knew I would resent her if having a child was not part of the life plan. Marla writes me a letter every year at Christmas and it is usually my best present. That year the last piece of the letter she wrote [was], "I am now ready to have a baby together." We bought our house together the previous July and we now felt ready to have a child. We quickly started making doctors' appointments and getting the necessary referrals.

K: *Is the biological father involved in any way?*

ML: No, we used an anonymous donor at the clinic here in Moncton.

K: *Despite there being no father in the picture, Marla is still prevented from adopting Keigan?*

MK: Yeah, that's right. In New Brunswick, a second-parent adoption is only permitted if you are legally married, whether you are gay or straight.

K: *So that will create an interesting challenge because you are married.*

ML: Exactly—that's why we have a complaint in front of the human rights commission. It is moving very slowly. Because we both work in the criminal justice system, we can't be as radical as the activist who chained himself to a chair and got arrested.

K: *When you first met, was it love at first sight, or did it take time to mature?*

MK: We met over a Web site called Groovy Annie's. I was scrolling through to see if there was anybody on there that is interesting and I came across Michelle's message. I e-mailed her on September 26. We e-mailed back and forth before exchanging phone numbers and then met in person a week or so later. Michelle had asked for my phone number because she wanted to confirm that I actually was a woman. When I told her where I lived, she immediately said, "Oh, there is a prison there." I thought, "Why does she know that there is a prison there?" I felt very cautious—perhaps she was a crazed psycho killer or something. We met in Moncton for breakfast one morning and ended up spending the whole day together. I went back home and immediately called my cousin. I said, "I met this person, I really like her, but should I call her?" My cousin said, "Don't call her tonight because then you would be pressuring her and you don't want to do that." Well, I opted to call anyway and I left a message saying that I hope you made it home safely. We ended up going to Halifax for Thanksgiving weekend, and the rest is history.

ML: It started that week and we spent every subsequent weekend together until we started cohabitating in December 1998. We spoke and e-mailed each other every day. Our attraction to each other was very quick. We were soon completely enamoured with one another. I felt like I could not go more than five days without seeing her.

K: *Have there been times when either of you thought of ending the relationship?*

ML: Not seriously, but there have been times in the heat of a fight where it has been like, "Oh, I can't stand that," but at those times you are so wound up that you aren't thinking clearly.

MK: Even in spite of Michelle's pushing! But I hate to admit it; the pushing has always turned out to be okay, except for three dogs. They sometimes drive me crazy.

K: *You have three dogs?*

MK: Yeah, we have three. When we first moved in together, there were times when I asked myself what I had gotten myself into. Michelle was still at school, I was working for the federal government, so I became the main breadwinner. I thought that I was taking a step backwards for this person who was still in school. There were times when I felt that I never would have moved that quickly without her pushing me, but in the long run, it has worked out very well.

ML: Marla has moved 360 degrees since we first met. She was barely out then, and when we moved to Moncton, we didn't know anybody. I thought that we should go to PFLAG and meet some interesting people and maybe we can help somebody who is trying to come out. Marla was like, "No way can I go." Now she is the one who does TV interviews, and she is in the one in the newspapers, and she is the one who writes letters to the editors. We have reversed roles a bit in that regard.

K: *Are the two of you comfortable with showing public displays of affection?*

MK: I am cool with it, but Michelle has issues around it.

ML: I don't want to make others uncomfortable. I know that is my own issue and I am working on changing that.

K: *What would you like to be able to do publicly, Michelle?*

ML: I would like to feel comfortable holding hands. If you saw us together, we would look like sisters. When we are at places where other gay people are, I am a totally different person. Clearly part of me suggests that I would like to be a person who touches more. I would like to be comfortable so that I could always hold her hand.

   We already kiss goodbye every day when I drop her off for work and we hold hands in movie theatres where nobody can see us. The other day when I dropped Marla off at work, we saw two lesbians kiss goodbye and thought, "Oh, good—we are not the only two girls who do the kiss and drop in the morning." We have had times when we have looked around at other people who have been standing there and thought, "Should we do this?", and we always have.

MK: We have had discussions around the topic of public displays of affection. When we were pregnant, we talked about whether we wanted to do anything that would give our child the impression that there is something to be ashamed about in being together. We decided that if we are having a baby, then we have to be comfortable kissing and holding hands in public so that our child knows that we are not any different from any other couple. We are getting there, but it isn't easy. Even when we go to Michelle's parents at Christmas, I don't feel I can sit too close to her on the couch. If I accidentally touch her, she will move over a little so that there is an inch between us.

K: *What advice would you give to other gay couples that are thinking about getting married?*

MK: I know that given the political climate right now, some people are thinking that same-sex marriage is cool, so let's do it. Don't do it just for political reasons. I would say the same thing, regardless of whether you are gay or straight. Make sure that you are on the same page as the person that you are going to make that commitment with. If you are going in opposite directions, your relationship will have some problems.

ML: Make sure you are compatible. Talk about your goals, your values, whether you are going to have kids, how you are going to parent, how are you going to handle money and family traditions, and all that stuff. I have noticed that with some of our straight friends, once they have a kid, suddenly they are fighting over issues like whether the child will be baptized. You should know this before getting married. Make sure that you have a complementary parenting style.

MK: That has been our approach and Michelle and I balance each other out quite well. My strengths go hand in hand with her weaknesses, and vice versa. We didn't find that out by accident: we found that out by talking about things. We aren't the best communicators either, but it is one of the areas that we continue working on in our relationship. Human communication is a complex issue. Instead of running away when things have gotten rough, we have done a lot of work to build our relationship.

ML: We have had a few rough spots along the way. Because we both work in the same field, sometimes I will say things like, "Don't talk to me about anger management because I know all about it." As a result, I think sometimes we come across as insincere to each other when that is not our intent.

K: *Is there a metaphor, image, movie or piece of music that speaks to your feelings or thoughts about same-sex marriage?*

ML: Both of us independently came up with the song, "Power of Two," by the Indigo Girls. The words are very meaningful to us.

K: *What would you put in a "hope box" for gay people? What do you think still needs to happen within our gay community?*

ML: Can you bottle acceptance? I think we get divided over stupid things. We have as many gay friends as we have lesbian friends, and a couple of our male friends are conflicted because they don't think they are supposed to hang out with us because they have other friends that say to them, "Why do you want to have anything to do with those lesbians?" We have very similar values and we are on the same page, so that kind of reaction makes little sense to me.

Same-Sex Marriage

K: *So you are saying that the gay male and lesbian communities are separate, and you wonder why this occurs?*

ML: Yeah, for sure. I also think we are divided as young and old, and in New Brunswick, we are divided French and English as well.

MK: We are divided economically so that the ones with more money can't necessarily hang out with the ones with less money. Some people reject us because we are too political for them.

K: *What day do you celebrate as an anniversary?*

ML: We were married on June 17, 2003, and we have decided that we are going to have two parties; one on June 17 and the other on September 26. We have been together five years. For me, there is some status that comes with time, and I think that other people give some legitimacy to time as well. I think that is where my mother was coming from when out of the blue [she bought] us a big-ticket item. I think she waited to ensure that we were going to remain together.

K: *Those are all of my questions. Do you think that we have dealt with this topic thoroughly enough, or does something need to be said that I have missed?*

MK: Straight people often think that we are significantly different from them. An interesting incident occurred on the day that they had the national sanctity of marriage march in Moncton. At the same time, the gay community rallied some people together. There were about four or five hundred people marching against same-sex marriage, along with a small group of thirty queer individuals and their supporters. ... Michelle and I were there with Keigan, and our other friends were there with their kids too. I noticed a woman walking beside the organizer, who was right behind us, and I overheard her say, "I think I am in with the wrong group." The organizer said, "Really?", and she said, "Yes, I think I am." He said, "Well, it's hard to tell, isn't it?" She replied, "You are right—it really is hard to tell."

Then she moved to the other side and kept on walking. I think that really sums it up because people couldn't tell by looking at us. In fact, as the traffic passed along, people were screaming to the entire group, "You fags burn in hell!" The sanctity of marriage...[was] being targeted...as well because the driverbys were noticing the pride flag being carried by some of the queer ralliers.

ML: It was great fun for a Sunday afternoon.

K: *Let me thank you both for taking part in this interview.*

Julie, Annie and Hillary Goodridge
photo © 2003 Marilyn Humphries

Our Love is Here to Stay
Hillary and Julie Goodridge

Date: October 14, 2003
Time: 10:20 am
Place: Telephone Interview (Boston, Massachusetts)

I'm setting up to begin the telephone interview with Hillary and Julie. So far I have been amazed by how much I have learned from each couple. You would think by now I'd heard everything. Yet, Hillary and Julie are unique individuals as I think you will agree after you read their interview.

J: It's been both wonderful and difficult over the course of the sixteen and a half years that we have been together. We actually met eighteen years ago through a mutual friend at an evening talk about [the South African divestiture movement]. A few months after meeting Hillary, I realized that I was madly in love with her. It took me the remaining time until we got together to convince her to go out with me. Although we had both been involved with men in the past, we were both lesbians. I had felt that I was a lesbian since I was about twenty-one years old. Our relationship really began in June 1987, and it progressed slowly at first. We had a variety of things happen to us during the course of our relationship—mostly deaths, I'm afraid.

As a consequence of many deaths and tragic events, we have become quite resilient as a couple. [The experiences have] cemented our relationship. We started living together in November 1988 in my condominium. In 1993, we bought a house a couple of blocks away from our condominium. I was self-employed at the time and I worked from home. Hillary was working at a foundation gig down the street, so it was a perfect location for us. The house, unfortunately, was a disaster and we had to fix it up. We did that together, and during that same year, Hillary was trying to get pregnant. Hillary had been trying to get pregnant without success for two years; so then I tried with much better success. I was finally able to get pregnant with our daughter, Annie. She was born in 1995, so I got pregnant about a year after we bought this house. Our fix-up job made it liveable.

Along the way, we've been private people. When we decided to have a commitment ceremony, we [held it] in private in our backyard. We've always worked hard on our relationships with people and with each other. We have gone for couples therapy to work through our different communication styles and improve our relationship.

K: *When you fell in love with Hillary, were you both available for dating each other?*

H: Neither of us were.

J: ...but that had never stopped me before! (*Laughter.*)

K: *Let me move over to you for a few moments, Hillary. At what point would you say that you were falling in love with Julie?*

H: Probably about five or six months into it. After we met, Julie started calling me during a time that I was seeing other people. I thought she was fantastic, but I also thought she was going to be high maintenance. I finally decided that I was ready for that much work. By the time we started going out in 1987, I had developed a strong friendship with her already. We had known each other for about eighteen months and we had worked on several projects together. I just thought Julie was fantastic, and I still think she is the most wonderful person I know.

K: *You said you knew she was going to be a challenge. Is that something you can talk about?*

H: Yes I can. I'm from New York and I moved to Boston in the early 1980s after my parents went through a messy divorce. My grandparents also died around this time as well. I needed to get away from my parents. I didn't think I could deal with a whole lot more excitement. Julie was somebody who didn't let things rest: she was persistent, challenging and emotional. She was also very funny and very smart.

K: *At what age did you come out, Hillary?*

H: I was nineteen years old and in college.

K: *Tell me about the circumstances around when you first met.*

H: We met at a seminar at Harvard University in November 1985. I was working for Haymarket People's Fund, which is a foundation based in New England that raises money and makes grants for social change projects. We were hosting an event at Harvard that connected [with] the divestment movement from South Africa. We had invited a speaker by the name of Amy Domini, who had written a book called *Ethical Investing*. She was, and is, a leader in the field. Julie and Amy were working closely together, and Amy had been saying to me for some time, "I really want you to meet this person, Julie Wendryck," which was her name at the time. Amy brought Julie to this event. She also had a professional interest in it, and we met. The joke at the time was that I thought Julie looked like a young Republican, wearing a plaid skirt and a Shetland sweater—but there was something compelling about her.

K: *You mentioned before we started the tape that the last name you both have now is not the last name that either of you were born with.*

J: Right. I had thought about changing my last name because of family differences early on in our relationship. Hillary's last name used to be *Smith*, which was my mother's maiden name, so I wasn't going to switch it to that either. We knew that we were going to have children, so we decided to adopt the same last name. We looked through our family trees and the only decent name was *Goodridge*. We asked our lawyer to legally change our names for us because I think partly, we were two women raising a child, which is still somewhat unusual. I felt that if we had the same last name, there would be fewer reasons to deny us access to each other or to our child. I was concerned about school, going to the doctors, or an emergency room situation. With the same last name, we would at least be considered related to each other in some way.

K: *You mentioned that the two of you had a commitment ceremony. Tell me more about that.*

H: We had our commitment ceremony in August 1995, and Annie was born by a planned caesarean section on September 1, 1995. Julie was very pregnant when we had the commitment ceremony, so we wrote something for each other and included some poetry and readings. We had rings made up that we exchanged at that time. We had them specially made, but as we said, we are really private. We were getting a ton of attention because of the lawsuit, but we really wanted it to be just the two of us. Our next-door neighbour did come over in the middle of it, not realizing what was going on. He asked to borrow our pruning shears. (*Laughter.*)

K: *What did it mean to you to have a private ceremony?*

H: Well, she was eight-months pregnant, and I had to make an honest women out of her! (*Laughter.*)

K: *Did it work?*

H: It sure did. You know, for me, I had been through lots of friends' weddings and I had been a bridesmaid several times too. The idea of a big public event wasn't that interesting to me. I didn't want a toaster oven either. What was interesting and important to me was having Julie know that I am completely committed to her and that I will stay with her.

J: I didn't feel like I wanted to say what my commitment to Hillary was in front of anybody. It didn't feel like something I wanted to do. However, now that we're trying to get married in Massachusetts, this has made our love more public. Fighting for same-sex marriage is not about my commitment to Hillary, because I have already made that commitment to her. This is about trying to secure the legal protections that people who are married have in this country.

K: *Does that mean that in your minds, hearts and souls that the commitment ceremony between you was in fact a marriage?*

H: I do.

J: Yes, although we're obviously both aware that the commitment ceremony doesn't provide us with the legal protections of real marriage. If some people choose to get married to show that they love and support each other or whatever, in sickness and in health, then we've done that part already. If getting married meant that we needed to stand up in front of three hundred of our closest friends, at this point we would do it. Ideally, however, it would be the state of Massachusetts giving us a marriage licence and the two of us going off and finding somebody to marry us again.

K: *So basically, you are taking the state of Massachusetts to court?*

J: Right. Two and a half years ago, we went down to city hall to apply for a marriage licence. We knew we weren't going to get one, but on another level, I was hoping we would. Part of that was because our daughter had been asking us if we were married since she was five years old. She wasn't harping on us or anything, but it made us start thinking about what it really means to be married. Although Annie was just asking the way five-year-olds do, the expression, "Are you married?" began to resonate. We started doing a lot of thinking and talking to our friends about it, and it turned out that there were a lot of reasons that we should be married.

We had gotten blood tests and had the application fee ready, but of course we were denied the marriage licence. We knew that some of our friends had talked to *Gay and Lesbian Advocates and Defenders* (GLAD), which is a group of lawyers in Boston who run an organization that provides legal services to lesbian, gay, bisexual and transgendered individuals. GLAD was interested in the marriage issue and…had been involved in the civil union case that occurred in Vermont a couple of years earlier. When we called them, we discovered that there had been several other couples that they had been talking to. We talked to GLAD about being involved in a marriage case.

That is basically what happened in April 2001. We filed suit in one of the superior courts of the state of Massachusetts, challenging the Department of Public Health's…preventing us from getting marriage licences. There is not a law in Massachusetts that says that marriage must be one man and one woman. We felt that we should not be automatically excluded.…

K: *Are there other gay couples that also have a lawsuit against the state?*

J: Yes, there are seven couples together in the lawsuit.

K: *I just heard a little bit about President Bush's stance and his desire to change the constitution. If he was successful in doing that, would that block every state from pushing forward with same-sex marriage?*

J: Yes, if [he] were able to amend the U.S. Constitution, which I sincerely doubt is going to happen. Amending the U.S. Constitution would…prohibit gay and lesbian couples from accessing the federal protections and benefits [of] social security, pension funds, etcetera. It would be devastating.

However, I think there are a lot of Republicans who would be very concerned about states' rights, and about amending the Constitution to specifically exclude something. That has never been done before.

H: Remember that the press sensationalizes stories as well. If you do a Google…search on same-sex marriage, the stuff that comes up would make you think that 99% of Canadians are picketing against gay marriage. I understand how it probably sounds from your end about what's going on in the United States right now.

K: *I think that's an accurate observation. When will this go to court?*

H: We filed suit in April 2001, and the case was heard in May 2002. The single Justice denied our request on the basis that marriage is about procreation. We appealed, and it would have immediately gone to an appellate court, but the Supreme Judicial Court picked it up instead because it involves Massachusetts' constitutional issues. The case was presented to [the Court] on March 4, 2003. Usually the Massachusetts Supreme Judicial Court issues [its] decision within 130 days of being heard, but [it] filed for an extension. [It] still [hasn't] made [its] decision.

K: *Can you tell me what it is like to be lesbian and also to be parents in Boston right now?*

H: It is a constant process of coming out. At the grocery store, for example, people will say, "Are you the *real* mother, or which one is the real mother?" We constantly are saying that we are both Annie's parents. There are only four other gay and lesbian families in the private school that Annie attends, so when we first placed her there, it was a big process of educating the school about gay and lesbian family issues. The faculty has actually been fantastic. Massachusetts is one of thirteen states that has co-parent adoption, so I adopted Annie a long time ago. The fact that I have a legal relationship with Annie is a huge comfort for us.

K: *Is there a biological father involved with Annie's care?*

J: Yes, we have a friend who became our sperm donor and he is Annie's biological father. He is involved in our life, and we talk to him several times a week and see him once a week on average.

K: *For the adoption to occur, did he have to relinquish his parental rights?*

J: Yes, and he knew and accepted that. He needed to be okay with this because it was part of the deal.

K: *When Annie sees him, does she refer to him as dad?*

H: Yes, and her dad spends time with her regularly. We've all gone on vacation together, which has worked out beautifully. He has a really full, busy life, but they just adore each other: they have a great relationship.

K: *Do you ever get a really negative reaction when people realize that you are a lesbian couple and you have a daughter that you are raising?*

H: No, I don't think we do. If [people] have a negative reaction, they've done a good job of keeping it to themselves. I think if we were going to face negativity, the main place it would come up would be at Annie's school where some people have lived sheltered lives in the suburbs. Some of these people don't know any gay people. My experience has been that for the vast majority, they get over their negativity quickly, and then they're fine. I think most people are that way. This year, Annie's teacher is a lesbian herself, and she is simply terrific. During [Annie's] first two years at school, some of the other children seemed a little confused as they asked, "Oh, you have two mummies?" They would just shrug their shoulders and keep playing: it is simply not a big deal to them.

K: *Children are malleable. If they grow up having this awareness, and other kids are also aware that there are people who get together of the same gender, then it's not a big deal.*

H: Exactly: Annie is loved and that is what matters.

J: Annie is fine with it. I don't know if when she becomes a teenager…she will drag up the lesbian thing as part of her rebelliousness from us. I suspect she will just hate us as her parents like most kids.

K: *Of course not every adolescent goes through that phase.*

J: Right.

K: *What advice would you give to gays and lesbians thinking about getting married?*

J: Know that any relationship is incredibly difficult, and it doesn't get any easier just because you're married—it doesn't get any harder either. I don't think Hillary and I have a lot of things in common, except that we are both pigheaded and we work really hard at whatever we do. Together, we have worked incredibly hard over the last sixteen and a half years to get through the difficult things that have come up, whether it's communication problems, strong wills, parenting issues, intimacy, childhood experiences, or issues with extended family. Also recognize that no relationship is ever going to be perfect. You always have to work at the relationship and keep communicating. If you get stuck, seek out some external help.

You can't assume that it's ever going to be a picnic, but you need to know that when the going gets tough, you will be able to work through it. That's what we have been doing. When it seems like you're overwhelmed in your relationship, try to deal with the issues and figure out whether you are still interested [in] making your life work together.

H: I certainly know from heterosexual relationships that just having children doesn't save an otherwise bad marriage. In some ways, having children complicates one's life. I think it is easy to leave relationships, but it takes real courage to see them through and work on what comes up. If you don't, it will come up again later.

...

J: Another thing I wonder about is people who have commitment ceremonies when they are still in their early twenties. I can't imagine still being with the person I thought I was in love with in my early twenties. Maybe people can stick it out if they have a good sense of themselves and they were honest to begin with. I wonder if part of the high divorce rate among traditionally married couples is because people haven't had enough life experience to figure out what their connection is to the person they have married.

So another piece of advice is to wait until you really know that your partner is part of your family and you really want to have that be the case for the rest of your life. I wouldn't encourage every person who has just finished college to marry their college sweetheart. Many people do it and it does work out sometimes, but I would be very cautious.

K: *That raises an interesting question that I haven't asked any other couple. Do you have an inner sense of what would be a good age for gay men and lesbian women to marry?*

J: I would say around age thirty-two.

H: I would probably put it at around thirty. Part of that is because it still takes time to deal with being gay in the world. That process may take a couple of years or longer. I think it is entirely appropriate to go through a couple of relationships while you do that necessary psychological work.

You might [come from that rare place where everyone] knows that you are 100% queer…since you had your first breath. For most people, however, there is a bell curve of sexual orientation. It blows my mind to think that in my parents' generation, most people married in their early to mid-twenties. I think it is better to be a bit older and more mature.

J: Plus when you are first getting involved with someone, you are all "lovey-dovey" for the first six months to a year, and then it gets kind of old. That is when you need to figure out that there is other stuff to support the relationship. If you get married after a year, you don't have a clue who the other person is.

K: *One is usually still in the honeymoon phase at that point. We need to get through our first major fight together to see how the other deals with conflict and controversy. How long do you think a gay couple should be together before they talk seriously about marriage?*

H: A couple of years—that's what I would say to friends.

J: Yeah, and I think I would say the same thing to heterosexuals. I would also recommend a couple of years, and I think that living together is a really good idea too. As I talk about this, it makes me reflect on the fact that Hillary and I have been together for sixteen and a half years, and we still have absolutely no legal relationship to each other, yet heterosexual couples can meet in a bar on Friday night and decide to get married the next day. That is absolutely insane.

You know, some people talk about how same-sex marriage is going to ruin the family, or that marriage as an institution will be ruined. How is family or marriage going to be ruined by people like us? We already have a family, and we have a bond that is already stronger than many if not most married couples' [bonds].

K: *Exactly. The fact is, you were married a long time ago in your hearts, but your government has denied you. What public displays of affection are comfortable for the two of you?*

H: We show public affection very rarely. We have a little place in Provincetown, which is an extremely gay town. Everyone walks around Provincetown holding hands or with their arms around each other. We'll do that on occasion, but not often.

K: *Do you think that if the marriage suit goes through, things like public affection will change for the two of you?*

H: I think it will in the long run. There is still a part of me that doesn't want to get shot. I think it will take time for the average person to become accustomed to seeing lesbians and gays holding hands and kissing in public. ...[A] queer individual in Boston [was recently] murdered. Not long ago, there was a lesbian couple camping in either West Virginia or Virginia and they were shot, and one of them died. Boston also has had its share of gay bashings and killings. That is always in my head.

K: *So it's with good reason you would be concerned about walking hand in hand in most areas of Boston.*

J: You know, I cannot tell you how much it affects my awareness of who I am when I am with Hillary. The last time we were in Provincetown, I saw two women kissing. Annie and I were driving by them and Annie was just staring. I just thought, "Wow, they're being so obvious about their relationship and their love for each other." I can't even imagine that, and that's one of the really sad things about all of this. I don't want to put Hillary, Annie or myself at risk.

K: *People in Canada and the U.S., so long as they are male and female, can neck and hold hands and no one bats an eye. However, a gay couple holding hands would also be in possible jeopardy in Calgary, Alberta, where I live. I've only seen it twice in Calgary, both times they were young gay guys holding hands, and I was scared for them. My first thought was, "I'm scared for you," and I am also proud of you, but I am more scared than I am proud right now.*

J: Right, and I see that all the time in Jamaica Plain, which is the neighbourhood of Boston where we live. I see young lesbians with multiple piercings holding hands and kissing on the sidewalk, and you know, I'm just scared for them. Sometimes you can't tell their gender, so that makes it less obvious, and therefore safer.

K: *Is there a metaphor, image, movie or piece of music that speaks to your feelings or thoughts about same-sex marriage? Broaden that to include your long-term relationship with each other.*

J: There is a piece of music that [our friends] Linda and Myana sang at their commitment ceremony that speaks to us. It's a Gershwin song called "Our Love is Here to Stay."

K: *What would you put in a "hope box" for gay people? What do you think still needs to happen within the gay community?*

H: Gays and lesbians are not 100% in agreement that marriage is the thing we should be fighting for. I really respect people that have other issues that they are working on. For example, you can still get fired in all fifty states of the United States for being gay. You can still lose your housing in many states and you can lose your child. Those issues and civil rights are deeply connected and include the same-sex marriage challenge. All of these issues and rights are incredibly important.

K: *I wasn't aware that you could lose your job and rental housing in fifty states.*

J: Some municipalities, states and companies have laws that provide protections around sexual orientation. Federally speaking, however, there is no protection. We can also be dishonourably discharged from the military for being gay, and that primarily affects low-income people and people of colour. These are the individuals primarily recruited for the military.

...

J: We know a couple of guys living in Canada who have two children, both by surrogate implant. One of the guys is the biological father. These two guys been together for over twenty-five years. When we saw them in Provincetown this summer, they said that they didn't know if they would get married. We didn't know exactly what to make of that, but we assumed they were concerned about the expectation of monogamy that marriage represents.

I would place in the hope chest that gay people in long-term committed relationships not kid themselves regarding the lack of protection that results from not being married. We knew a couple of gay people who died in the September 11 attacks on New York. One lesbian woman lost her life partner in the attack, and absolutely nothing was in her name or in a joint name with her partner. The things that she considered to be joint assets—the home, the car—it was all taken away from her. You need to think about how you are going to protect your relationship and how to protect yourself in the context of that relationship. I don't believe most gay people think about it, and they are deceiving themselves.

H: We don't like to think about the horrible things that could come up in our lives—who wants to? Unfortunately, it's when bad things come up, like death, disability or disease, that you realize, "Oh my god, I'm not protected!" I assume that if Julie died, I'd get to keep the house. Maybe I would, but I would have to pay taxes on the value of half of it, and that would be a lot of money.

Everybody thinks, "Oh, the house is in both our names, so no problem." These are not issues you think of when you are falling in love and thinking about getting married in your twenties and thirties, but these questions do come up in your forties and fifties.

K: *Very true. These are all the questions I wanted to ask the two of you. Is there anything that you think I should have asked you, but didn't?*

H: No, I think you've asked really great questions.

K: *Let me thank you both for our interview today.*

the Future
Queering/   /Marriage

The struggle for queer marriage outlined in this book has taken place at every level of human existence. As the stories of the couples interviewed for Part II of this book so richly illustrate, the marriage movement has not simply been a movement about abstract political and legal demands—it has been an expression of the lived experiences and deepest desires of lesbian and gay people who have had the courage to seek love in the face of sometimes complete social and legal erasure.

Like the incredible paradigm shifts that occurred when women were pronounced to be 'persons' within the meaning of the Canadian constitution, and when the U.S. courts decreed that African-Americans could be considered to be 'citizens,' and when racist and anti-semitic signs bearing slogans like 'whites only' were prohibited by human rights laws in Canada, the extension of marriage to same-sex couples has dismantled major barriers to the full expression of the humanity of lesbian and gay couples and their families.

To underscore this point, it is not 'the law' that has changed. What has changed is how some courts and some legislatures have begun to interpret the law and their understanding of which human beings are permitted to enjoy the benefit and protection of the law.

That 'the law' has not changed at all is perfectly clear on the face of the historical record:

1) In 1975, county clerks in Boulder, Colorado, and Phoenix, Arizona, had begun to hand out marriage licences to queer couples after the clerks realized that state marriage laws permitted 'any two persons' to marry. State officials stopped these marriages by simply decreeing that lesbian and gay couples were not in fact 'any two persons.'

2) In the 2000s, when the Dutch and Belgian parliaments, the courts in Ontario, B.C. and Massachusetts, and the City of San Francisco opened marriage to same-sex couples, they did it with another simple decree: that lesbian and gay couples *can be* 'any two persons' who can marry.

The legal status of marriage has not changed. What has changed has been the perception that lesbian and gay couples are fully equal with other adult couples who wish to form the durable and intimate relationships known as 'marriage' today.

The seeming simplicity of this change belies the incredible efforts that have had to be made in order to bring it about. During the three decades between the 1970s and the 2000s, lesbian, gay, bisexual, two-spirited, transgendered, intersex and transsexual people have had to assert their full rights within virtually every dimension of human existence in order to persuade the state to perceive their essential humanity.

In 1969, the popular *Everything You Always Wanted to Know About Sex, But Were Afraid to Ask* by David Reuben, M.D., summed up gay male existence as being focused literally on 'the penis, not the person.' Canada joined the new trend toward decriminalizing queer sex in 1969, but as demonstrated by the New York Stonewall Rebellions in that same year and similar raids in Toronto in the 1970s and 1980s, police still felt free to harass queers who congregated in public spaces. Similarly, the American Psychiatric Association continued to view homosexuality as a mental disorder until 1973—but even after the removal of that diagnosis, U.S. psychiatrists known as conversion or reparative therapists have continued to treat lesbian and gay persons as mentally ill.

Every minority group has encountered what queers have faced to a greater or lesser degree: stereotyping; pressure to conform to dominant ideals; pressure to disappear (the 'spiral of silence' effect); even internalized stereotyping and self-hatred. Stereotypes concerning sexuality meant that at the time Reuben published his book, the majority of people in Canada and the U.S. generally viewed gay men and lesbian women as sick, demented and criminal. With 'homosexuality' classified legally as a crime and medically as a disease, queer relationships were actively suppressed—gay and lesbian individuals could not form meaningful commitments with each other without facing the risks of imprisonment and/or institutionalization in a mental hospital.

For years, these legal and psychiatric norms reinforced each other and the barriers to 'coming out' as queer. In a way, the breaking down of these barriers has had to begin in the heart of every single queer who ever rejected being labelled as 'sick,' 'demented' or 'criminal.' Like other aspects of the queer civil rights movement, the queer marriage movement has been both a reclamation of full civil rights and a refusal of these stereotypes.

As you read in Part II of this book, some gay and lesbian couples reached beyond these images to establish deep commitments to each other even before 1969. Other couples dared to demand that their relationships be recognized in the same mundane ways that modern states recognize heterosexual relationships in modern life, or even challenged religious views that only heterosexual marriages are spiritually blessed. Their fight continues today.

The new legal context brought about by the recent changes in Dutch, Belgian, Canadian and U.S. marriage laws is rich with the layered histories of why and how queers have demanded to be considered to be full 'persons' in life and in the law. In this process, the heterosexual paradigm has been shaken to the core. Now that important courts in Ontario, B.C., Quebec and Massachusetts have all taken more or less the same route to the conclusion that lesbian and gay couples can be 'any two persons' in law, officials elsewhere—in California, New Mexico, New Jersey, Oregon and New York—are taking this proposition not to court, but directly into life on the basis that to continue to exclude queer couples is undemocratic and discriminatory. These actions have of course triggered reactive litigation. However, the fact that local officials have begun to proactively read neutral laws to *include* queers signals that a paradigm shift is taking place.

As this new era unfolds, there is much to be learned from the stories we have told. Heterosexual individuals can learn from lesbian and gay marriages that true love surpasses both gender and gender roles. They may even arrive at the shocking discovery that the same stereotypes used to put down queers—'fag,' 'butch,' 'dyke'—have also helped construct the tyranny of heterosexual stereotypes in which gendered roles constrain the full humanity of each partner. True equality in relationships may well become more conceivable instead of remaining merely exceptional.

At the same time, lesbian and gay individuals can learn from their own experiences as recent outsiders to marriage how the institution of marriage suits them. As queers search for and find common ground with heterosexual couples, the state can more effectively do its job, which is to make sure that legal policy remains fitted to changing social realities instead of using the force of law to fit people into pre-existing legal categories.

Filling in the gaps in the new patchwork quilt of inclusive marriage laws will take time. But this task, the completion of the revolution, will now be carried out in a transformed political and social reality. Yes, some of the most powerful forces of homophobia are now searching for new ways to block queer marriage. The Catholic Pope began his campaign in the summer of 2003 in response to the Canadian court decisions, calling on politicians and judges to exercise their power to enforce Catholic religious doctrine. The U.S. President is seeking amendment of the U.S. constitution to prohibit recognition of same-sex marriages across the U.S. Even Hollywood's

'Terminator' in the form of California Governor Arnold Schwarzenegger has been deployed to 'stop those marriages.'

Even though we cannot predict how these renewed political attacks on queer marriage will work themselves out, we do know that there are now important new truths in the world about same-sex couples and their families. Forty years ago, at the beginning of the queer marriage movement, this day was just a dream even to those who dared to imagine what full equality might eventually look like.

The journey toward same-sex marriage has brought us not just to our destination, but to another important beginning as well. The first decisive steps toward recognizing the full humanity of queers will now in turn shape how people everywhere think about life and about law. As human beings around the globe continue to struggle with what it means to fully integrate queers into all aspects of life, we believe that queer marriage will promote that integration through the simple yet profound process of inviting celebration by all.

Further References

J.A. Lee, 'Going Public: A Study in the Sociology of Homosexual Liberation' in *Journal of Homosexuality*, 3, 49-78, 1977.

D. Reuben, *Everything you wanted to know about sex, but were afraid to ask*, New York: Bantam, 1969.

Acknowledgements

We would like to acknowledge the commitment and pride that led lesbian, gay, bisexual, transgendered and transsexual couples around the world to challenge the inhuman rigidities of legally-defined sex and marriage. We particularly thank the couples who agreed to be interviewed. Some of them have been among the first pioneers in this marriage movement, others have carried the struggle to its fruition in Ontario, British Columbia, Quebec, the Netherlands, Belgium and (hopefully soon) Massachusetts. Your courage and your stories move us to tears. By participating in this project, you have given voice to the special love you have for your partner. We want you to know that your accomplishments have changed the world we now live in.

We would also like to acknowledge the many lawyers, judges, legislators and activists who made this flowering of the marriage movement, described by some as the 'greatest civil rights movement of this generation,' imaginable. Key participants are identified throughout these pages, but we would particularly like to single out some heroes here. Evan Wolfson, now executive director of Freedom to Marry, with his co-counsel Dan Foley, convinced the Hawaii courts in 1993 to rule for the first time in the world that denying queers the right to marry violates their constitutional rights. The brilliant record put before the Hawaii courts enabled those judges to see that there never really have been any genuine legal barriers to same-sex marriage, that same-sex couples are obviously just as much 'any two persons' as are heterosexuals. A decade later, Martha McCarthy and Joanna Radbord then convinced the Ontario Court of Appeal in its historic decision of June 10, 2003, to strike the ban on same-sex marriage, and at the same time, Doug Elliott obtained the ruling that same-sex marriages performed by the Metropolitan Community Church of Toronto two years earlier were legally valid. The powerful decisions obtained by Mary Bonauto from the Vermont and Massachusetts appellate courts have had a similar effect. Gavin Newsom, Mayor of San Francisco, and Jason West, Mayor of New Paltz, New York, authorized same-sex marriages in February 2004 on the strength of the Massachusetts court ruling. Jason West has since been criminally charged with nineteen counts of marrying couples who do not possess valid marriage licences under New York law, and has been ordered by a court to not perform any more same-sex marriages at the price of facing harsher consequences. Other county officials in Oregon and New Mexico have put their careers on the line as they have extended marriage to same-sex couples because they could not in good conscience engage in discrimination.

Legislators, government officials and policy experts have also played key roles. The then Canadian Minister of Justice Martin Cauchon changed the course of history when he decided that the Ontario and British Columbia court decisions should not be appealed, and when he proposed legislation to extend same-sex marriage to the whole of Canada. The City Clerk of Toronto and the Attorney General of British Columbia, Andrew Petter, made the courageous decisions back in 2000 to initiate legal proceedings after being told by the federal government that they could not issue marriage licences to lesbian and gay couples. Terry Hancock worked tirelessly with the Canadian Bar Association, Ontario Bar Association and Law Society of Upper Canada to educate lawyers and judges on the many forms of discrimination faced by queers in contemporary society, many of which flowed from the marriage bar. Without these and many other efforts, this movement would doubtless have remained stalled for another decade or two.

We thank Richard Almonte, then editor at Insomniac Press, for suggesting the idea of this book to us. All three of us have been amazed at how quickly this book went from its inception to your hands.

On a more personal level, we would like to thank our own institutions for supporting this work. The University of Calgary Conjoint Research Ethics Board provided valuable input into the interview format. We would also like to thank those couples who were interviewed but whose stories do not appear in these pages. Part of doing ethical research, particularly research that does not use pseudonyms, is allowing interviewees to retract their stories before the book goes to print. No explanation is required and no penalty of any kind occurs. Two lesbian couples decided to retract their stories before the book went to print, and before publication it also became necessary to remove an additional four stories due to length constraints. Kevin would like to thank the couples who gave of their time and whose stories do not appear: Jim Sanyshyn and Lyle Jones, Douglas Saunders and Michael Bartholomew, Kam Wong and Morag Misselbrook, and Albert and Gerhard Berkenhoff van Dijk. We made contact with most of these couples ourselves, but we received additional assistance from Egale Canada, and for this we are very grateful.

Kevin would like to thank the following angels who helped transcribe the taped interviews: Dolores Clarkson, Heidi Chorzempa, Paige Marshall and Amanda McLane. You each did an amazing job, and learned more than you expected. While Kevin kept worrying about how he would possibly make sense of all the transcripts once they were ready, some of the same angels, and a few others, joined him in an eventful task on November 8, 2003. They spent a day together extracting the themes of what could be learned about same-sex marriage from a more holistic perspective. Kevin thanks the coders of the transcripts: Misty Brigham, Heidi Chorzempa, Erin de Denus, Alexander Lam, Amanda Loates, Amanda McLane, Kimberly Miller, Tracy Quayat, and Angela Spohr. Kevin has never felt such support from a group of students before.

Queen's University's Faculty of Law has long been in the forefront of progressive legal education and lawyering; the many students, staff and faculty members who contributed to this work in many ways include Vyvien Vella; Dean Alison Harvison Young; Professors Mark Walters, Martha Bailey, Nick Bala, Kim Brooks, Beverley Baines, Mark Weisberg and Stan Corbett; and researcher Morgan Camley, Law '04. Funding from the Social Science and Humanities Research Council of Canada supported the writing of *Are We 'Persons' Yet? Law and Sexuality in Canada* (University of Toronto Press, 1999), which provided the legal and strategic framework within which much of the Canadian litigation was formulated.

We would also like to thank our families for believing in the importance of this work. *Kathy:* I have had the great privilege of being the mother of two wonderful daughters who have taught me more about the realities of family and commitment than I ever realized I could know. Kate and Michèle, the story told in this book is your story too. I am sad that it has fallen partly to you to help show other people the inherent worth of queer families. I am immensely proud that you have not let this burden stop you from becoming incredible young women who embody faith in human potential. I have also had the gift in my life of being loved more than I thought anyone could be loved by my family, by my friends, and by my partner Maggie. It is unbe- lievably difficult for relationships to thrive in societies that ignore or stigmatize them. Maggie and I have been fortunate to find in each other the deep love and mutual regard that has enabled us to live with those realities. I would also like to thank my parents Edward Lahey and Evelyn Lahey Roney for teaching me how to value family and commitment, my brothers Tom and Mike Lahey for their strong and loving support, and my sister Linda Jensen for helping me make sense of the paths we are walking.

Kevin: I cannot write a book without thanking my ex-wife, Bess, for always believing in me, even when I couldn't believe in myself. Without question, she is my deepest friend. We share in the love of our two children, two individuals who inspire me to become more of who I am. Finally, I thank my partner, Kevin Midbo, who has challenged me and loved me more than anyone I know. I stand in awe of his presence, and I cry at times in his absence, my own celebration of the love I feel for him. Ours is not a conventional relationship, and as we continue to forge ahead, I never know if looking forward will be as good as looking back. Kevin gave me the space I needed to write this book. As every author knows, one's home life suffers as a higher purpose temporarily takes over. I suspect this is a spiritual journey. Thank you, Kevin, for understanding it. You are *my* mustard seed.

March 21, 2004
Kingston, Ontario, and Calgary, Alberta

Index

Kathleen A. Lahey was the lawyer for three of the B.C. couples who won the right to marry from the B.C. Court of Appeal as of July 8, 2003. She is the author of *Are We 'Persons' Yet? Law and Sexuality in Canada* (University of Toronto Press, 1999), and has published and consulted on a wide range of legal issues relating to equality and human rights. The founding editor of the *Canadian Journal of Women and the Law*, she has also served on various advisory boards, including the Sexual Orientation and Gender Identity Committee of the Ontario Bar Association, Egale Canada, the Ontario Advisory Council on Women's Issues, and the Ontario Fair Tax Commission. She lives in Kingston, Ontario, where she is a professor at Queen's University Faculty of Law.

Kevin Alderson is an assistant professor of counselling psychology at the University of Calgary. His areas of research interest include all aspects of human sexuality, gender studies and gay identity. Throughout his career, Dr. Alderson has counselled hundreds of gay men and lesbian women. He currently maintains a part-time private practice. Before joining the university in July 2001, he was the Head of Counselling and Health Services at Mount Royal College in Calgary. He has published two previous books, *Beyond Coming Out: Experiences of Positive Gay Identity* (Insomniac Press, 2000) and *Breaking Out: The Complete Guide to Building and Enhancing a Positive Gay Identity for Men and Women* (Insomniac Press, 2002).